D0707191

Germany
Beyond the Enchanted Forest

Germany

Beyond the Enchanted Forest

A Literary Anthology

Edited by Brian Melican

Signal

**Signal Books
Oxford**

First published in the UK in 2013 by
Signal Books Limited
36 Minster Road
Oxford
OX4 1LY
www.signalbooks.co.uk

© Brian Melican, 2013
Foreword © Philip Oltermann

To be read in conjunction with p. 231 which constitutes an extension to this copyright page.

All rights reserved. The whole of this work, including all text and illustrations, is protected by copyright. No parts of this work may be loaded, stored, manipulated, reproduced or transmitted in any form or by any means, electronic or mechanical, including photocopying and recording, or by any information, storage and retrieval system without prior written permission from the publisher, on behalf of the copyright owner.

A catalogue record for this book is available from the British Library

ISBN 978-1-908493-77-4 Paper

Production: Tora Kelly
Cover Design: Tora Kelly
Cover Images: Wikipedia Commons
Images: Wikipedia Commons
Printed in India

For Thomas Scheele and Mark McDonald,
two people to whom I wish I could still give a copy personally

Contents

Foreword by Philip Oltermann...x

Introduction..xiii
Of Saxons and Saxe-Coburg-Gothas...xiii
From Rustic to Regimented xiv
About This Anthology..xvi

1.Triple Dutch: Teutons, Alemans and Germans 1589 - 1700.......................1
At the Birth of Travel Writing..2
Germany: A New Word for an Old Place 3
Henry Wotton, *Letters*..4
Fynes Moryson, *An Itinerary*..6
Thomas Coryate, *Coryat's crudities*...9
John Taylor, *Taylor his travels*...11

2.From Berlin to Coswig: New Pomp and Old Squalor 1700 - 1800.........15
Men of Letters...17
Petty Princes and Courageous Kings..18
Joseph Addison, *Letters*..19
Mary Wortley Montagu, *Letters*...20
David Hume, *Letters*...21
James Boswell, *The Journal of his German and Swiss Travels*.....................24
David Garrick, *Letters*...26
Nathaniel Wraxall, *Memoirs of the Courts of Berlin, Dresden, Warsaw, and Vienna*........27
John Moore, *A View of Society and Manners in France, Switzerland and Germany*.........29

3.The Call of the *Kulturnation* Germany and the Romantics 1787 - 1817................32
The First Germanophiles 34
Great Men in Mediocre Surroundings 35
Dorothy and William Wordsworth, *Letters*..36
Samuel Taylor Coleridge, *Letters*...39
Henry Crabb Robinson, *Letters*..41
Mary Wollstonecraft-Shelley and Percy Bysshe-Shelley, *History of a Six Weeks' Tour*......45
Mary Wollstonecraft-Shelley, *Frankenstein; or, The Modern Prometheus*.......................47

4.Echoes of Goethe on the Eve of Bismarck 1820 - 1860............................50
From Worthy Learners to Merciless Satirists..52
The Last Nap of the "Sleepy" Germans..53

William Meredith, *A Tour to the Rhine* 54

William Makepeace Thackeray, *Letters* 56

Francis Bond Head, *Bubbles from the Brunnens of Nassau by an Old Man* 59

Thomas Hood, *Letters* 61

Thomas Hood, *Up the Rhine* 62

Elisabeth Gaskell, *Letters* 64

Herman Melville, *Journal of a Tour to London and the Continent* 67

George Eliot, *Letters* 69

5. "The German" Replaces Germans: The Rise of Jingoism 1860 - 1900 72

Funny Foreigners—and Funny English-speakers 74

Enchanted Forests and Prussian Soldiers 75

Henry James, *Letters* 76

Mark Twain, *A Tramp Abroad* 79

Thomas Stevens, *Around the World on a Bicycle* 82

Albert Morris Bagby, *Miss Träumerei* 86

Jerome K. Jerome, *Three Men on the Bummel* 89

6. Close Connections and Opposing Policies 1900 - 1920 93

Masterpieces of English Literature about Germany 95

Germans: Lucullans against Draconians 96

D. H. Lawrence, *The Prussian Officer* 97

T. S. Eliot, *Letters* 98

Evelyn Princess Blücher, *An English Wife in Berlin* 100

Ford Madox Ford, *The Good Solider* 104

Joseph Conrad, *Notes on Life and Letters* 107

Robert Graves, *Goodbye to All That* 109

7. From 1920s Bohemia to 1930s Germania 1925 - 1935 111

The Weimar Republic: From Zenith to Nadir 113

Delayed Publication 114

Stephen Spender, *The Temple* 115

Christopher Isherwood, *Goodbye to Berlin* 116

Gerald Hamilton, *Mr. Norris and I* 118

Patrick Leigh Fermor, *A Time of Gifts* 119

Martha Dodd, *My Years in Germany* 121

Unity Mitford, *Letters* 125

8. Writing through the Nazi Stranglehold 1935 - 1939 128

Diaries and Columns 130

Germanophiles in the Shadow of Censorship 131
Virginia Woolf, *Diary*..132
Samuel Beckett, *German Diaries*..133
Thomas Wolfe, *I Have a Thing to Tell You* 134
W. E. B. Dubois, *Forum of Fact and Opinion (Pittsburgh Courier)*............137
Richard Hillary, *The Last Enemy* 140
William Shirer, *Berlin Diary: The Journal of a Foreign Correspondent* 142

9. From the Darkest Hour to *Stunde Null* 1940 - 1950.........................145
Journalists, Civilians, Combatants 147
Rabid Nazis and Reluctant Soldiers..148
Howard K. Smith, *Last Train from Berlin*...149
Harry Flannery, *Assignment to Berlin*..151
Michael Burn, *Yes, Farewell*..155
Christabel Bielenberg, *The Past is Myself* 157
Evelyn Waugh, *Diary*..160
Michael Howard, *Otherwise Occupied*..162

10. Spy Fiction and the State of the Nation 1950 - 1983........................164
Observers of the New Germany 166
From Excitement to Routine..167
Tony Benn, *Diaries*...168
Anthony Sampson, *The New Europeans*..170
Leon Uris, *Armageddon* 172
John le Carré, *The Spy Who Came in from the Cold*..............................175
Harry Flannery, *Which Way Germany?*...176
Patricia Highsmith, *The Boy Who Followed Ripley*................................179
Bob Larson, *Your Swabian Neighbours* 181
Len Deighton, *Berlin Game*..182

11. A Dying Dictatorship and Instant "Ostalgia" 1982 - 1999................185
Caught by Surprise in 1989...187
The Return of Light-heartedness 188
Gordon Craig, *The Germans*...189
John Ardagh, *Germany and the Germans*..191
Michael Skinner, *USAREUR: The United States Army in Europe*............193
Bill Bryson, *Neither Here nor There* 196
Dave Rimmer, *Once Upon a Time in the East*.......................................197
Timothy Garton Ash, *The File*..199

12.Berlin Hype, Globalization and the Role of History 2000 - 203
Academics, Journalists, Authors...205
Robert Ford, *Rhapsody*..208
James Carroll, *Secret Father*...209
Steven Ozment, *A Mighty Fortress: A New History of the German People* 212
Michael Gorra, *The Bells in Their Silence: Travels Through Germany*............................213
Roger Boyes, *A Year in the Scheisse* 215
Ben Donald, *Springtime for Germany*..217
Anna Winger, *This Must Be the Place* 219
Philip Kerr, *A Quiet Flame*...220
Ingrid Anders, *Earth to Kat Vespucci*..222
Esi Edugyan, *Half-Blood Blues*...223

Bibliography and Further Reading...226

Acknowledgements...231

Index..232

Foreword

IF A MARTIAN were to use this book to bone up on the character of the German people ahead of a holiday, he would quite possibly be left sitting on a bit of volcanic rock, scratching his head in confusion. What a strange bunch of people this is. These humans are supposedly terrible at cooking (raw cabbage with bacon dusting is a particular favourite) and at the same time brilliantly gastronomically gifted, producing meals that are both bland and "rich and spicy", including "rye bread, dark pine-honey and huge ice-cream puddings". Germany's countryside, meanwhile, is marked by "Waste & Decay", but also "beautiful, well cultivated Plains". Are the Germans desolately poor or stinking rich? It's hard to say. Are they "inferior in creative intellect" or uniquely erudite? Cold and distant, or hyper-sexualised and touchy-feely? All these assessments of the German character can be found in this rich and varied collection. The Germans, it seems, have traditionally been regarded by visitors from Britain and America as a walking collection of paradoxes, "the politest people on earth" who are also "a warlike race", a people both "modern and impressive" but also "unmodern, almost primitive". The only reconciliation lies in the fact that those Germans who have come the other way have hardly been less puzzled.

Considering the geographical proximity between Great Britain and Germany, considering how much history they share, it is curious how frequently meetings between these two Northern European nations have ended in misunderstandings. In fact, one of the most beautiful ironies in the history of Anglo-German relations is that the two countries who can claim to have given birth to Romanticism have found it notoriously hard to kindle romance between each other. Two poets closely associated with the Romantic movement illustrate this. Both at least tried to bridge the culture gap: William Wordsworth, featured in this collection, travelled to Germany in 1789. The German poet Heinrich Heine went the other way in 1827. Both had nurtured a fascination with the country they were visiting and both wanted to meet their idols: Wordsworth admired the "German Milton" Friedrich Gottlieb Klopstock, while Heine was keen to seek out the radical publicist and radical William Cobbett.

In the end, neither of them quite found what they had been looking for. Wordsworth met Klopstock but seems more struck by the ageing man's grotesque physical appearance than his intellect. Hamburg, where he and his sister Dorothy arrive, is "a sad place", and Goslar, where they end up, marooned by snow and ice, is an "old decaying city". The seminal poem he produces in the Harz mountains is less inspired by the German landscape than by his homesickness for the English countryside.

Heine's encounter is even more crushing. At the Crown and Anchor Tavern off the Strand, he looks on with despair as Cobbett engages in a shouting match with a group of politicos. His verdict is damning:

Poor old Cobbett! Dog of England! I have no love for thee, for every vulgar nature my soul abhors; but thou touchest me to the inmost soul with pity, as I see how thou strainest in vain to break loose and to get at those thieves who make off with their booty before thy very eyes, and mock at thy fruitless springs and thine impotent howling.

If the accounts assembled in this anthology are so fascinating to anyone with a personal history that bridges German and British culture, it's because we recognise in encounters like the two above a familiar pattern: high hopes, dashed on the rocks of hard fact, and—sometimes—a reconciliation with reality.

Are Britain and Germany getting better at getting on with each other? Are our expectations these days less overblown and more realistic? The optimist in me would like to think so. One distinctive trend noticeable in these British and American accounts of Germany is that after decades of belittling the Germans, a century of distrust and a decade of noticeable disinterest, we are currently witnessing a revival of "the good German" in English-language writing.

US-born travel writer Bill Bryson's account of his visit to Germany may well turn out to be ahead of its time in that respect, calling the Germans "the new Americans—rich, ambitious, hard-working, health-conscious, sure of their place in the world" and concluding that "I was happy to hand them my destiny". This is even more considering that passage was written in 1991: a year after the reunification that was watched with such unease in Britain, after a painful defeat in a World Cup semi-final and after Margaret Thatcher's industry secretary Nicholas Ridley had described the European Monetary Union as "a German racket designed to take over the whole of Europe".

In 2013, British politicians and journalists are more likely to echo Bryson's sentiments than Ridley's. The Germanophile rhetoric of the current Labour leaderships has been so enthusiastic as to earn it the moniker "Neue Labour", while the Trades Union Congress has published a pamphlet called "German Lessons". On the directly opposite side of the political spectrum, the Tory MP Elizabeth Truss has made a plea to "rebuild Britain's economy the German way", while former Conservative defence secretary Liam Fox has argued that "Britain must learn from Germany—not France and Greece". "If there is one alliance in Europe that makes sense, it has always been between Britain and Germany," *Guardian* columnist Simon Jenkins wrote earlier this year. Even the tabloids are getting in on the act: after David Cameron's speech on an in-out referendum for

British membership of the EU, both *Bild* and the *Sun* published lists with ten reasons why they really loved their North Sea neighbours.

It remains to be seen whether Germany can live up to so many divergent expectations at once. But perhaps we should enjoy the romance while it lasts—if Brian Melican's perceptive anthology teaches us anything, it's that our current views are unlikely to stay the same for long.

Philip Oltermann

Introduction

IN A SPORTING METAPHOR much loved by journalists, confrontations between the English-speaking and Germanophone peoples over the course of history have taken on something of a derby character. In the United Kingdom, Germany is the preferred foe for everything from football to bagging sun-loungers on that great Mediterranean outpost of northern Europe, Mallorca; and during the long decline from its early-twentieth-century geopolitical and industrial zenith, Britain has continually looked to its military victories over Germany for reassurance of its resilience. For the United States, too, Germany is a country against which measures of military muscle have an important societal role, albeit as part of the national narrative of how America became, for a period in the late twentieth century, the greatest country in the world. Canada, Australia, India: all of these outposts of the English language have taken up arms against Germany in the last hundred years, too.

Of Saxons and Saxe-Coburg-Gothas

Yet this rivalry is by no means as immutable as many English-speakers would think. For much of their history, the old enemy of the English has been the French. In fact, to rephrase this slightly: ever since the English stopped being German, they have been fighting the French. At the Battle of Hastings, the King of England who was defeated was a Saxon. Saxony today, of course, is a region of Germany.

The Saxons spoke a dialect of Old German, which in turn became Old English as it mixed with Old Norse (itself also a Germanic tongue); it became the English we speak today only after a few centuries of close and continued interaction with French. Words which were in use before 1066 tend to be cognates in modern English and German: bed and *Bett*, before and *bevor*, bread and *Brot*, to name but a few. In some regions of England there is no difference in pronunciation between the two languages: English-speakers from Newcastle diphthongize several words in the same way as modern German—just listen to a Geordie and a German say the words beer and *Bier*. If Britain and America are two nations divided by common language, Germany and Britain today are two nations united by a different language.

As, of course, are America and Germany. The sheer scale of German immigration into America led to a second period of interaction between (what had now become) the two languages in the nineteenth century. The United States loves its "brats"—nothing less than a contraction of *Bratwurst*—as well as its frankfurters and wieners, sends its kids to kindergarten and freely uses

Yiddish words like schmuck, which also have their roots in German. Other, less obvious links are also present: if you ever wondered why Americans sometimes call Santa "Kriss Kringle", the German "Christkindl" provides the etymology. German immigration also led to old German words that were present but little-used in British English becoming standard in America: "dumb" instead of stupid (from *dumm*) or "wagon" for almost all kinds of four-wheelers (*Wagen*). While that old story about German almost becoming the official language of the USA is certainly apocryphal, the influence of German on US English should not be underestimated.

In fact, for much of its early life America was ruled by German kings—by virtue of the fact that Britain was, too. From 1714 onwards the British royal family was Hanoverian: George I was imported from Hanover as a suitable Protestant monarch and refused to learn English. When the Founding Fathers declared America's independence from the British king, they set themselves up against George III, the grandson of the Elector of Hanover. In 1837 the direct Hanoverian line in Britain came to an end as Queen Victoria succeeded to the throne, only to marry her cousin Prince Albert of Saxe-Coburg-Gotha and immediately reintroduce German-born royalty to Britain.

None of this interaction between Britain and Germany was considered abnormal. In fact, so relaxed was the attitude towards all things German that the British royal family only changed its name from Saxe-Coburg-Gotha to the somewhat more patriotic variant "Windsor" in 1917—i.e. towards the end of the First World War. Americans, too, were in little hurry to distance themselves from Germany and German influences, with significant German-speaking communities enjoying an easy coexistence with Anglophone Americans in large industrial cities such as Cincinnati or Pittsburgh well into the twentieth century. For both Britain and America, the sheer brutality and the horrific nature of German crimes in the Second World War seem to provide a clearer caesura in terms of attitudes.

From Rustic to Regimented

The writers in this anthology provide detailed documentation both of this historically less complicated relationship—and of the change to the fear and mistrust that came to characterize it. In writing from the sixteenth and seventeenth centuries the tone about Germany is matter of fact: writers such as Fynes Moryson and Thomas Coryate experience the states of the Holy Roman Empire as simply another area of the very complicated patchwork of early-modern Europe, of which England too was an integral part.

Even as England and Scotland became Great Britain and pulled away from the Continent both in economic and intellectual terms in the eighteenth century,

Germany did not become an enemy. Its backwardness was lamented, its divided and autocratic states and principalities were a subject of pity, only to become part of the old-world charm in search of which the Romantics such as Mary Wollstonecraft Shelley and later writers like William Makepeace Thackeray and Herman Melville cruised the Rhine in the nineteenth century.

By 1850 Germany had garnered itself a stereotype as a bumbling land of country simpletons too busy drinking beer and eating large quantities of pork to actually form a modern nation-state. The occasional brilliant writer or philosopher à la Goethe or Kant as well as low living costs made it and its language attractive to generations of young intellectuals, but travellers to the country were shocked again and again by what they saw as the coarseness and laziness of its general population.

If foreign opinion of Germany is a pendulum capable of oscillating between indulgence of rustic yokels and fear of regimented armies, it was at its furthest point towards the former in the mid-nineteenth century. The rise of Prussia precipitated the swing towards the latter, but so deeply ingrained was the image of the bumpkin *bon vivant* that even after the unification of Germany under "Kaiser Willy" and "Iron Chancellor" Bismarck in 1871, round-the-world-cyclist Thomas Stevens still wrote that "the average German would much rather loll around, sipping wine or beer, and smoking cigarettes, than impel a bicycle across a continent". It would take until the early 1940s when the Wehrmacht was impelling entire Panzer divisions across Europe for the pendulum to reach its furthest point in the direction of fear.

The metaphorical role of the forest in this transformation is vital. Germany has for centuries been known for its woodlands; the country's entry into recorded history is Tacitus' description of the forest ambush on Varus' legion. This event would later be used by German nationalists as a rallying call, and the forest spoken of in symbolic terms as "the source of the power of the German race", a mendacious mythologizing tendency which Patrick Leigh Fermor gently mocked at its frightening ideological height in the 1930s: "A number of Brownshirts—I'd forgotten all about them for the moment—was scattered among the congregation, with eyes lowered and their caps in their hands. They looked rather odd. They should have been out in the forest, dancing round Odin and Thor, or Loki perhaps."

English-language writers have seen Germany's forests variously as simple features of its landscape to be walked through (or cycled over by Thomas Stevens, for instance), as the typical site of fairy-tales and the Romantic uncanny (Elisabeth Gaskell and Mark Twain are examples here) or indeed through the ideological lens as a suspect site of pilgrimage for dangerous nationalists. As the view of Germans altered from one of innocent peasants and crafters of wooden cuckoo clocks to that of sinister soldiers gathering in shadowy clearings to commune with the ancestors of a debased Germanic mythology, so too did the meaning of the German forest.

The writing in this anthology traces this swing in metaphorical meaning, and shows continuous exceptions to it; writers often question rather than accept *idées reçues*, yet they are inescapably locked into the framework of perception of their age. A good way to read many of these texts is therefore to look for preconceptions the authors in question may be writing against: David Hume makes it quite clear that the general view of Germany on the British Isles in the eighteenth century was such that he expected to find a nation bent double under the weight of greedy absolutists; Coleridge and the Wordsworths, meanwhile, were expecting a country of friendly, slightly slack-jawed locals, and are consequently surprised when they are swindled out of a pretty penny in Hamburg. This way of reading is at its most applicable in the period following the Second World War through to today, where many writers more or less explicitly take it upon themselves to explain that not all Germans can be written off as Swastika-saluting lunatics. This work wants to allow readers to go beyond the forest and start seeing the wood for the trees.

About This Anthology

If the overriding aim of an anthology is to open up new perspectives to readers on a given topic, the reality of producing one seems to consist more often than not in closing off expansive views. For every text the reader finds in these pages, there is another one that was not included; and for every sentence of an extract, there are another two cut elsewhere.

As painful as this process sometimes was, it is, of course, in the very nature of an anthology. Rather than simply presenting a list of 77 texts on Germany that the editor thinks should be read, this collection offers the reader the opportunity to delve a little into each one before going to the (sometimes considerable) trouble of accessing it for him or herself. What is more, the reader may simply be looking for a compact overview of what has been written about Germany by British and North American authors, and this anthology provides such a guide.

Especially if the reader is placing his/her trust in the editor to supply this overview, he/she will doubtless have some important questions about how he went about compiling this anthology. Which writers and what kind of writing is in here? What was left out—and why? How were the extracts selected? If you are looking for answers, what follows is a brief guide to the principles behind this anthology (and several indications of where they may have been contravened).

Starting at the beginning, the first question is surely about the timeframe: why 1587? Is there no writing available about Germany before? The answer is that there most certainly is, but probably not composed in English, which brings us to an important point: all of the work in this collection was written in English. None of it is in translation, which explains why the reader might not find some authors he/she might perhaps expect to—from Tacitus, author of the first known text about Germany, to Thomas Mann, one of the wittiest, most incisive and internationally read commentators on his home country. This anthology limits itself to the perspectives English-speaking writers have had of Germany, and this is something which, before the printing press, would have been limited entirely to monasteries and courts.

This observation brings with it the next question: whose perspectives? What is a writer for the purposes of this anthology? Although this collection is literary, this does not mean that only literary fiction about Germany is present here—because that would make for a very short and uninteresting book. Many of the greatest authors in the English language have spent time in Germany, but without translating this directly into their works; many very insightful, well-travelled commentators, meanwhile, were simply not authors of fiction: and since limitations would deprive us of a great deal of interesting material, I decided not to impose any. The only real criterion beyond the sheer fact of having written about Germany in English, whether in fiction, diaries, letters, essays, or newsprint, was that the writing be interesting to a reader looking for perspectives on Germany.

Nonetheless, this criterion of intrinsic quality alone means that the majority of texts are written either by literary figures, or at least by people accustomed to writing for a wider readership. There are exceptions, however: Unity Mitford, while clearly lacking both literary merit and any semblance of commonsense, offers such a unique glance into the 1930s Nazi milieu—and the extension of its tendrils into the English aristocracy—that it would seem wrong not to include her letters. I have also included published material that is in no way intended to be literary, such as the extract taken from Michael Skinner's 1989 guide to American armed forces in Europe, an unlikely but deeply rich source.

These questions about what has been included bring with them as many questions about what has not—and why. Firstly, there are several references to Germany in diaries, journals and novels which, on further investigation, are fleeting. James Howell's *Instructions and Directions for Forren Travell* of 1650, for example, which I quote in the introduction to the first chapter, is simply too short on Germany to provide an extract worth including. Several other "go to" texts for anthologies that deal other places skip Germany altogether: Edward Daniel Clarke's *Travels in Various Countries of Europe* of the early nineteenth century, for example, or Maurice Baring's *Round the World in Any Number of Days* a century later.

Sometimes, I have not included extracts because they are already very well known: is there anyone interested in Germany who has yet to come across Mark Twain's essay on *The Awful German Language?* Since Twain produced plenty of other interesting material on Germany, it would seem a shame to stick with the obvious here. Furthermore, I have taken, where possible, actual descriptions of places: especially on a topic like Germany and the Germans, there is no shortage of pontificating and punditry available, and much of the more interesting, less prejudiced writing comes out of detailed spatial observation. I have made some exceptions where warranted: I could not find anything by the late Gordon Craig, for instance, that would have made an engaging extract about a given place, but his analysis of the development of the German language was too precise and too informative to miss.

Other notable omissions have occurred for more prosaic reasons. Copyright laws, for instance, have been a hindrance: the Ernest Hemingway Foundation levies heavier fees for reproduction of his work than most other copyright-owners, so I have been limited to quoting from his letters here. Sometimes I simply could not get to potentially interesting material in time, such as a book about the early years of Weimar Germany called *The Revolver Republic*, written by British foreign correspondent Eric Geyde (continuously unavailable at the British Library) or poems about Germany by W. H. Auden, who was part of the Oxford Bohemian crowd and visited Christopher Isherwood and Stephen Spender in Germany (unpublished at the New York Public Library).

Finally, a word on the chronology of the extracts, which is a complicated point. It is not always possible to date writing precisely, not even diary entries, which are provided with both a date of creation and, within the framework of a printed edition, a date of publication: William Shirer, for example, doctored his diary entries at some point between leaving Germany in late 1940 and publishing them in 1941. Stories, too, can lie in drawers for years before being published, and thus ordering this anthology strictly by the date of publication of the extracts would lead to some off-putting distortions: much writing about the 1930s and 1940s, for instance, has either been created after 1960, or at least has not appeared until then. In order to give the reader a collection of views of Germany at each stage of its development, therefore, the extracts are generally ordered based on the moment in history about which they are written. This, too, has its odd effects, and there are some unclassifiables, such Leon Uris' entirely imagined but thoroughly researched novel about the end of the Second World War and the Berlin Blockade written and published in 1963, or Esi Edugyan's 2011 story about a jazzman returning to today's Berlin but remembering the city as it was in the 1930s—but this modus operandi paradoxically produces the least confusing, most coherent structure.

Coherent in my opinion, at least, and that is the final point about the way this anthology is constructed. As much as anything, the extracts are a matter of personal choice, and the results of personal hobbyhorses, which include a strong interest in food and drink and a liking for ships and trains. Thankfully enough, this fits the remit of an anthology about travelling really rather well.

I personally had more than a few moments of what the Germans would call *Erkenntnis*—that flash of sudden insight—while compiling this anthology. The one I would be most keen to share is that the world is indeed small—and pretty much always has been. Although technology is undoubtedly making this fact clearer than it ever has been, it is certainly not the case that our past is less international than the present. In this anthology you will find John Taylor, in 1620, helping an English widow return from a few decades spent in Central Europe with her husband, a master brewer attracted abroad by good pay. You will also witness Hermann Melville, in 1848, coming across a German who has just returned from a stay in St. Louis, on a boat on the Rhine. Then there is Francis Bond Head (Chapter 4), who wrote about trekking across the Andes in the 1820s and was later a governor of Upper Canada, dying on Duppas Hill in Croydon, the rather nondescript part of South London from which I hail, and where D. H. Lawrence (Chapter 6) spent three years teaching before eloping to Germany with the wife of a modern languages professor.

This is before we get to the tragic coincidences of the First World War, in which a school friend of Robert Graves (also Chapter 6) shoots down one of his German cousins, , or before we delve into the rich seam of intertextuality: when she crosses into Germany, Virginia Woolf is reading *Aaron's Rod* by D. H. Lawrence. Richard Hillary (Chapter 8) is also at the centre of a nexus of personalities both within and outside of this anthology: in a passage not quoted here, Christabel Bielenberg (Chapter 9) sees an illicit copy of his book when visiting one of the Stauffenberg plotters in Berlin in 1944. Moreover, before his death in 1943 Hillary had been in love with a woman named Mary Brooker, who then met and married Michael Burn (also Chapter 9). Burn, meanwhile, had had a flirtation with Nazism in the 1930s and had once lunched with Unity Mitford (Chapter 7) in Munich before going on to a Nuremberg rally. While writing the novel anthologized here, Burn was at Colditz, where he received a Red Cross Parcel from Ella van Heemstra, an old Dutch acquaintance, to whom he repaid the favour upon release, thus helping van Heemstra through the food shortages of 1945/6 and supplying her with cigarettes which she could barter for penicillin to treat her seriously ill daughter. Her daughter was Audrey Hepburn.

It is a strange, small world we live in, and one which has long been more intertwined than many would imagine. This anthology shows some of the long history of interaction between speakers of English and German, from when

Henry Wotton called what was spoken in Germany "the cousin-german to the English", hinting at a very common past, through to the present day.

A brief word on language to close: given the sheer variety of the texts in terms of the time at which they were written and according to which (lack of) rules of orthography, I have refrained from standardizing them to the greatest possible extent. To enhance readability, I have changed some letters in the oldest extracts (e.g. old-type v to u, f to s) and occasionally adapted punctuation (many nineteenth-century authors use long dashes in place of full stops). Where authors have made errors, I have tended to leave them, and there are some wild differences in spelling of German places and words; this cornucopia of international errors and adaptations is, as far as I am concerned, all part of the enjoyment.

1

Triple Dutch:
Teutons, Alemans and Germans
1589 - 1700

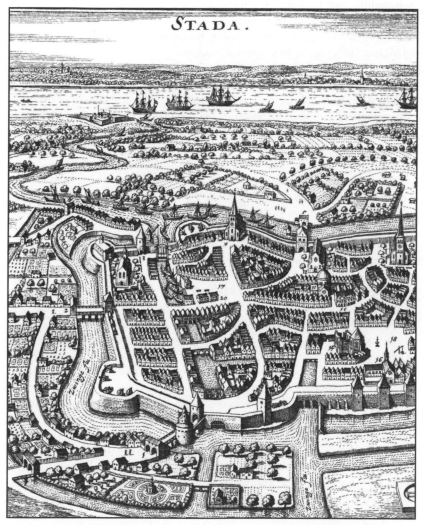

Once a major maritime metropolis, Stade today is a sleepy commuter town near its one-time commercial rival, Hamburg.

AT THE END of the Middle Ages, what we today call Germany was part of the much larger Holy Roman Empire, an entity at once as monolithic as it was messy, as powerful as it was vulnerable. Composed of hundreds of states, principalities and fiefdoms, the empire that covered so much of Central Europe was frequently consumed by internecine squabbles between royal houses, a state of affairs that had only been made worse by the Reformation of 1517, initiated by Martin Luther in the heartlands of Saxony.

The religious schism came on top of a range of regional allegiances and rivalries which produced almost continuous rebellion and low-level conflict, as well as often explosive economic town-country inequality: there was the 1523 peasants' revolt in Frisia, for example, followed by the much larger German peasants' war in the south in 1524. These uprisings flowed seamlessly into the religious fighting which went on until the Peace of Augsburg in 1555. Serious violence broke out again in the 1580s around Cologne as competing archbishops of opposing religious allegiance were elected. Soon the competing kingdoms of Palatinate and Bavaria were joining in, and within the year most of Europe was involved in what became a proxy war fought between Spain on one side and England and the Dutch provinces on the other. This kind of spiralling conflict foreshadowed that great Armageddon of early-modern Europe, the Thirty Years' War, which would lay waste to Germany between 1618 and 1648.

At the Birth of Travel Writing

If there is one thing all readers of travellers' accounts are looking for, it is adventure. Whether these are adventures of the more sedate kind, such as Peter Mayle losing a few days' extra pay to wiley Provençal builders, or of the more extreme physical variety found in the stories of explorers such as Shackleton: a travel story without some form of undesired or unforeseen event is about as much use as a cart without wheels.

The writings of the four Englishmen we shall accompany into seventeenth-century Germany are certainly not without adventure. The thin strip of sea separating England from continental Europe was, at the time, far from mastered: travellers across the Channel were pitted both against the elements and against hostile ships. Meanwhile, the sweeping lands of Germany were often filled with renegade soldiers between jobs as mercenaries in another internal mini-war, thieving bandits armed with their cast-off weaponry, or crooked locals ready to take foreign folk for all they were worth.

Just before the dawn of the seventeenth century in 1589, Henry Wotton (b.

1568), travelling at the age of 21 in preparation for a diplomatic career, was forced to circumnavigate Bremen due to marauding mercenaries and feared for his safety more than once on his way to commence his studies in Heidelberg. He was nevertheless lucky enough to experience a swift and pleasant Channel crossing—afeat unusual enough for him to comment on in the letter he sent to his brother.

However, Fynes Moryson (b. 1566), travelling in 1591, needed eight days at sea just to get to Heligoland, some of this time under pursuit by pirates. He spent the following decade on endless peregrinations through Europe, which he later made the subject of *An Intinerary*, published in 1617. Moryson is considered by many scholars to be the first English writer to have travelled with no other purpose than to record the observations he made on his journey—or, in other words, to be the first travel writer in English literature.

Thomas Coryat (or Coryate, b. 1577), a member of the court to the eldest son of James I, was also a pioneer of the idea of the travelogue as an end in itself. True to his age, his *Crudities* of 1611 actually begin with nothing other than a rustic description of an awful Channel crossing: "I was imbarked at Dover... and arrived in Calais about five of the clocke in the afternoon, after I had varnished the exterior parts of the ship with the excrementall ebullitions of my tumultuous stomach, as desiring to satiate the gormandizing paunches of the hungry Haddcocks."

Ironically enough for the self-styled "Thames water poet" John Taylor (b. 1578), his aquatic adventures of 1620 do not take place in English waters. Taylor, taking the idea of the travelogue a step further, persuaded subscribers to pay in advance to read about a journey he was planning to make. One such trip recorded in *Taylor his travels* was to Prague, and on the journey back he and an English widow were forced to steer their vessel a few hundred miles down the Elbe by themselves after their boatman jumped ship just before Dresden.

Germany: A New Word for an Old Place

Taylor's boatman fled because his ruler, the Duke of Bohemia, was at war against Saxony. This incident is revealing of the state of Germany at that time in two ways: firstly, it was a collection of princedoms, duchies and city states that were continuously squabbling, politicking and fighting among themselves; secondly, Germany was an ill-defined and ever-changing geographic entity, and would essentially remain so until 1990.

Taylor did not at any point use the name Germany, something of a neologism at the time, or mention the Czechs, speaking simply of Bohemia, Saxony and the various bishoprics and dukedoms he crosses along the way. Writing one hundred years later, however, Mary Wortley Montagu (see Chapter 2) would even include

Bohemia and Prague under the title of Germany. Meanwhile, Henry Wotton mixed and matched various spellings of Germanie/Germanye with older words such as Allemaign, while calling the language "Dutch", which he divides into High and Low.

In the seventeenth century speakers of the dialects in what are today northern Germany and the Netherlands referred to their mutually intelligible language as "Low Dutch" while those in the south called their tongue "High Dutch", all using some variant of the modern word *Deutsch*. For a long time this usage also influenced English words for the German language and, by extension, Germany: in his *Instructions and Directions for Forren Travell* of 1650, for example, James Howell refers to the language as "German", "Teutonique" and "Dutch" within the space of one page. It was only much later in the seventeenth century, when the Union of Utrecht had become a truly distinct political entity, that English speakers stopped considering the Netherlands part of Germany and stopped, oddly enough, referring to the rest of the continent's German speakers as "Dutch".

This indistinctness is why, in the extracts below, Taylor records distances in "Dutch miles" and Fynes Moryson refers to "Dutch Inns" at Stade, about a hundred miles away from today's Netherlands. On the topic of inns, Thomas Whythorne, who wrote in the 1570s about his travels in Europe, describes the "vice of drunkenness I perceived to reign as well in Germany, and high Alman as in the low Duchland." In the seventeenth century Germany could be anything from Amsterdam and Antwerp to Augsburg and the Alps—but was known, then as now, as an excellent destination for drinkers.

*

Henry Wotton, *Letters*

Stade, Nov. 1, 1589

My ever most dear Brother,

Here are my first commendations out of Germany, which I send you with a soul that wishes you, and all those that wish you well, the world's perfect happiness. I have at this present lesser time than mind to write, and yet so much of both as shall let you understand briefly how it runs with me. I departed London the day of my last letter's date unto you, to Leigh, where I lay four days for a south-west; and then blew the wind so light and fair, as the fourth day following, which was the 28th of October, we made good the coast of Germanie. Our passage I thank God was pleasant and safe; and what it is to be sick at the sea I cannot tell you, besides some two or three odd qualms, with their appurtenances. I have, since my arrival, lived in this town Stode[1] three days, where there is nothing to be had but alla borso alla borsa. My stay hath been merely for want of company, which I now have gotten to my farthest desire, and am travelling toward Basill this 2nd of November. I determined once to have passed to Bremen, there to fall into the acquaintance of Doctor C. Piscelius, the principle divine in all Germanye, but the Malcontents come often up and sweep the stakes by the way, and a younger brother's ransom is twenty thousand crowns – this caused a great variation in my compass. I have, since I came hither, seen a great piece of justice done upon certain witches; their manner of arraignment did much differ from England; their death was all one. This town is able, out of his own provision, to refute fifty Mr. Reginold Scotts.

(…)

The dearest thing and most pinching that I find is drink, 2d. sterling the poor pint of English beer. But my hope is that the change of the English mercanteria from Antwerpe hither, hath raised the price; and so in the higher country I shall find it fallen, where it is less desired and used. I laugh at many things, and especially at the women, which, believe me, are the most pitifully attired of any creatures since the fall of Adam. The clowns here are scarce animalia; all possessed with so not-understanding a spirit, as the best taught of them cannot make a leg. My High Dutch is yet very Low; but it comes so near my reach, as I find the tongue of the Germans to be cousin-german to the English.

(…)

Heidelberg, Dec. 14, 1589

I am at this present 14th of December at Heidelberge, unto which place I came the 26th of November. The cause of my coming so late in the month hither is this: upon the 1st of November I departed Stoade with two English, bound for Venice, and an High Allemaign, whose farthest was to Erdforde; we kept together up the countrys as far as Brunswick, the chief city under the Duke of that name. Thither came we on the 5th of November. That town divided us; the three taking to Norremberge, and myself, the fourth open to accept all occasion to Franckforde. But here fortune crossed my hasty spirit, and laid a pause upon me of eight days. All the coaches and company for Franckforde were gone the day before; and I must live there and expect my chance, or hire a coach for my single self. I could bargain to no price under twenty-six dollars, in English money 5li. 15s. 8d. The sum was full of persuasion to make me stay, which I did

---

[1] Today a forgotten backwater in Hamburg's commuter belt, Stade (variously Stode and Stoade in seventeenth-century English) was once a harbour of considerable importance; all English trade passed through the port and English currency was accepted everywhere. Its harbour became too small for newer ships in the course of the 1700s and this lack of strategic importance meant that the beautiful old town survived the conflicts of the twentieth century happily unscathed.

eight full days; and then found I two companions good for nothing but to take down the price of travel; believe me, my dear brother, two of the worst natures in the worst part of Germanye, and against whom I had nothing to keep myself safe, but to imagine them to be worse than they were. Their company, with all their ills, brought the twenty-six dollars to eight; so casting my expense in the time of my resting – which came to two dollars and one half – I find myself wealthier than I should have been by fifteen dollars and a half. When we came to Franckforde, my companions did me the pleasure to let me alone, and so I cast about for new company, but could find nine in two days. And a worse ill, every meal stands a traveller in the third of a dollar in that town. This made me hire a coach myself alone, rather than multiply my charges by sitting still. My way was short, for I came to Heydleberge in two days; and yet did that cost me largely as much as any five days before.

(…)

I have apparelled and booked myself, and am in this wiser than I was before, that I have hitherto been afool, and am to begin the world at one and twenty, with more settled care of my life. We have in this place three Professors of Law, all doctors; they read twelve times every week, and we have twice disputations. The doctors teach so as we may weigh every syllable. I am of this opinion that a student in the Laws of five years beyond the seas, may leave a doctor in England of ten years behind, if there be an equality of wit in both. In this place how long I shall live I cannot assure you (my most dear brother) – this persuade yourself, my mind is from all changeableness free.

Fynes Moryson, *An Itinerary*

At last, in the beginning of the yeere 1591, and upon the first day of May, I tooke ship at Liegh, distant from London twenty eight miles by land, and thirtie six by water, where Thames in a large bed is carried into the Sea. Thence we set saile into the maine, and the eight day of our sailing, the Merchants Fleet of sixteene ships being dispersed by a fogge and tempest, two Dunkerke Pirats followed our ship, till (by Gods mercy) the fog being cleared after some few houres, and two of our ships upon our discharging of a great Peece drawing towards us, the Pirates despairing left to pursue us. That they were Pirates was apparant, since as wee for triall turned our sayles, they likewise fitted themselves to our course, so as wee though flying, yet prepared our selves to fight, till God thus delivered us. The ninth day towards night, wee fell upon an Iland called the Holy-land (vulgarly Heiligland), and not daring to enter the River Elve before the next morning, wee strucke all sayles, and suffered our ship to bee tossed too and fro by the waves all that night, (which Marriners call lying at Hull.) This

Iland hath onely one Port capeable of some sixe ships, in the forme of the Moone decreasing, and lying open to the East. On the North side is a great Rocke, and the rest of the shore is all of high Cliffes. It is subject to the Duke of Holste, and by that title to the King of Denmarke; but the inhabitants are so poore, as they yield no other tribute then stones for the Dukes building. It is in circuit some three miles, and hath about one hundred Families.

The tenth day we entred the River Elve, and landed at Stode. This is an ancient Citie, and one of the Empires free Cities[2], and one of those Sea-Townes, which from the priviledge of traffick with their Neighbours, are called Free Cities (vulgarly Hansteten), but of late was become so poore, as they had sold the priviledge of coyning money, and some like Rights to Hamburg; till the English Merchants removing their seate of trafficke from Hamburg to Stode, it began lately to grow rich, not without the envy and impoverishment of the Hamburgers. In the Dutch Inns I paid for each meale foure Lubeck shillings and an halfe, and in the English Innes eight pence English. In the great winding and troubled Streame of Elve, which ebs and flowes as high as Luneburg, certain Booyes are laid to shew the channels and sholes of the River, and the maintaining of each of them cost 40 pounds yeerely, and of all a thousand pounds at the least, at the common charge of Stode and Hamburg: but after frosts begin, they are taken up, and reserved to the next Spring. Of old when Stode flourished, this charge belonged onely to it, taking some contributions of the other Cities for the same. This free Citie had then chosen the Bishop of Breme for their Protector, and had but small scattered revenewes, to the value of ninety pounds sterling by the yeere; but the soile is so fertile, as they milke their Cowes thrice each day. Of late the Hamburgers had in vaine attempted by Navall forces to forbid the arrivall of the English at Stode, whom as they had grieved having their seate with them, as well with exactions, as with forbidding them free exercise of Religion, so now sometimes by faire treaties, sometimes by force, they laboured to draw backe unto them. Those of Stode have by priviledge the pre-emption and choice of Rhenish Wines passing by them. This Citie might be made strong, if the workes they have begun were perfected. The fields of the North and East sides may bee drowned, and because the high Hilles towards the West and South(though somewhat distant) seemed to threaten danger, they had on those sides raised an high and broad wall of earth, fastned on the out-side with Willowes, in which place an armory for all munitions was built; but the gates of the Citie, for ridiculous ostentations of strength were furnished with Artillery of stone

---

[2] Within the structure of Holy Roman Empire, free cities were not subject to rule by one of the many princedoms and duchies of which it was composed; they were subordinate only to the emperor. Many of the free cities were in turn part of the Hanseatic League, that immensely powerful trading alliance which dominated late medieval northern Europe.

painted over. The territory without the City belongs on the West side to the Bishop of Breame, and on the East side to the Earle of Scheneburg and the Duke of Hoist. From Stode to Hamburg are five miles. In a Waggon hired for five Lubecke shillings each person, wee passed two miles, then crossing the Elve (not without danger in respect of the shallow places and present storme) wee hired another Waggon for foure Lubeck shillings each person, and through thicke woods passed the other three miles to Hamburg. The passage by water to Hamburg had beene much easier, especially for a stranger, and a boat daily passeth from Stode thither in some three hours space, if the winde bee not contrary, wherein each man paies three Lubecke shillings for his passage: but all Passengers without difference of condition must help to rowe, or hire one in his stead, except the winde bee good so as they need not use their Oares; besides that the annoyance of base companions will easily offend one that is any thing nice. (...)

Hamburg is a Free Citie of the Empire, and one of them which (as I said) are called Hans-steten, and for the building and populousnesse is much to be praised. The Senate house is very beautifull, and is adorned with carved statuaes of the nine Worthies. The Exchange where the Merchants meet is a very pleasant place. The Haven is shut up with an iron chaine. The Citie is compassed with a deepe ditch, and upon the East and North sides with a double ditch and wall. Water is brought to the Citie from an Hil distant some English mile, by pipes of wood, because those of lead would be broken by the yce, and these pipes are to bee seene under the bridge, whence the water is convaied by them unto each Citizens house. The Territory of the Citie extendeth a mile or two, and on one side three miles out of the walles. It hath nine Churches and six gates called by the Cities to which they lead. It is seated in a large plaine and a sandy soyle, but hath very fatte pasture ground without. On the South side and some part of the West, it is washed with the River Elve, which also putteth a branch into the Towne, but on the North and somewhat on the East side, the River Alster runneth by towards Stode, and falleth into the Elve. The streets are narrow excepting one which is called Broad-street (vulgarly Breitgasse.) The building is all of bricke (as in all the other Sea-bordering Cities, lying from these parts towards Flanders) and all the beautie of the houses is in the first entrance, having broad and faire gates into a large Hal, the lower part whereof on both sides is used for a Ware-house, and in the upper part lying to the view of the doore, the chiefe houshold-stuffe is placed, and especially their vessell of English Pewter, which being kept bright makes a glittering shew to them that passe by; so as the houses promise more beauty outwardly then they have inwardly. Here I paid each meale foure Lubeck shillings, and one each night for my bed. The Citizens are unmeasurably ill affected to the English, to whom (or to any stranger) it is unsafe to walke out of the gates after noone, for when the common people are once warmed with drinke, they are apt to doe them injury. My selfe one day passing by some that were unloading and telling of Billets, heard them say these words: Wirft den zehenden auff des Englanders kopf, that is, cast the tenth at the Englishmans head. But I and my companions knowing well their malice to the English for the removing their trafficke to Stode, were content to pass by as if we understood them not.

Thomas Coryate, *Coryats crudities*

It is exceeding difficult for a stranger to enter into one of the Germane Princes Courts (as I have before said in my description of Turlowe) except he hath some friend living in the same, which I found verified by mine owne experience at the Count Palatines Court. For I could not possibly be admitted without some speciall and extraordinary favour, which was this. Master Gruterus understanding by my owne report that I was acquainted with our noble Ambassador Sir Henry Wotton then resident with the Signiorie of Venice, the same of whose excellent learning and generose qualities hath greatly spread itselfe in Heidelberg (for there hath he beene heretofore, and honourably entertained at the Princes Court) counselled me to goe to a learned Doctor of the Civill Law dwelling in the City, whose name was Master Lingelfemius, heretofore Tutor to Fredericke the fourth, who was then Count Palatinate when I was in Heidelberg, (can therefore the better able to procure his friend accesse to the Court) and a familiar acquaintance of Sir Henry Wotton. Whereupon I repaired to his house, insinuating my selfe partly with a token from Master Gruterus, and partly by the meanes of Sir Henry Wottons name[3], which was so acceptable unto him, that he entertained me after a very debonair and courteous mancr, and sent one of his men with mee to the Prefect of the Princes Court, who gave me admittance into the Palace; I noted the situation thereof to be very pleasant. For it seated at the South side of the Citie upon the side of an eminent hill, having as sweete an ayre as any Palace whatsoever in all Germanie. (…)

There is a notable thing to be seene in this Palace, the sight whereof it was not myne to enjoy, because I heard nothing of it before I went out of the Palace: a matter of great antiquity. Namely certain ancient stony pillars, in number five, which the Emperor Carolus Magnus above eight hundred and fifty years since brought from the City of Ravenna in Italie, and placed them afterward in his Palace of Ingelheim, a place of high Germany within a few miles of the City of

---

[3] It would appear that, following his studies in Heidelberg, Henry Wotton (above) left behind such a good impression that it was in and of itself a recommendation.

Mentz, where he was borne, and oftentimes kept his Court. The same pillars were of late years removed from the said Ingelheim to Heidelberg by the Prince Philip of whom I have before made mention in my discourse of the Church of the holy Ghost who erected them in this Palace whereof I now speake, and are there shewed for a principall ancient monument to his day.

But some of the Gentlemen of the Princes family did sufficiently recompence my losse of the sight of these ancient pillars by shewing me a certayne peece of worke that did much more please my eies then the sight of those pillars could have done. For it is the most remarkable and famous thing of that kinde that I saw in my whole journey, yea so memorable a matter, that I thinke there was never the like fabric (for that which they showed me was nothing else than a strange kind of fabrick) in all the world, and I doubt whether posterity will ever frame so monstruously strange a thing: it was nothing but a vessel full of wine. Which the Gentlemen of the Court shewed me after they had first conveighed me into divers wine cellars, where I saw a woundrous company of extraordinary great vessels, the greatest part whereof was replenished with Rhenish wine, the totall number containing one hundred and thirty particulars. But the maine vessel above all the rest, that superlative moles unto which I now bend my speech, was shewed me last of all standing alone by it selfe in a wonderfull vast roome. I must needes say I was suddenly strooken with no small admiration upon the first sight thereof. For it is such a stupendous masse (to give it the same epitheton that I have done before to the beauty of St. Marks streete in Venice) that I am persuaded it will affect the gravest and constantest man in the world with wonder. Had this fabric beene extant in those ancient times when the Colossus of Rhodes, the Labryrinth of Ægypt and Creta, the Temple of Diana at Ephesus, the hanging gardens of Semiramis, the Tombe of Mausolus, and the rest of the those decanted miracles did flourish in their principall glory, I thinke Herodotus and Diodorus Siculus would have celebrated this rare worke with the their learned stile as well as the rest, and have consecrated the memory miracle. For indeed it is a kinde of monstrous miracle, and that of the greatest sise for a vessel that this age doth yield in any place whatsoever (as I am verily persuaded) under the cape of heaven, Pardon me I pray thee (gentle Reader) if I am something tedious in discoursing on this huge vessel. For as it was the strangest spectacle that I saw in my travels: so I hope it will not be unpleasant unto thee to read a ful description of all the particular circumstances thereof. (…)

When the Cellerer draweth wine out of the vessel, he ascendeth two severall degrees of wooden staires made in the forme of a ladder which containe seven and twenty steps of rungs as we call them in Somersetshire, made in the forme of a spout, wherewith he draweth up the wine, and so poureth it after a pretty manner into the glasse or &c. out of the same instrument. I myself had experience of this matter. For a Gentleman of the Court accompanied me to the toppe together with one of the Cellerers, and exhilarated me with two sound draughts of Rhenish Wine. For that is the wine that it containeth. But I advise thee gentle reader whatsoever thou art that intendest to travel into Germany, and perhaps to see Heidelberg, and also this vessel before thou commest out of the City: I advise thee (I say) if thou doth happen to ascend to the toppe thereof to the end to tast of the wine; that in any case thou dost drinke moderately, and not so much as the sociable Germans will persuade thee unto. For if thou shouldest chance to over-swill thyselfe with wine, peradventure such a giddinesse wil benumme thy braine, that thou wilt scare finde the direct way downe from the steepe ladder without a very dangerous precipitation.

John Taylor, *Taylor his travels*

Sunday the 26 of Auguste we set sayle from Gravesend and with various windes, some large and some scarce, we happily past the seas, and sayled up the river of Maze, by the Brill, and on the Wednesday following I arrived at Rotterdam in Holland, at which time the worth regiment of the right honourable Colonell Sir Horace Veare, and the two noble Earls of Essex and Oxford departed from thence in Martiall Equipage toward the Pallatinate Country, whose Heroick and Magnanimous endeavours I beseech the Lord of hosts, and God of battells to direct and blesse.

The same day I went to the Hage, and from thence to Leyden, where I lodged all night, and the morrow being thurseday the 30 of August, I sayled from Leyden, to Amstersam, where I saw many things worthy the noting, but because they are so neere and frequent to many of our Nation, I omit to relate them to avoid teadiousnes: but on the friday at night I got passage from thence towards Hambrogh, in a small hoy, in the which wee were weather-beaten at sea three days and nights before wee arrived there.

Saterday the eight of September I left Hambrogh, and being carried day and night in wagons, on the mundasy night following I came to an ancient towne called Heldeshim. Heldesheim, it standeth in Brunswick land, and yet it belongeth to the Bishop of Collin, where I did observe in their Domme Kirke, of Cathedrall Church, a crowne of silver 80 foote in compasse, hanged up in the body of the Church, in the circuit of which crowne were placed 160 wax candles, the which on festival days, or at the celebration of some high ceremonies are lighted to lighten their darknesse, or their ignorance, chuse yee whether.

Moreover there I saw a silver bell in their steeple, of six hundred and 30 l. weight, and the Leades of their steeple, shining and sparkling with the Sun beames, they did affirme to mee to bee gold, the truth of which I am doubtfull of.

In this towne I stayed foure days, and on friday the 14 of September, I went six dutch miles to the strong towne of Brunswick, where by reason of my short stay, which was but two hours, I observed nothing worthy of memory, but their triple walls and double ditches, their artillery and fortifications, which they thinke to be impregnable; besides, there I saw an old house of the Duke of Brunswicke, with the statue of a golden lyon, of a great bignesse, standing aloft upon a piller, with the broken walls, and houses, which the Dukes Cannon hath left there six yeares since, as tokens and badges of his fury and their rebellion.

From thence on the morrow I went one dutch mile further, to an ancient towne called Wolfenbuttle, where the Duke of Brunswicke keeps his court, in the which I and my fellow could get no further admittance, then over a bridge into his outermost, or base court; for his soldiers, seeing us with swords and pistols, were fearefull, belike, that wee would have taken the fortresse from them, and therefore though wee were but two Englishmen, yet they durst not let us enter, which made mee call to rememberance the frequent, and dayly egresse and regresse, that all people and nations have to his Majesty royal Court of great Brittaine, where none that are of any good fashion or aspect are debar'd entrance: when those inferior Princes houses are garded with hungry Halbediers, and reverend rusty bil-men, with a brace or two of hot shots, so that their palaces are more like prisons then the free & noble courts of commanding potentates.

After two days entertainement at Wolfunbuttle, with an English Merchant residing there, of good fame and credit, named Master Thomas Saskville, I with my brother, my fellow Tilbery, and another man in my company departed from thence on foote onward on our journey towards Bohemia, in which travel, what occurrences happened, and what things of note I saw were as followeth. Passing with many weary steps, through the townes of Rofondink, Remling, Sootem, Hessen, Darlum and Halverstadt, which is all in Brunswicke land, but this towne of Halverstadt[4] belong to a Bishop so stiled, who is Duke Christian brother to the now Duke of Brunswick, a long dutch mile (or almost six English) is a small towne or a Bleck called Groning belonging to the Duke, in the which place I observed two things worthy of remembrance.

First a most stately Pallace with a beautiful Chappell, so adorned with the image and forms of Angells and Cherubins, with such quantities of arcs, with such industry of carving, graving, guilding, painting and paving, with such

---

4 Today Halberstadt, this once thriving market town has had, like Stade, the good fortune of being superseded by its neighbours. It survived the Second World War intact and years of neglect in communist East Germany left it gloriously unimproved.

superexcellent workmanship of organes, pulpit and font, that for curiosity and admirable rarenesse, all the buildings, and fabricks that ever I beheld, must give it preheminence. I confesse that Henry the Sevenths Chappell at Westminster, Kings Colledge Chappell in Cambridge, and Christs Church in Canterbury, are beyond it in heigh and workmanship of stone: for indeed this Chappell is most of wood gipps, and plaster of Parris; but it is so guilded as if it had bin made in the golden age, when gold was estemmed as drosse, so that a man had need to weare a vaile over his dazeling eyes, or else he can hardly looke upon it.

The carving and painting seeme to outgo the arts of Pigmalion, Apelles, or Praxiteles; the paving of chequered blacke and white marble, and the windows glassed with Christall: but all this great cost and shew is very little to the honor of God, or the propagation of the Ghospel, the edification of the ignorant. For in this Chappell of case, there is Service. If the painted pulpit could preach, the dumbe images might (perhaps) have a sermon now and then; for scarce at any time there comes any body into the Chappell, but a fellow that shewes the beauty of it for two pence or three pence apiece.

In the same house, in a place or celler built of purpose, is a great tonne or vessel of wood, that was 7 years in making, and hath used to befilled with Rhenish wine: it is sayd to bee twiece as bigge as the vessel at Heidelberg, and the hoopes of it are twelve inches thick, and the staves or bordes of it being as much: I went up to the top of it, with a ladder of 18 stepps, hee that keeps it faith it will hold 160 tonnes. My fellow Tilbery did creepe in at the tap hole; it is in length 32 foote, and in breadth acrosse 19, and verily I thinke that bable cost more mony the making, then would have built a good ship, or founded an almes house for 6 poore people.

(…)

From Groning wee travelled to a towne called Albers Leaven, to Albeleaven, to Kinderne, to Hall, and so to Leipzig, which is one of the chiefest townes in Saxony, being famous for a yearely Mart that is yearely held there, where to Merchantes and other people from the most part of Christendom have annual concourse: in this towne we stayd two days, and taking our leave then of some English Merchants, who used us kindly, we there would have hired a coach or wagon to Prague, but all Saxon coach-men and carters were afraid to looke upon any part of Bohemia, because their Duke is a profest enemy in armes against the Kind of Beame, so that we were forced to hire a fellow with a wheelebarrow two days to carry our cloakes, swords, guns, pistols, and other apparel and luggage which were our necessaries, to a towne called Boorne, to Froburge, and so to another towne called Penigh, where wee cashierd our one-wheel'd coach, and hired a cart with two, which carried both us and our baggage to Chemniut another towne in Saxony, from whence to a place called Shop, wee were faine to bee our owne sumpter horses, walking on foote to the last towne in Saxony, called Marienburg.

(…)

Thus having stayd in Prague almost 3. weekes, I returned from thence homeward, on Tuesday, the 26 of September, having in my company three Gentlemen, a widow (and foure small children) whose husband being an English man, and the Kings Brewer for Beere, deceased, and was buried there in Prague whilst I was there: the good desolate woman having received reward after seven years service there and at Heidelberg, being desirous to retire to her countrey (England) came with us, with my brother , and my fellow Tilberry. We tooke two Coaches at the Castle of Prague, & in a day and halfe, we were carried seven Duch miles, to a Towne in Bohemia (standing on the river of Elve) called Leutmeritz, at which Towne we all layd our moneys together, and bought a boate of 48. Foote in length, and not 3 foote in bredth, and because we did not know the river, wee hired a Bohemian waterman to guide us 15. dutch miles, to the Towne of Dreason in Saxony. But 4. miles short of that Towne, which was the first Towne in the Saxon Countrey, called Pirne, where we were stayed 5. houres without the gates, til such time as the Burgamaster wold be pleased to examin us: in the meane space our waterman (not daring to abide the terrible trial of examination, because the Duke of Saxon was in Armes against the King of Beame) hee ran away, and left us to bring the boate downe the river, 600. English miles our selves to Hamburgh.

But not to close up all, I will relate what rare dyet, excellent cookery, and sweete lodging we had in our journey in Germany: first for our comfort, after very hard getting of houseroome, our lodgings was every night in straw, where lying together well littered, we honestly always left our sheetes behind us: then at our suppers at table square, and so broad, that two men can hardly shake hands over it, we being some twelve about it, Our first dish being a raw cabbadge, of the quantity of halfe a packe, cut and chopped small, with the fat of resty bacon powred upon it instead of oil; which dish must be emptied before we could get any more: Our second dish perhaps, a peck of boylde Apples and honey, the Apples being boyled skins, stalkes, cores, and all: Thirdly, 100. Gudgeons, newly taken perhaps, yet as salt as if they had beene three years pickled, or twice at the East Indies, boyled with scales, guts and all, and buried in Ginger like sawdust: a fresh pike as salt as brine, boyled in flat milke, with a pound of Garlick. This was the manner of the most part of our dyet; and if we did aske them why they did salt their meate so unreasonably, their answere was, that their beer could not be consumed, except their meat were salted extraordinarily.

2 From Berlin to Coswig:
New Pomp and Old Squalor
1700 - 1800

When not expanding Prussian territory, the Francophile philosopher King Frederick the Great liked nothing better than to play the flute at his imposing Sanssouci Palace in Potsdam.

ONCE THE DUST of the Thirty Years' War in Europe and the Civil War in England had finally settled somewhat towards the end of the 1600s, both Germany and Britain had changed drastically. On the Continent, the fragile balance of power between the German states making up the Holy Roman Empire had been shattered once and for all, to the benefit of big and the detriment of the small. What had before been a generally pluralistic grouping of states and territories started to coalesce ever more around two poles at opposite ends of the compass: Habsburg Austria in the south and Hohenzollern Prussia in the north.

During the Thirty Years' War, Prussia had been nothing more than a small duchy under the Swedish crown in what is today Lithuania and the Russian enclave of Kaliningrad. It was acquired in 1657 by the Elector of Brandenburg, the area around Berlin, in no small part due to the fact that it lay outside the Holy Roman Empire; as such, it was a territory of which an ambitious monarch nonplussed by the idea of being the subject of the Holy Roman Emperor might one day crown himself king. In 1701 his son Frederick did just that, albeit under the caveat imposed by the Hapsburg emperor that he be King *in* Prussia rather than *of*. Over the course of the century Brandenburg swallowed up the surrounding territories while Prussia crept steadily westwards through Polish lands. Under Frederick the Great (b. 1712) Prussia grabbed Silesia from Hapsburg Austria and became powerful enough for Frederick to crown himself King *of* Prussia in 1772.

Yet while Prussia's military rise was meteoric, its economy remained comparatively weak, and far wealthier areas of Germany too suffered under the continuous infighting. By the end of the eighteenth century Bavaria was exhausted from fighting Austria, while Saxony, having spent years as an unfortunate buffer zone between the latter and Prussia, was battered and impoverished. The smaller bishoprics, electorates and principalities along the Rhine, meanwhile, were weak and divided by bickering, making them attractive pickings for an increasingly rapacious France.

The British Isles at the beginning of the eighteenth century, on the other hand, were fast becoming the powerhouse of Europe: the differences between England and Scotland were settled, the Enlightenment was getting underway and a new, sophisticated writing style emerged for the purposes of the growing coffee house literati of London.

Men of Letters

Almost all travel writing about Germany in the eighteenth century comes in the form of correspondence between London society figures. Joseph Addison (b. 1672) was typical of the new type of travel writer: touring Europe on a royal stipend with a view to becoming a diplomat, Addison was an educated gentleman who took advantage of the new channels of postal communication across the Continent. Whereas only a hundred years before the likes of Moryson and Coryate had not written up their experiences until their return from years of comparative isolation abroad (and producing sprawling, baroque compendia) there is something distinctly more modern about the crisp style and everyday chatter of Addison's letters back from Germany in 1703.

Mary Wortley Montagu (b. 1762), too, writing letters back to England in 1716, nonchalantly mixed small talk about London society with descriptions of what she saw on her way through Germany bound for Turkey, where her husband was to take up his position as an ambassador to the Ottoman Empire. Often credited as the first woman travel writer in the English language, Montagu's *Letters from Turkey* created a sensation when circulated after her return to England in 1718.

Another author accompanying someone on a diplomatic mission to the East was David Hume (b. 1711). As an assistant to a Scottish general on the latter's journey to Vienna in 1747, he took almost exactly the same route as Montagu, cutting straight through Germany as the quickest route to south-eastern Europe. Despite the already rather mundane nature of international letter writing, Hume clearly saw it as his duty to pack his missives full of serious reportage.

Such was the all-pervasiveness of letters in educated eighteenth-century circles that even diaries, too, often read like well-composed correspondence. Hume's countryman James Boswell's (b. 1740) journal, kept while he was in Germany in 1764, for example, has a distinctly epistolary taste to it. Even the odd intimate thought about his fight with depression would not seem out of place in a letter to a loved-one.

The letters of David Garrick (b. 1717) to his brother, also of 1764, are more cheerful—and far more banal—in tone. Travelling in his late forties with his German wife, Eva Marie Veigel, Garrick comments as much on what one might call the "inconveniences" of his journey as on the places he passes through. Garrick's wife was one of the early health tourists, returning through her home country from a spell in Italy; as we shall see in later chapters, countless German towns would soon be attracting the sickly and wealthy to take a "cure" in their waters, a trend which would go on to inspire works of imaginative fiction.

Yet in the eighteenth century writing about Germany remains entirely dominated by letters. Even the growing class of those who actually earned their living from writing, such as John Moore (b. 1729), preferred the letter format to all others: although his *A View of Society and Manners in France, Switzerland and Germany* (1780) was aimed at his broad readership, it was composed in the form of letters personally addressed to the reader.

As was Nathaniel Wraxall's (b. 1751) *Memoir of the Courts of Berlin, Dresden, Warsaw and Vienna,* published in 1799 on the basis of a trip made in 1778. This was, after all, the epoch of the epistolary novel, an age in which readers were considered more likely to believe an account—or believe in a story—if it appeared as correspondence.

Petty Princes and Courageous Kings

Indeed, Germany in the 1700s was home to some sights that would have already become quite unbelievable to British readers. With the power of the monarchy severely reined in following the English Civil War, the writers of the eighteenth century were experiencing unheard civil freedom—and gaining the self-confidence to match it. Even in David Hume's barbed comment that the Germans' situation is "not very much inferior to the English, notwithstanding all the Airs the latter give themselves," there is still tacit recognition of the progress made in Britain. Even if many Germans did enjoy some freedom, they enjoyed it, as John Moore observes, at the absolute mercy of their rulers, and as both Hume and Boswell recount, rulers could not always be relied upon to spend wisely.

Lady Montagu, too, becomes aware of the geographical lottery affecting eighteenth-century Germans: in the free cities she sees prosperity and contentedness, while the smaller princedoms are impoverished, desperate and intimidated by foolish leaders. Moore's encounter with the Margrave of Baden, however and, to some extent, Wraxall's observations concerning Frederick the Great of Prussia show the seductive side of successful enlightened absolutism.

Frederick's capital Berlin is the big story in the eighteenth century. Made capital of Prussia in 1701, Berlin began the century as an unimportant town in an area considered to be a barren wasteland, but finished it as the gleaming new capital of Europe's most triumphant new kingdom. If Germany before Berlin had been considered quaint and outdated, a land of higgledy-piggledy houses, Holy Roman Emperors and comedy-sized vats of wine, Berlin's classicizing grandeur showed that there was no reason why a European power of the distinctly modern sort could not arise here.

*

Joseph Addison, *Letters*
(31) To George Stepney

Dresden, Sunday, 3rd January, 1703

Sir,

If I trouble you with another Letter so soon after my last you must impute it to the frequency of the favours I receive from you. It is to them we owe all the pleasures we find at Dresden as well as what we met with at Vienna. Since our leaving Prague we have seen nothing but a great varietie of Winter pieces, so that all the account I can give you of the country is that it abounds very much in snow. If it has any other beauties in it this is not a time of year to look for 'em when almost everything we see is of the same colour and scarce any thing we meet with except our sheets and napkins that is not White. I find very little difference in the Straw-beds of Saxony and Bohemia. About three nights ago we had the honour of a Cow for chamber-fellow that bore with our company for the convenience of a stove. We are very seldom without the company of a cock that roosts under the same Roof and has bin as troublesome to us as ever he was to St. Peter.

(32) To Charles Finch, Third Earl of Winchelsea

Hamburg, March 1703

My Lord,

I can no longer deny my-self the honour of troubling your Lordship with a Letter tho Hamburg has yet furnish me with very few materials for it. The great Business of the place is commerce and Drinking: as their chief commoditie, at least which I am best acquainted with, is Rhenish wine. This they have in such prodigious Quantities that there is yet no sensible dimunition of it tho Mr Perrot and my-self have bin among 'em above a Week. The principal curisotie of the town and what is more visited than any other I have met with in my Travails is a great cellar filld with this kind of Liquor. It holds more Hogsheads than others can bottles and I believe is capable of receiving into it a whole Vintage of the Rhine. By this cellar stands the little English Chappel which your Lordship may well suppose is not all-together soe much frequented by our Countrymen as the other. I must however do 'em Justice as they are all of 'em Loyal Sons of the Church of England to assure your Lordship that her Majestie can have no Subjects in any part of her Dominions that pray more heartily for her Health or drink to it oftener. We are this Evening to take a Bottle with Mr Wyche and Strafford. To draw us in they tell us it shall be my Lord Winchelsea's Health. I dare not let you know, My Lord, how often we have already made this an Excuse for a meeting least at the same time that I would show our Zeal for your lordship I should give you a very small opinion of our Sobrietie: But as all here are extremely disappointed in not having the honour of your company at Hambourg they think this the only way they have left of showing their high Esteem for your Lordship. I hoped my stay at Hambourg would have given me occasion to have written a much Longer Letter but as I can find no better a subject to entertain your Lordship with I am sensible I have already made it too long. I am my Lord with all possible respect Your Lordship's &c.

Mary Wortley Montagu, *Letters*
Letter IV
To the Lady ---

Cologn, August 16, O. S., 1716

If my lady —— could have any notion of the fatigues that I have suffered these two last days, I am sure she would own it a great proof of regard, that I now sit down to write to her. We hired horses from Nimeguen hither, not having the conveniency of the post, and found but very indifferent accommodations at Reinberg[1], our first stage; but it was nothing to what I suffered yesterday. We were in hopes to reach Cologn; our horses tired at Stamel, three hours from it, where I was forced to pass the night in my clothes, in a room not at all better than a hovel; for though I have my bed with me, I had no mind to undress, where the wind came from a thousand places. We left this wretched lodging at day-break, and about six this morning came safe here, where I got immediately into bed. I slept so well for three hours, that I found myself perfectly recovered, and have had spirits enough to go and see all that is curious in the town, that is to say, the churches, for here is nothing else worth seeing. This is a very large town, but the most part of it is old built. The Jesuits church, which is the neatest, was shewed me, in a very complaisant manner, by a handsome young Jesuit; who, not knowing who I was, took a liberty in his compliments and railleries, which very much diverted me. Having never before seen any thing of that nature, I could not enough admire the magnificence of the altars, the rich images of the saints (all massy silver) and the *enchassures* of the relicks; though I could not help murmuring, in my heart, at the profusion of pearls, diamonds, and rubies, bestowed on the adornment of rotten teeth, and dirty rags. I own that I had wickedness enough to covet St Ursula's pearl necklaces; though perhaps this was no wickedness at all, an image not being certainly one's neighbour's; but I went

---

[1] In 1739 Wortley Montagu was to have a vicarious encounter with the almost-homonymous town of Rheinsberg about 300 miles to the east, in Prussia. Along with the English courtier John Hervey, Montagu had become engaged in a bizarre bisexual love-triangle with the colourful Italian intellectual Francesco Algarotti. As she sped towards his home city of Venice in July 1739 hoping to edge out her rival, Algarotti himself was bound for England, from whence he was invited to visit the Crown Prince of Prussia—later Frederick the Great—at his Rheinsberg estate.

yet farther, and wished the wench herself converted into dressing-plate. I should also gladly see converted into silver, a great St Christopher, which I imagine would look very well in a cistern. These were my pious reflections: though I was very well satisfied to see, piled up to the honour of our nation, the skulls of the eleven thousand virgins.[2] I have seen some hundreds of relicks here of no less consequence; but I will not imitate the common stile of travellers so far, as to give you a list of them; being persuaded, that you have no manner of curiosity for the titles given to jaw-bones and bits of worm-eaten wood.—Adieu, I am just going to supper, where I shall drink your health in an admirable sort of Lorrain wine, which I am sure is the same you call Burgundy in London.

Letter V
To the Countess ---

Nuremberg, August 22, O. S., 1716

After five days travelling post, I could not sit down to write on any other occasion, than to tell my dear lady, that I have not forgot her obliging command, of sending her some account of my travels. I have already passed a large part of Germany, have seen all that is remarkable in Cologn, Frankfort, Wurtsburg, and this place. 'Tis impossible not to observe the difference between the free towns and those under the government of absolute princes, as all the little sovereigns of Germany are. In the first, there appears an air of commerce and plenty. The streets are well-built, and full of people, neatly and plainly dressed. The shops are loaded with merchandise, and the commonalty are clean and cheerful. In the other you see a sort of shabby finery, a number of dirty people of quality tawdered out; narrow nasty streets out of repair, wretchedly thin of inhabitants, and above half of the common sort asking alms. I cannot help fancying one under the figure of a clean Dutch citizen's wife, and the other like a poor town lady of pleasure, painted and ribboned out in her head-dress, with tarnished silver-laced shoes, a ragged under-petticoat, a miserable mixture of vice and poverty. They have sumptuary laws in this town, which distinguish their rank by their dress, prevent the excess which ruins so many other cities, and has a more agreeable effect to the eye of a stranger, than our fashions. I need not be ashamed to own, that I wish these laws were in force in other parts of the world.

David Hume, *Letters*

Cologne 23rd March, 1747

We came hither last Night & have travelled thro an extreme Pleasant Country

---

[2] The first of several references to this gory relic; both Thackeray and Gaskell comment on it in the next chapter. The authors' estimates of the precise number of skulls vary wildly.

along the Banks of the Rhine. Particularly Cleves, which belongs to the King of Prussia, is very agreeable, because of the Beauty of the Road, which are Avenues bordered with fine Trees. The Land in that Province is not fertile but is well cultivated. The Bishoprick of Cologne is more fertile &adorn'd with fine Woods as well as Cleves. The Country is all very populous, the Houses good & the Inhabitants well cloath'd& well fed. This is one of the largest Cities in Europe, being near a League in Diameter: The Houses are all high: And there is no Interval of Gardens or Fields. So that you wou'd expect it must be very populous. But it is not so. It is extremely decay'd, & is even falling to ruin. Nothing can strike one with more melancholy than its Appearance where there are Marks of past Opulence & Grandeur, but such present Waste & Decay, as if it had lately escap'd a Pestilence or Famine. We are told, that it was formerly the Centre of all the Trade of the Rhine, which has been since remov'd to Holland, Liege, Frankfort & c. Here we see the Rhine in its natural State; being only a little higher (but no broader) on account of the melting of the Snows. I think it is as broad as from the Foot of your House to the opposite Banks of the River.

Bonne, 24th March

This is, about six Leagues from Cologne, a pleasant well-built little Town, upon the Banks of the Rhine, and is the Seat of the Archbishop. We have bestow'd half a day in visiting his Palace, which is an extensive magnificent Building; & he is certainly the best lodg'd Prince in Europe except the King of France. For, besides this Palace, & a sort of Maison de Plaisance near it (the most elegant thing in the World), he has also two country Houses very magnificent. He is the late Emperor's brother; and is, as they say, a very fine Gentleman; a man of Pleasure, very galant& gay: he has always at his Court a Company of French Comedians and Italian Singers. And as he always keeps out of Wars, being protected by the Sacredness of his character, he has nothing to hope & nothing to fear; and seems to be the happiest prince in Europe. However, we cou'd wish he took a little more care of his high Ways, even tho his Furniture, Pictures, & Building were a little less elegant. We are got into a Country where we have no Fires but Stoves; and no covering but Featherbeds. Neither of which I like, both of them are too warm and suffocating.

Coblentz, 26th March

We have made the pleasantest Journey in the World in two days from Bonne to this Town. We travel all along the Banks of the Rhine; sometimes in open, beautiful, well cultivated Plains: At another time sunk betwixt high Mountains, which are only divided by the Rhine, the finest River in the World: One of these Mountains is always covered with Wood to the Top; the other with Vines:

And the Mountain is so steep, that they are obligd to support the Earth by Walls, which rise one above the other like Terrasses, to the length of forty or fifty Stories. Every Quarter of a Mile, (indeed as often as there is any flat Bottom or Foundation), you meet with a handsome Village, situated in the most romantic manner in the World. Surely there never was such an Assemblage of the wild and cultivated Beauties in one Scene. There are also several magnificent Convents and Palaces to embellish the Prospects. This is a very thriving well built Town situated at the Confluence of the Moselle & the Rhine, & consequently very finely situated. Over the former River, there is a handsome Stone Bridge: Over the latter, a flying Bridge; which is a boat, fixd by a Chain: This Chain is fixt by an Anchor to the bottom of the middle of the River far above, & is supported by seven little Boats placd at Intervals that keep it along the surface of the Water. By means of the Rudder, they turn the head of the large Boat to the opposite Bank & the Current of the River carriers it over of itself. It goes over in about 4 Minutes, and will carry four or five hundred People. It stays about five or six Minutes, and then returns: Two Men are sufficient to guide it; And it is certainly a very pretty Machine. There is the like at Cologne. This Town is the common Residence of the Archbishop of Treves; who has here a pretty magnificent Palace. We have now travelld along a great Part of that Country, thro which the Duke of Marlborough marchd up his Army, when he led them into Bavaria. Tis of this Country, Mr Addison speaks when he calls the People Nations of Slaves, by Tyranny debas'd: Their Makers Image more than half defacd. And he adds that the Soldiers were *Hourly instructed, as they urge their Toyl, To prize their Queen & love their native Soil.* If any Foot Soldier cou'd have more ridiculous national prejudices than the Poet, I shou'd be much surprised. Be assurd, there is not a finer Country in the World; nor are there any Signs of Poverty among the People. But John Bull's Prejudices are ridiculous; as his Insolence is intolerable.

Frankfort, 28th March
Our road from Coblentz to this passes thro' a great many Princes Territories: Nassau, Hesses, Badens, Mentz& this Republic &c. And there is as great a Diversity in the Nature of the Country. The first Part of the Road from Coblentz to Weis-Baden is very mountainous & woody: But populous & well cultivated: In many places, the Snow is lying very thick. The Road is disagreeable for a Coach. Sometimes you go along the Side of a Hill with a Precipice below you, & have no an Inch to spare; & the Road hanging all the Way towards the Precipice; so that one had need to have a good Head to look out of the Windows. Nassau, the Prince of Orange's Capital, is but a Village, & one of the most indifferent I have seen in Germany. Betwixt Weis Baden & Frankfort we travel along the Banks of the Maine, & see one of the finest Plains in the World. I never saw such

rich Soil, nor better cultivated; all in corn & sown Grass. For we have not met with any natural Grass in Germany. Frankfort is a very large Town, well built & of great Riches & Commerce. Around it, there are several little Country Houses of the Citizens the first of that kind we have seen in Germany: For every body except the Farmers, live here in Towns. And these dwell all in Villages. Whether this be for Company, or Protection, or Devotion, I cannot tell: But it certainly has its Inconveniences.

(…)

The Danube, 7th April

Thus we have finished a very agreeable Journey of 860 Miles (For so far is Vienna from the Hague.) I have past thro many a Prince's Territories, & have had more Masters than many of these Princes have Subjects. Germany is undoubtedly a very fine Country, full of industrious honest People: & were it united, it would be the greatest Power that ever was in the world. The common People are here, almost everywhere, much better treated, & more at their Ease, than in France: and are not very much inferior to the English, notwithstanding all the Airs the latter give themselves. There are great Advantages in travelling, & nothing serves more to remove Prejudices; for I confess I had entertained no such advantageous Idea of Germany; and it gives a Man of Humanity Pleasure to see that so considerable a Part of Mankind as the Germans are in so tolerable a Condition.

James Boswell, *The Journal of his German and Swiss Travels*

Wednesday 4th July, 1764

At nine the Inspecteur of the gallery at Sans Souci waited on me & I carried him in a coach to the Retreat of the Great Frederic. The King has here apartments for himself & four friends. The Building is light and elegant. But the Gallery is truly superb. It is very long very lofty & very richly finished. The Collection of Pictures is not as yet very numerous, but they are all fine pieces, and I was told by Lord Marischal that there is not a better collection in one place. I was unlucky enough to be gloomy, & could not relish this rich scene as Boswell himself relishes Beauty. I speculated on the ennui of terrestrial existence. I waited on Lord Marischal, who, as one of the King's particular friends, is lodged here. I then saw the foundation of an immense Palace which the King is building near this. I returned to Potsdam, din'd quiet, journalised and walked & chatted till Bedtime.

Thursday 5th July

I hired Post-Horses for My Lord's Coach, & set out free and happy to conduct Madame de Froment to Berlin. We had a pleasant jaunt, & arrived about two at *Rufin's* in the *Post Straas*. Here we found M. de Froment, a lively frenchman pretty much mellowed, and Lieutenant Lauchlan Macpherson late of Frazer's Highlanders. He is son to Breckachie. He is a fine, honest, spirited fellow. We dined & then I drest& Macpherson accompanied me to Mr. Mitchel's the British envoy, & to my Bankers; but we found none of them at home. I was struck with the Beauty of Berlin. The Houses are handsom and the streets wide long and straight. The Palace is grand. The Palaces of some of the Royal family are very genteel. The Opera-House is an elegant Building, with this Inscription: Fridericus Rex Apollini et Musis. At night we sauntered in a sweet walk under a grove of Chesnut-trees by the side of a beautifull Canal, where I saw a variety of Strangers. The foul fiend fled.[3]

Friday 6th July

I went to my Bankers, and found Mr.Schickler a fine jolly generous fellow and young Splitzerber a good bluff dog; he had been three years in London. He went with me to look for lodgings, but I found none to my mind. He then carried me in his coach to the Campagne of Heer Schickler that is to say a house & Garden. We dined in a handsom Summer-house which projects upon the River, and commands a view of Berlin and it's beautifull vicinity. We were fifteen or Sixteen at table. I was enlivened by seeing the hearty Germans. After being three hours together at table, we played at nine-pins. I then took a tour in Schickler's Boat. At nine we had a cold collation & good wine. Splitzberger carried me home in his elegant coach & sung many English Songs in The Jovial Crew, Artaxerxes etc. I was firm & gay and sound as ever. Am I indeed the dull dog of Utrecht.

Monday 24th September

About noon I arrived at Coswig, the residence of the Prince of Zerbst, who is a strange wrong-headed Being. He has got his troops forsooth to the number of 150 foot and 30 horse, and during the last war, he took a fancy that the King of Prussia was coming to attack him. So, he put in readiness his little Battery of Cannon, and led out his 180 to make head against the armys of Frederic. He was not here at present, but at Vienna, as he has a Regiment in the Austrian Service. So I had no opportunity of paying my court to him. The appearance of his dirty little town, his castle and his Sentinels with Sentry boxes painted in Lozenges of different colours like the stockings of Harlequin diverted me a good deal. I walked about & to have a little German talk I asked every Sentry vie veel troepen hebt der Furst. One Soldier whose head resembled that of his Prince had

---

[3] Here Boswell refers in familiar terms to his depressive nature, which he seems to have shaken off briefly during his summer tour of Germany. As a whole, his diary entries give the impression of a young man captivated by the beauty of the country—and by that of its charming young ladies.

marked me with serious political Attention & dreading that a foreign Spy had got into his Highness's dominions and that a Conspiracy was forming against the state, followed me close & at last when I came to the Grenadier before the Castle-Gate, he laid hold of me charged the Sentry with me, & bringing a Party, conducted me to the Main Guard. I was heartily entertained with this adventure & marched with all the formal composure of a State Prisoner. When I arrived at the Guard, there was a hue & cry around me, as if I had entered a Kennel of Dogs. I could not explain myself well enough in German and stood for some time like the Stag at Bay. At last a Blackguard dog of a Soldier said 'Dominus forsitan loquitur latine.' I told this fellow that I was a Stranger a Gentleman of Scotland, and that I supposed I had done no harm. He repeated this in German, & most of the troops seemed content. But my foolish fellow of an accuser would see more into the matter, and so away they carried me before the Burgmeester, while I laughed & cried Beast. My interpreter repeated my defence to the Burgmeester & this judicious Magistrate smiled at the fellow and dismist me immediatly.

David Garrick, *Letters*
To George Garrick

Munick the Capital of Bavaria
Aug 5th 1764

My dear George,
We are got here in our way to the Spaw, & are oblig'd to stop for a few days, for my Wife is very bad still with her lameness, & has been in great pain. We fear that we must put on a blister, & try the cold Bath, which will detain us 7 or 8 days. I am very uneasy that we cannot remove the Rheumatism, it is very obstinate, indeed, considering that she has gone through a fiery trial for 5 Weeks in ye Muds at Abano. I have sent to Selwyn & Foley at Paris, to send my Letters to Stugard from whence I shall go directly to Spaw, if I have the least hope of meeting You there, if not, we shall go either to Paris, or some other part of France, till I hear farther from You. I don't Expect that You will venture your Carcass on this Side the Water, tho I think the little voyage from Dover to Calais, & back again, would clear your bowels for you. I am very much rejoyc'd that we came thro' Germany; for ye Prospects of the Tyrol are Superiour to any thing I have Ever yet seen. Eating, drinking, & Beds Exceed those in Italy, & their neatness is equal to the Inns (almost) in England. Pray tell Townley (with my Love to him), that I never, since I left England, till now, have regal'd Myself with a *good house of Office*, or as he calls it, a *Conveniency*. The holes in Germany are generally too large, & too round, chiefly owing I believe to the broader bottoms of the Germans, for they are *swingers* indeed all thro' Bavaria. We have

a little English Gentleman with us, who Slipt up to the Middle in one of the holes, & we were some Minutes before we could disEngage him – in short You may assure Townley, (Who loves to hear of the state of these Matters) that in Italy the People *do their Needs*, in Germany they *disembogue*, but in England (& in England only) they *Ease* themselves. I must desire you to remember me in a very Particular manner to Mr Fitzherbert when you see him. Pray let me know how he is & direct to me chez Messrs Selwyn and Foley at Paris. You shall hear soon from Me again.

Nathaniel Wraxall, *Memoirs of the Courts of Berlin, Dresden, Warsaw, and Vienna* Letter III

Berlin, 19th October, 1777

I must here premise, that I have not been presented to his Prussian Majesty; a misfortune, as well as a distinction, for which I am indebted to the "Tour round the Baltic". The freedom with which I ventured to animadvert in that work on the partition of Poland, and particularly on the treatment of the city of Dantzic by Frederic, have excited his resentment. It was signified, through the medium of his minister, to the British Envoy Mr. Elliot, that my being presented at Court would not be agreeable. I am at a loss to determine whether I ought to consider such an exclusion as a subject of pride, or of mortification; since I certainly cannot either repent, or retract the sentiments which have occasioned it. But the friendship of Prince Frederic has procured me an occasion of seeing him more agreeably than at his Levee, by sending an officer who conducted me, a few mornings ago, to the Princess Amelia's Palace, in the "Rue Guillaume," where his Majesty breakfasted. I had there the gratification of considering him for a few minutes, divested of the restraint imposed by the forms of a Court. The King of Prussia, unlike most of the other Sovereigns of Europe, is neither to be seen, except on particular occasions; nor is it at Berlin that his character can be studied, nor his actions investigated. So limited and restrained is the communication between this metropolis and Potzdam, that scarcely any thing transpires here which is transacted there, till several days afterwards. The King may be dangerously indisposed, without its generally being known, or without the nature of his illness being well understood. At Vienna, and at Dresden, they are often better acquainted with the private transactions of Frederic, than in his own place of residence. Such is the policy, and such are the precautions of that able and extraordinary Prince!

Before, however, I enter on the examination of his character, and the leading events of his reign, I must say a few words relative to Berlin. They shall be few, in compliance with the principle which I have laid down, of describing men, not cities. Unlike Paris, London, or Madrid, this place recalls to the beholder at every step, the image, the genius, and the actions of the reigning Sovereign. It is a mirror in which Frederic is perpetually seen, either as the General, the Architect, or the Master, Peter the Great is not more constantly present to the imagination at Petersburgh, than the present King of Prussia at Berlin. He is besides, the Palladio of his own Capital. I have seen him riding slowly through the principal streets, accompanied only by his nephew Prince Frederic of Brunswic, a General Officer, and three or four attendants; giving exact directions relative to every structure, and examining with his glass at his eye, the progress of the works undertaken for its embellishment.

Like Petersburgh, this city is magnificent, regular, and has sprung up since the beginning of the present century. It existed indeed previously; but, only eighty years ago, it contained no more than twenty-five thousand inhabitants. They estimate the population now at above a hundred and twenty thousand. In the centre of Berlin, a stranger finds himself completely surrounded by a groupe of palaces or public buildings, of the most striking kind. Several owe their construction to the present King; and on the front of the Opera House, which he built at the beginning of his reign, we read the short and classic inscription affixed by himself, "Fredericus Rex, Apollini, et Musis." His universal and creative genius has however been constantly intent on maintaining the spirit of military enthusiasm, in the midst of peace, and among all the display of architecture, taste, or magnificence. We never cease to recollect that we are in a country, where from the sovereign to the peasant every man is born a soldier. But it is in the Garrison Church, that those feelings are peculiarly awakened, animated, and called into action.

(...)

If, however, Berlin strikes by its regularity and the magnificence of its public buildings, it impresses not less forcibly with a sentiment of melancholy. It is neither enriched by commerce, enlivened by the general residence of the Sovereign, nor animated by industry, business, and freedom. An air of silence and dejection reigns in the streets, where at noon-day scarcely any passengers are seen except soldiers. The population, much as it has augmented during the present reign, is still very unequal to the extent and magnitude of the city. Ostentation and vanity, more than utility or necessity, seem to have impelled Frederic to enlarge and embellish his capital. The splendid fronts of the finest houses frequently conceal poverty and wretchedness. A colonnade, hardly inferior to the Louvre, proves when inspected, to be only a casern, or barrack. We are first disappointed, and in the end disgusted with this deception. Petersburgh, though situated in a much more inclement latitude, has a thousand natural and political advantages which are sought in vain at Berlin. The Neva itself, at the former city, flowing majestically from the lake Ladoga into the gulf of Finland, is at once a sublime and pleasing object, covered with ships, and exhibiting a scene perpetually varying as well as gay. Here the little river Spree creeps along, unnoticed and forgotten. Like London, Berlin is composed entirely of brick; for there are, unfortunately, no quarries of stone in its vicinity. They mask indeed the exterior of the houses with plaster or stucco; but it soon falls off, and betrays the original meanness of the materials. The King too appears to be more fond of constructing than of repairing, though he compels such of his subjects as build, to conform to the rules of architecture, and to the elevation or plan of the adjoining houses.

Nothing can be more destitute of beauty or fertility than the environs of Berlin. On every side stretches an expanse of sand, and as soon as a carriage passes the gates, it is buried up to the axle trees. Scarcely any trees, except firs, are to be seen; and even from hence to Potsdam, the intermediate country is almost a wilderness. The morass which surrounds Petersburgh is not so dreary; and the savage rocks, destitute of vegetation, amidst which Stockholm is built, are at least undulated, romantic, and picturesque. Even Hanover, though certainly not placed in a favoured position or in a fertile soil, yet is preferable in these respects to the Prussian capital. I shall say no more however upon it; nor should I have gone into so large a detail, if I did not consider it as intimately connected with the character and genius of the King. Other cities are constructed or embellished, at least in some degree, by the people, in proportion to the commerce, opulence, or grandeur of the State. But the most beautiful part of Berlin, the "Fredericstadt," is almost exclusively the work of Frederic.

John Moore, *A View of Society and Manners in France, Switzerland and Germany*
Letter XLI

Manheim

Upon crossing the Rhine we entered into the territories of the Margrave of Baden Durlach, which lie along the banks of that river immediately opposite to Alsace. At Rastade we were informed that the Margrave and his family were at Karlsruch. Rastade is the capital of this princes' dominions. The town is but small, and not very populous: The Margrave's palace, however, is sufficiently large. We made only a short stay to examine it, being impatient to get on to Karlsruch.

There is another very magnificent palace at Karlsruch, built in good taste. It was begun many years ago, and has lately been finished by the reigning prince. The town of Karlsruch is built on a regular plan. It consists of one principle street of above an English mile in length. This street is at a considerable distance in front of the palace, and in a parallel direction with it. All the other streets go off at different angles from the principle one, in such a manner as that whichsoever of them you enter, walking from it, the view is terminated by the front of the palace. The length of these smaller streets is ascertained, none of them being allowed to approach the spacious area, which is kept clear before the palace.

The principle street may be extended to any length, and as many additional streets as they please may be built from it, all of which, according to this plan, will have the palace for a termination.

The houses of this town are all as uniform as the streets, being of an equal size and height, so that one would be led to imagine that none of the inhabitants are in any considerable degree richer or poorer than their neighbours. There are indeed a few new houses, more elegant than the others, belonging to some of the officers of the court, built at one side of the palace; but they are not, properly speaking, in the town.

Having announced in the usual form, that we wished to have the honour of paying our court to the Margrave, an officer waited on the D_ of H_ and conducted us to the palace.

(...)

The German Princes are minute observers of form. The same establishment for their household, the same officers in the palace, are to be found here, as in the court of the most powerful monarch in Europe. The difference lies more in the salaries than in the talents requisite for these places; one Paymaster for the forces has greater emoluments in England, than a Grand Marechal, a Grand Chamberlain, two Secretaries of State, and half a dozen more of the chief officers of a German court, all taken together.

The Margrave of Baden has body guards who do duty in the palace, foot guards who parade before it; also horse guards and hussars, all of whom are perfectly well-equipped and exactly disciplined; a piece of magnificence which seems to be adopted by this prince, merely in conformity with the custom long established in his country.

He keeps on foot no other troops besides the few which are necessary for this duty at the palace, though his revenue is more considerable, and his finances are in much better order than some princes in Germany who have little standing armies in constant pay. He has too just an understanding not to perceive that the greatest army he could possibly maintain, could be no defence to his dominions, situated as they are between the powerful states of France and Austria: And probably his principles and dispositions prevent him from thinking of filling his coffers by hiring his subjects to foreign powers.

If he were so inclined, there is no manner of doubt that he might sell the persons of his subjects as soldiers, or employ them in any other way he should think proper; for he, as well as the other sovereign princes in Germany, has an unlimited power over his people. If you ask the question, in direct terms, of a German, he will answer in the negative; and will talk of certain rights which the subjects enjoy, and that they can appeal to the great council or general diet of the empire for relief. But after all his ingenuity and distinctions, you find that the barriers which protect the peasant from the power of the prince, are so very weak, that they are hardly worth keeping up, and that the only security the peasant has for his person or property, must proceed from the moderation, good sense, and justice of his sovereign. Happy would it be for mankind if this unlimited power were always placed in as equitable hands as those of the Margrave of Baden, who employs it entirely for the good of his subjects, by whom he is adored!

The prince endeavours, by every means he can devise, to introduce industry and manufacture among his people. There is a considerable number of English tradesmen here, who make Birmingham work, and instruct the inhabitants in that business.[4] He has also engaged many watch-makers from Geneva to settle here, by granting them encouragements and privileges of every kind, and allows no opportunity to slip unimproved, by which he can promote the comfort and happiness of his people: A prince of such a character is certainly a public blessing, and the people are fortunate who are born under his government: but far more fortunate they who are born under a government which can protect them, independent of the virtues, and in spite of the vices, of their sovereign.

---

[4] In their race to catch up with industrially pioneering Britain, German towns in the first half of the 1800s regularly focused on attracting skilled manufacturers from across the Channel. As competition between Prussian Germany and Britain heated up later in the century, this practice was replaced with industrial espionage. The now legendary "Made in Germany" label was introduced in the 1880s by the British parliament in an effort to make second-rate German products recognizable at market, and it was during this period of German catch-up that the ironically derogatory use of *Ersatz* began in English.

3 The Call of the *Kulturnation*
Germany and the Romantics
1787 - 1817

One of the longest-lived literary giants the world has ever seen, Goethe started—and outlived—the influential *Sturm und Drang* and Romanticism movements, finishing his life's work in Weimar.

THE COMPLEX, FRAGILE mesh of the Holy Roman Empire, already stretched by the disproportionate and growing weight of Prussia and Austrian in its east, was torn apart by the French Revolutionary Wars. From 1792 onwards France began swallowing up the array of small Rhenish states along its borders in ever larger gulps, and after Napoleon smashed the Austrian army at Austerlitz in 1806 the Hapsburg Holy Roman Emperor abdicated and the empire ceased to exist.

After integrating the north-west into its empire, France reorganized much of the remaining German territories into *départements* after its own republican model, turning them into client states of the Confederation of the Rhine in its war against Prussia—and against Britain, which was embargoed from 1806 until the collapse of Napoleon's empire in 1813/14. At first, the French occupation was welcomed by some Germans as an improvement on the rule of petty absolutist princes and endless internal squabbling; yet disenchantment grew in proportion to Napoleon's megalomania as French forces were foisted upon poor country towns and trading cities struggling after being cut off from many of their overseas partners.

To the disappointment of many politically progressive Germans, the result of the Congress of Vienna following Napoleon's defeat in 1815 was not to produce a strong, secular state on German soil, but to simply consolidate the number of duchies, principalities and kingdoms from a three to a two-figure sum and organize them in the loosely-bound German Confederation within which only Prussia, Austria and—at a pinch—Saxony and Bavaria were able to yield any kind of clout,

Yet culturally German-speaking lands were becoming ever more united under the aegis of the monolith Johann Wolfgang von Goethe (b. 1749). Courted by an ever-changing coterie of controversial younger writers such as Schiller, Novalis and Kleist (b. 1759, 1772 and 1777 respectively), Goethe stormed to European notoriety and took German literature with him. It was the age of the *Kulturnation*, in which a common cultural identity stood in for the absent nation-state. Henry Crabb Robinson, an extract from whom is to be found in this chapter, quotes Schlegel in the first years of the nineteenth century: "Germany has two national theatres—Vienna with a public of 50,000 spectators, Weimar with a public of fifty." Even if the Netherlands were now no longer considered part of Germany (and the word "Dutch" had become attached to them), many other parts of Europe were still potentially part of the pan-German state many wished for, and for which hopes were already settling on Prussia.

After the final defeat of France, Prussia's rise to power continued, and economic and military interests started to converge increasingly on Berlin; but the undisputed centre of Germany in cultural terms was Weimar. Foreign visitors to Britain have almost always passed through London, whether their reasons for travelling were economic, diplomatic or literary; visitors to Germany could simply by their choice of destination wear their interests on their sleeve.

The First Germanophiles

This can best be illustrated by a look at the year 1798. While Nathaniel Wraxall was compiling his diplomatic memoir of Berlin and Dresden twenty years before (see Chapter 2), a completely different, much younger type of writer was becoming interested in Germany: in the autumn of that year, William Wordsworth (b. 1770) left for Germany in the company of his wife, Dorothy Wordsworth (b. 1771), and his friend Samuel Taylor Coleridge (b. 1772).

This might be considered the first incidence of a primarily educational journey. While writers in the previous two centuries certainly hoped to learn something from their travels in Germany, they considered themselves educated before they arrived: especially for the men of letters of the eighteenth century, a mastery of Greek, Latin and French was more than sufficient. Yet the Wordsworths and Coleridge went to Germany with the express aim of learning German and gaining an appreciation of German literature, as is shown by the discussion between them about the quality of Goethe in their letters.

Henry Crabb Robinson (b. 1775), following in 1800, was also in Germany to learn, going on to spend five years studying there before working as a correspondent for *The Times* in Hamburg in 1807. In his letters back to his brother Robinson gave a fascinatingly rich view of Germany, where he travelled widely, meeting much of the literary establishment of the day from grandees like Goethe and Schiller (with whom he discussed Coleridge's translation of *Wallenstein*) to the young Romantic Clemens Brentano. In later years back in London society, he would indulge his lasting enthusiasm for Romantic German literature with none other than Samuel Taylor Coleridge and the Wordsworths. By translating, recommending and discussing German poetry and drama, all three were to be instrumental in furthering the cause of German Romanticism in Britain.

The Romantic period of German literature is considered to have begun with Goethe's *Sturm und Drang* works such as *Götz von Berlichingen* und *The Sorrows of Young Werther* in 1773/4 and not to have ended at least until his death in 1832. This made Goethe and German literature a living, lasting source of inspiration not just for one, but for several generations of British Romantics. Born in 1797 while the Wordsworths and Coleridge were wintering in Germany,

Mary Wollstonecraft Shelley would later go on to make three visits to Germany and publish twice about her travels there and in France, Switzerland and Italy. It is her first travel narrative, *History of a Six Weeks' Tour*, published with her husband Percy Bysshe Shelley (b. 1792) in 1817, which is reproduced here, as well as an extract from *Frankenstein; or, The Modern Prometheus* (1818) in which Victor Frankenstein writes of his journey down the Rhine to reach England. Some of the text is taken almost word for word from the History, showing how directly Mary Shelley's experience of the Rhine flowed into her fiction.

Great Men in Mediocre Surroundings

For the Shelleys, Germany's literary reputation preceded the reality of the place, and this led to no small amount of sobering disappointment. The Rhine especially, with its ruined castles à la Drachenfels, had already gained a reputation as a literary landscape. William Beckford eulogized it in his 1783 record of the Grand Tour, and in 1791 John Gardnor produced an illustrated account. After the Continental Blockade of 1806-1814, pent up enthusiasm for the Rhine was able to flow freely, as it did in the Third Canto of Byron's (b. 1788) *Childe Harold's Pilgrimage* (verse 55).

The castled crag of Drachenfels
Frowns o'er the wide and winding Rhine.
Whose breast of waters broadly swells
Between the banks which bear the vine,
And hills all rich with blossomed trees,
And fields which promise corn and wine,
And scattered cities crowning these,
Whose far white walls along them shine,
Have strewed a scene, which I should see
With double joy wert *thou* with me!
(...)

The river nobly foams and flows,
The charm of this enchanted ground,
And all its thousand turns disclose
Some fresher beauty varying round;
The haughtiest breast its wish might bound
Through life to dwell delighted here;
Nor could on earth a spot be found
To Nature and to me so dear,
Could thy dear eyes in following mine

Still sweeten more these banks of Rhine!

Yet despite terming it a "paradise" in terms of its landscape, the Shelleys' account of their voyage down the Rhine is marked by the somewhat un-poetic, post-lapsarian nature of the rowdy German passengers accompanying them and the frustratingly slow rate of progress. The Romantics who preceded the Shelleys, too, were often struck by the difference between the Germany of literature and the sometimes impoverished, often downright downtrodden early nineteenth-century society they experienced.

In scenic terms, too, disappointment often seemed the order of the day. The Wordsworths' encounter with the mythical Brocken of Goethe's *Faust* fame left them distinctly nonplussed. Henry Crabb Robinson, meanwhile, despite writing at length about his time visiting the provincial capitals of German letters such as Jena and, of course, Weimar, said precious little about these places: "Weimar is an insignificant little town, without an object of beauty or taste but its park; and even that among parks has no great excellence. It has been immortalized by many a passage in Goethe's poems." Despite his fondness for literature set in the German wildernesses, when he described places instead of people, Crabb Robinson opted for bustling cities.

One clear advantage of Germany's rather unspectacular small towns, however, was the low cost of living. For comparatively hard-up young poets like the Wordsworths and Coleridge, this was a (if not *the*) decisive ground for indulging their love of German literature. The Wordsworths' letters, for example, go into great detail about their financial situation and the benefits to it of spending some time in Germany. Even Henry Crabb Robinson, who enjoyed more financial freedom and was thus less interested in discussing money matters in his correspondence, remarked of Teplitz in Saxony: "my breakfast consisted of grapes and cream—and certainly I never lived at so little cost." In this sense, today's broke but bohemian Berlin, with its buzzing artistic scene, is the true heir to the Germany of Coleridge and the Wordsworths.

*

Dorothy and William Wordsworth, *Letters*
(93) D. W. to Mrs Rawson

Allfoxden 13th June (and Bristol 3rd July) 1798

My dear Aunt,

(…)

I think Mr. Rawson has correspondents in Germany; perhaps by their means I should be able to hear from you and write to you post free. Otherwise I fear letter-writing will be so expensive that I must very much abridge the quantity of letters which I write. In writing letters in foreign countries the expense is much more than doubled for one is obliged to pay both for the letters sent and received. Perhaps I shall be able to get letters sent by means of the Wedgwoods who are to give us letters of introduction to some Hamburgh merchants. At any rate I must so manage that when one of my friends hears from me the rest must hear either of or from me.

(…)

When I am just upon the point of concluding my letters I recollect that you may perhaps think that we are going upon an expensive scheme into Germany and that our income will not suffice to maintain us. I must put you to the expense of a double letter to explain this to you. Notwithstanding Mr. Montagu (from having changed the course of his application to the law) has not been able to fulfil his engagement respecting Basil, we have lived upon our income and are not a farthing poorer than when we began house-keeping. We can live for less money in Germany while we are stationary than we can in England, so that you see our regular income (independent of what we may gain by translation) will be sufficient to support us when we are there, and we will receive, before our departure much more than sufficient to defray the expenses of our journey, from a bookseller to whom William has sold some poems that are now printing.

(…)

(100) W.W. to Thomas Poole

Hamburg, 3rd October, 1798

My dear Poole,

It was my intention to have written to you from England to bid you farewell. I was prevented by procrastination and I now take up the pen to assure you that my sister and myself both retain the most lively recollection of the many kindnesses which we have received from you and your family. I believe my letter would be more acceptable to you if instead of speaking on this subject I should tell you what we have seen during our fortnight's residence at Hamburg. It is a *sad* place. In this epithet you have the soul and essence of all the information which I have been able to gather. We have however been treated with unbounded kindness by Mr. Klopstock the brother of the poet and I have no doubt this city contains a world of good and honest people, if one had but the skill to find them. I will relate to you an anecdote. The other day I went into a Bakers shop. Put into his hand two pieces of money for which I ought to have had five loaves but I thought the pieces had only been worth two loaves each. I took up four loaves. The baker would not permit this, upon which I took from his hand one of the pieces, and pointed to two loaves, and then re-offering to him the piece I took up two others: he dashed the loaves from my hand into the basket in the most brutal manner. I begged him to return the other piece of money, which he refused to do, nor would he let me have any bread into the bargain. So we left the shop empty-handed and he retained the money. Is there any baker in England who would have done this to a foreigner? I am afraid we must say, yes. Money, money is here the god of universal worship. And rapacity and extortion among the lower classes and the classes immediately above them, are just sufficiently common to be a matter of glory and exultation.

The situation of the town is upon the whole pleasant: the ramparts present many agreeable views of the river and the adjoining country. The banks of the Elbe are thickly sown with houses built by the merchants for Saturday and Sunday retirement. The English merchants have set the example, the style is in imitation of the English garden, imitated as Della Crusca might imitate Virgil. It is however something gained, the dawning of a better day.

We set off this evening by the diligence for Brunswick. We shall be two days and two nights constantly travelling in a vehicle compared with which Tanlin's long coach is a very chariot of the Gods – patience, patience. We have one comfort travelling in this way, a very great one for poor, viz. that we cannot be cheated. Coleridge has most likely informed you that he and Chester have settled at Ratzeburg. Dorothy and I are going to speculate farther up in the country.

I have seen Klopstock the poet. There is nothing remarkable either in his conversation of appearance, except his extreme gaiety with legs swelled as thick as your thigh. He is in his 74th years. He began his Messiah at 17. Not the composition for the plan employed him 3 years.

(110) D.W. & W. W. to S. T. Coleridge

Nordhausen, Wednesday evening
27th February, 1799

My dear Coleridge,

(…)

The peasants in the *plains* adjoining to Goslar are extremely well clothed and decent in their appearance. We had often seen in Goslar women inhabitants of the hills, but we did not imagine them to be so rude and barbarous a race as we found them. They carry enormous burthens in square baskets hung over their shoulders, their petticoats reach very little below their knees, and their stockings are dangling about their ankles without garters. Swellings in the throat are very common amongst them which may perhaps be attributed to the straining of the neck in dragging those monstrous loads. They rarely travel without a bottle of German brandy, Schnapps as they call it; many of them go weekly from Clausthall to Brunswick, they perform this journey, a distance of thirty five miles in two days, carrying ass loads, parcels, &c, and letters clandestinely. These

people are chiefly inhabitants of Clausthal, a large Hanoverian town cursed with the plague of a vicious population.[1] We arrived there in the dusk of the evening, found an excellent inn, with beautiful bed-linen, good coffee, and a decent supper. The charge was about the same rate as in England, perhaps a little cheaper. This town lies in the centre of the Hartz forest. We left it on sunday, a mild morning, saw little that was remarkable till we came to the decaying posts of an old gibbet. We had scarcely passed it when we were saluted with the song of the lark, a pair of larks a sweet, liquid and heavenly melody heard from the first time, after so long and severe a winter. I ought to have said that before this we had a view of the Brocken, the Mont Blanc of the Hartz forest, and the glory of all this part of Germany. I cannot speak of its height compared with any of our British mountains, but from the point of view from which we saw it, it had nothing impressive in its appearance. (D. W.)
(…)

My progress in German considered with reference to literary emolument is not even as dust in the balance. If I had had opportunities of conversing I should not have cared much if I had not read a line. My hope was that I should be able to learn German as I learn'd French, in this I have been woefully deceived. I acquired more French in two months, than I should acquire German in five years living as we have lived. In short sorry I am to say it I do not consider myself as knowing *any* thing of the German language. Consider this not as spoken in modesty either false or true but in simply verity. I cannot sufficiently thank you for your two valuable letters particularly upon the German Poets. Of the excellence of Lessing I can form no distinct idea. My internal prejudgements concerning Wieland and Goethe (of Voss I knew nothing) were, as your letter convinced me, the result of no *negligent* perusal of the different fragments which I had seen in England.

Samuel Taylor Coleridge, *Letters*
(254) To Mrs S. T. Coleridge
Wednesday afternoon, 4 o' clock (19th September 1798)
We are safe in Hamburgh – an ugly City that stinks in every corner, house, & room worse than Cabbin, Sea sickness or bilge Water! The Hotels are all crowded – with great difficulty we have procured a very filthy room at a large expense; but we shall move tomorrow. We get very excellent Claret for a Trifle – a guinea sells at present for more than 23 shillings here. But for all particulars, I must refer

---

[1] It is worth remembering at this point that the British kings of the day were the Hanoverian Georges, electors of Hanover called to the British throne to secure a Protestant succession after Queen Anne had died childless. This was doubtless a contributing factor behind the upswing in interest in Germany during the eighteenth and early nineteenth centuries.

your patience to my Journal – & I must get some proper paper.

(255) To Thomas Poole

Hamburg, Friday 28th September 1798

My dear dear Poole,

The Ocean is between us & I feel how much I love you! God bless you my dear Friend. Since I last wrote to Sara, I have been wandering about & about to find Lodgings. I have given up all thought of going to Eisenach or Weimar, and shall settle with Chester for three months or possibly four at Ratzeburg, 7 German (i.e. 35 English Miles) from Hamburg. We go tomorrow & my address is – Mr Coleridge, at the Pastor Unruke, Ratzeburg, Germany.

Get a German map and find me out. Ratzeburg is a most beautiful place and North-east of Hamburg. On Sunday Morning I begin my Journal, and you will receive, or Sara, the first Sheet by the next Mail. Did you receive my letter from Yarmouth? Did Sara receive the Bank note of £30 from London? The price of Lodging and Boarding is very high – we shall pay 36 marks a week for two rooms, for bread, butter, milk, dinner & supper – & find ourselves washing, tea & wine – this is at the rate of 60 pounds a year each, English money. We are not imposed on in this, but the Cheapness of Germany is a Hum! At least of the Northern Parts. Wordsworth & his Sister have determined to travel on into Saxony, to seek cheaper places.

(…)

(258) To Thomas Poole

26th October 1798

(…)

Since I last wrote, I have been on a tour to Travemunde on the Baltic Sea, & the places adjoining to which circumstance you must attribute my silence. My last landed me on the Elbe-stairs at the Baum-house, Hamburgh. While I was standing on the stairs, I was amused by the passage boat which goes once or twice a day from Hamburg to Haarburg, across the River. It was crammed with all people of all nations in all sorts of dresses, the Men with pipes of all shapes and fancies, strait and wreathed, simple and complex, long and short, cane, clay, porcelain, wood, tin, silver, and ivory – *one*, a mere hot-spice-gingerbreadcake-man's Stump Whiffer, and *many* with silver chains & with silver *bole*-covers.

(259) To Mrs S. T. Coleridge

9th November 1798

(…)

This was the Dinner, & all the Dinners I have seen, resemble it as nearly as

English Dinners resemble one another in different Houses. First – Soup (N.B. It was good *Broth*; but every Thing here is called *Soup*). A long Interval. Some hung Beef, with unsalted boiled Beef, cut out in slices & handed round in a plate – each man takes what he likes with his fork. Then two larges Dishes of Vegetables were handed round – The first, Carrots drest in Butter – not unpleasantly: & at the same time, great French Beans with their seeds in them, stewed in some condiment, I knew not what. The vegetables are never brought to Table *simple* as with us. Another long Interval – 'And Patience, at a German Ordinary, Smiling at Time!' (G. A. Bürger, *Lenore*, lines 101-2). Then were handed round in a plate as before Slices of roast-beef, roasted dry & ragged. A good Sallad – then Slices of Roast Pork with stewed Prunes, / other sweet Fruit stewed. Then cheese, and Butter, with plates of Orleans Plumbs by way of Desert: *and* – Apples. It appears from Shakespear's Plays that in his time the English drest their dishes as the Germans do now – as for instance, the Merry Wives of Windsor – 'Slender. I bruised my shin with playing with sword & dagger for a dish of stewed prunes; & by my Troth I cannot abide the smell of Hot Meat since.' So in the same piece: 'Evans. – I will come and make an end of my dinner: there's pippins & cheese yet to come.'
(…)

They change Plates often; but seldom or never the Knives and Forks – not even after Fish. I however always send away my knife and fork with the Plate and the Servants consider me as an Englishman. All the men have a hideous custom of picking their Teeth with their forks. Some hold up their napkins before their mouths while they do it – which is shocking – and adds a moral Filth to the action by evincing that the Person is conscious of the Filth of the Action. And the Top of their Teeth, the breadth of the Top, is commonly black & yellow with a Life's Smoking – the Women too have commonly bad Teeth. In *every* House every Person, Children & all, have always a folded Napkin put on the Plate, but it is not always very clean. Carpets are very uncommon. As far as my experience goes hitherto, I like the Stoves very well.

Henry Crabb Robinson, *Letters*

Frankfort sur Mein
11th May 1800
(…) The remark I before made on the houses of Altona applies to Hambro' and the Adjacent Country. They perpetually suggest the Idea that you are looking at England as it was a Century ago – The original model of a farm house (& farm houses were the primitive houses) as I have seen it in the wild parts of Hanover, is that of one immense room, with Chimney or division, the various parts are divided as a farmer lays his different seeds or fruits – At one corner the fire;

here beds, there the piggery; here some furniture and a good carriage way all thro' – Now the progress of refinement is this; after a time the sides are separated (like the King's Bench & Common Please in Wester Hall) glazed & adorned for the Women & children – but still the centre is unpaved – I have seen several respectable houses of this kind in the country near Hambro' – Refinement increases but still the old Hall remains as in ancient English mansions. Perhaps we have gone beyond the exact mark of propriety & through our proud love of retirement by converting our Halls into narrow passages & large parlours; have injured our houses as summer retreats & promoted the natural shyness of our tempers – In the Houses near Hambro' the genteelest families dine or drink coffee in their Halls & with the Doors open to observation & curiosity – In the Town too, most of the Houses have the narrow or gable end in front, which necessarily precludes the elegant uniformity of a Bath Street but at the same time allows of an infinite variety of ornament which gives an idea of distinctness to the mind & is I think an advantage – As the Stories rise, the curtain, if it may be so called, is narrowed till it terminates in a Pyramid – There is, it must be confessed, a great waste of room in the lofty halls & shops which you see in the front of the Hambro' houses. But perhaps it is more pleasing to witness resources & means of future improvements, as necessities may arise, than as in London to behold every inch occupied and Management & Economy put to their last shifts – The Dress of the Lower Classes confirms the suggestion that Germany is now what England was – Many a poor woman bears about her a tight black velvet bonnet like that in which Mary Q. of Scotts is painted – The Lutheran clergy appear to wear the cast-off ruffs of Queen Elizabeth, & the heads of the maid servants & country women are adorned with stiff perpendicular lappets, giving fierceness & rotundity to their square faces and on the crown of their heads they bear a profusion of gold and silver, that is yellow and white lace – So much for the outside of the Men and Women of the lower ranks – The higher orders dress differently. All the Gentlemen imitate the English, all the Ladies, the French. (...) *17-18*
(...) You would suppose from what I have yet said that there is great strictness in religious service – Yet on the first Sunday I was invited to dine with a party of near 30 at Mr Hagedorns and in the Evening Cards were introduced as of course – Afterwards I was invited to a Ball on the Lords Day, Virtue may not be an affair of Geography, but certainly the ceremonials of Religions, as well as the Decorums or ordinary life are, It would be ridiculous to scruple where even the most serious & strict lead the way. I mentioned Dinner – eating & drinking occupies so large a portion of human life that though it is a low subject you will expect me to say something about it – When I first dined at the Table d'hote (or ordinary) I was astonished at the schoolboy fashion in which we were

served – First Soup – Then some boiled meat then a dish of Vegetables (in which the Germans infinitely surpass us) with an entre met then roast Meat are given to you without a question being asked – this is at first unpleasant & subjects a person to inconvenience if he is dainty since he knows not what is coming he may repent of eating too much or too little – private tables are served much in the same stile – The Meat is brought on the table and taken off again to be carved – there is a pause between each course by which means much time is wasted & much food too, for one eats upon such occasion through ennuie – The Cooking is generally abused by Englishmen but in several respects I prefer it to ours – But roast meat is seldom good – and there are few puddings…

(…) *19-20*

But one other striking object remains to be noticed – Cassel the elegant & superb residence of a vulgar & savage tyrant, a dealer in man's flesh. One of the most unpleasant sights here, is the hard labour of the women – the peasants are all forced to be soldiers hence Agriculture is in a great measure carried on by the women – a military life is the destiny of all the males. And it is from the sale of them that prince derives his revenue – they are his property & he compels them to fight as other cattle are forced into the harness – Yet, strange perversity of man, this prince with a character as personally despicable as politically atrocious, is popular among his subjects…

Frankfort sur Mein
29th July 1800

(…) You know where Frankfurt lies, I doubt not pretty well, as you must have shewn it to at least 12 Gossips on your Atlass – You therefore perceive that I am within an Inch, on the aforesaid Atlass, of the provisional Department of Donnersberg in the french Republick – The Gazatteers, too, call it an ancient, rich, free, commercial, imperial Stadt or Town, each of which phrases is by no means insignificant & forms an important Circumstance in the History of the place and they luckily affoard me a Number of Heads or Divisions… Imprimis, then it is ancient: That is the Streets are narrow & wretchedly paved the Houses lofty, & irregularly built, the Churches mean & the whole without either dignity or beauty excepting one broad place which is called *Zeil* or straight line, though it is unluckily rather crooked 2nd & 4th it is rich & commercial – And in this character it holds a distinguished Rank in the Cities of the Empire. From its situation so near the Confluence of the Rhine and Maine and the singularly good Roads which are kept up between it and the great Cities higher in the Empire it has become the great Mart of Commerce with france – and on each Side with Holland – and Switzerland even down to Italy – That even the length of Land carriage is not a sufficient Impediement to this Trade, the Commerce of Mr. Aldebert's House is a proof, it consists principally in the Manufacture of Cotton

Goods at Manchester where Mr A. is now about to settle – and in the Sale of them in Italy where another member of the House resides. – As the balance of Trade is altogether against Germany – its exports being very inconsiderable – while it imports the Luxuries of politer france more industrious Holland & more enlightened England, the Patriots affect to consider the Town as carrying on an harmful and pernicious Trade – I leave to the Economist to determine what the Effect of this is upon the Empire – It does not make the Town more agreeable to me – It takes away all the distinctness & pleasing peculiarities of a national character & gives it only the mean vices of wealth – In the language of the Saints though not precisely in their Sense Frankfort is a dark Town there but Two Coffee Houses and they take no News Papers but the french and german Journals of the Town, That is two dirty mean little Quarto sheets published every day & sold for a penny which I have read constantly without being able to learn whether Napper Tandy is dead or alive whether Fox took a share in the Union debate or whether the Law is yet passed.

Of the Society of the place I am disqualified from yet speaking confidently. According to all report and all appearance, it is the reverse of enlightened. Here are no literary Characters – Yet it had a Lodge of Illuminati – I know one of that celebrated body and mean hereafter if you are interested in the Subejct to send you some Information which will better enable you to judge of the Abbé Baruel's & Robinsons Books. Here are no literary Institutions – No public Libraries but one belonging to the City and which is more a matter of form and a collection of antient books than a *useful* and *used* Library – The circulating Libraries, are like the English – Yet there is one Circumstance which it would be ungrateful in the Traveller to omit. Its Inns are some of the first in Europe – No Town of its Size can boast a moments comparison with it. Both in Number and Size they are very excellent they have not the tasty genteel Air of the Hotel at Caernarvon the Castle at Marlborough and our Angel but they are immensely large and very well built Houses – with the best accommodations – The *Tables d'Hote* are infinitely better attended than our Ordinaries – Ladies & Noblemen do not hesitate to join in the party. And before I fixed myself here I was amused by comparing them – for less than half a corwn you have really a sumptuous Entertainment generally of 4 courses including a Pint of Rhine Wine (in England commonly called Old Hock) fruit pastry fish &c. They are protected by the Magistrates in a way that seems illiberal to strangers – who can not go into private Lodging without a Licence. Besides these Inns which are some of the best Houses in the Town, there are other Houses very large & substantial, Not so far removed from the English Style as those of Lower Saxony – but by no means as elegant as ours. – Indeed though the place is wealthy there is not that display of luxury which is so offensive to those who are not rich – either in dress or furniture –

The Hours too here are better than those in England – Most persons breakfast between 7 & 8 – They dine at one, the play ends at 9 – And most honest people are in bed at 10 – There are no *Gentlemen* properly speaking – Indeed the remark might be extended to almost through Germany. The Wealth of the Country is divided between the little nobility and threat merchants, & as the former have sometimes more titles than revenues their resource is in the Army & Church – but now I ramble –

Mary Wollstonecraft-Shelley and Percy Bysshe-Shelley, *History of a Six Weeks' Tour*

Before we slept, S*** had made a bargain for a boat to carry us to Mayence,[2] and the next morning, bidding adieu to Switzerland, we embarked in a boat laden with merchandize, but where we had no fellow-passengers to disturb our tranquillity by their vulgarity and rudeness. The wind was violently against us, but the stream, aided by a slight exertion from the rowers, carried us on; the sun shone pleasantly, S*** read aloud to us Mary Wollstonecraft's Letters from Norway, and we passed our time delightfully.

The evening was such as to find few parallels in beauty; as it approached, the banks which had hitherto been flat and uninteresting, became exceedingly beautiful. Suddenly the river grew narrow, and the boat dashed with inconceivable rapidity round the base of a rocky hill covered with pines; a ruined tower, with its desolated windows, stood on the summit of another hill that jutted into the river; beyond, the sunset was illuminating the distant mountains and clouds, casting the reflection of its rich and purple hues on the agitated river. The brilliance and contrasts of the colours on the circling whirlpools of the stream, was an appearance entirely new and most beautiful; the shades grew darker as the sun descended below the horizon, and after we had landed, as we walked to our inn round a beautiful bay, the full moon arose with divine splendour, casting its silver light on the before-purpled waves.

The following morning we pursued our journey in a slight canoe, in which every motion was accompanied with danger; but the stream had lost much of its rapidity, and was no longer impeded by rocks; the banks were low, and covered with willows. We passed Strasburgh, and the next morning it was proposed to us

---

[2] Referred to by its French name Mayence in English at the time, the city of Mainz was and remains an important cultural centre on the Rhine. Other German cities which formerly had different names in English usage include Braunschweig (formerly Brunswick(e)), Frankfurt (Franckeford) and Karlsruhe (Karlsruch), as well as its modern-day suberb Durlach, formerly Turlowe. Even today, Köln is still referred to as Cologne, Nürnberg as Nuremberg, and München, of course, as Munich.

that we should proceed in the *diligence par-eau*, as the navigation would become dangerous for our small boat.

The country was uninteresting, but we enjoyed fine weather, and slept in the boat in the open air without any inconvenience. We saw on the shores few objects that called forth our attention, if I except the town of Manheim, which was strikingly neat and clean. It was situated at about a mile from the river, and the road to it was planted on each side with beautiful acacias. The last part of this voyage was performed close under land, as the wind was so violently against us, that even with all the force of a rapid current in our favour, we were hardly permitted to proceed. We were told (and not without reason) that we ought to congratulate ourselves on having exchanged our canoe for this boat, as the river was now of considerable width, and tossed by the wind into large waves. The same morning a boat, containing fifteen persons, in attempting to cross the water, had upset in the middle of the river, and every one in it perished. We saw the boat turned over, floating down the stream. This was a melancholy sight, yet ludicrously commented on by the *batalier*, almost the whole stock of whose French consisted in the word *seulement*. When we asked him what had happened, he answered, laying particular emphasis on this favourite dissyllable, *C'est seulement un bateau, qui etoit seulement renversèe, et tous les peoples sonst seulement noyès.*

Mayence is one of the best fortified towns in Germany. The river, which is broad and rapid, guards it to the east, and the hills for three leagues around exhibit signs of fortifications. The town itself is old, the streets narrow, and the houses high: the cathedral and towers of the town still bear marks of the bombardment which took place in the revolutionary war.

We took our place in the *diligence par-eau* for Cologne and the next morning (September 4th) departed. This conveyance appeared much more like a mercantile English affair than any we had before seen; it was shaped like a steam-boat, with a cabin and a high deck. Most of our companions chose to remain in the cabin; this was fortunate for us, since nothing could be more horribly disgusting than the lower order of smoking, drinking Germans who travelled with us; they swaggered and talked, and what was hideous to English eyes, kissed one another: there were, however, two or three merchants of a better class, who appeared well-informed and polite.

The part of the Rhine down which we now glided is that so beautifully described by Lord Byron in his third canto of *Childe Harold*. We read these verses with delight, as they conjured before us these lovely scenes with the truth and vividness of painting, and with the exquisite addition of glowing language and a warm imagination. We were carried down by a dangerously rapid current, and saw on either side of us hills covered with vines and trees, craggy cliffs crowned by desolate towers, and wooded islands, where picturesque ruins peeped from behind the foliage, and cast the shadows of their forms on the troubled waters, which distorted without deforming them. We heard the songs of the vintagers, and if surrounded by disgusting Germans, the sight was not so replete with enjoyment as I now fancy it to have been; yet memory taking all the dark shades from the picture, presents this part of the Rhine to my remembrance as the loveliest paradise on earth.

We had sufficient leisure for the enjoyment of these scenes, for the boat-men, neither rowing no steering, suffered us to be carried down by the stream, and the boat turned round and round as it descended.

While I speak with disgust of the Germans who travelled with us, I should in justice to these borderers record, that at one of the inns here we saw the only pretty woman we met with in the course of our travels. She is what I should conceive to be a truly German beauty; grey eyes, slightly tinged with brown, and expressive of uncommon sweetness and frankness. She had lately recovered from a fever, and this added to the interest of her countenance, by adorning it with an appearance of extreme delicacy.

On the following day we left the hills of the Rhine, and found that, for the remainder of our journey, we should move sluggishly through the flats of Holland: the river also winds extremely, so that, after calculating our resources, we resolved to finish our journey in a land diligence. Our water conveyance remained that night at Bonn, and that we might lose no time, we proceeded post the same night to Cologne, where we arrived late; for the rate of travelling in Germany seldom exceeds a mile and a half an hour.

Mary Wollstonecraft-Shelley, *Frankenstein; or, The Modern Prometheus*

After some days spent in listless indolence, during which I traversed many leagues, I arrived at Strasbourg, where I waited two days for Clerval. He came. Alas, how great was the contrast between us! He was alive to every new scene, joyful when he saw the beauties of the setting sun, and more happy when he beheld it rise and recommence a new day. He pointed out to me the shifting colours of the landscape and the appearances of the sky. "This is what it is to live," he cried; "how I enjoy existence! But you, my dear Frankenstein, wherefore are you desponding and sorrowful!" In truth, I was occupied by gloomy thoughts and neither saw the descent of the evening star nor the golden sunrise reflected in the Rhine. And you, my friend, would be far more amused with the journal of Clerval, who observed the scenery with an eye of feeling and delight, than in listening to my reflections. I, a miserable wretch, haunted by a curse that shut up every avenue to enjoyment.

We had agreed to descend the Rhine in a boat from Strasbourg to Rotterdam, whence we might take shipping for London. During this voyage we passed many willowy islands and saw several beautiful towns. We stayed a day at Mannheim, and on the fifth from our departure from Strasbourg, arrived at Mainz. The course of the Rhine below Mainz becomes much more picturesque. The river descends rapidly and winds between hills, not high, but steep, and of beautiful forms. We saw many ruined castles standing on the edges of precipices, surrounded by black woods, high and inaccessible. This part of the Rhine, indeed, presents a singularly variegated landscape. In one spot you view rugged hills, ruined castles overlooking tremendous precipices, with the dark Rhine rushing beneath; and on the sudden turn of a promontory, flourishing vineyards with green sloping banks and a meandering river and populous towns occupy the scene.

We travelled at the time of the vintage and heard the song of the labourers as we glided down the stream. Even I, depressed in mind, and my spirits continually agitated by gloomy feelings, even I was pleased. I lay at the bottom of the boat, and as I gazed on the cloudless blue sky, I seemed to drink in a tranquillity to which I had long been a stranger. And if these were my sensations, who can describe those of Henry? He felt as if he had been transported to fairy-land and enjoyed a happiness seldom tasted by man. "I have seen," he said, "the most beautiful scenes of my own country; I have visited the lakes of Lucerne and Uri, where the snowy mountains descend almost perpendicularly to the water, casting black and impenetrable shades, which would cause a gloomy and mournful appearance were it not for the most verdant islands that believe the eye by their gay appearance; I have seen this lake agitated by a tempest, when the wind tore up whirlwinds of water and gave you an idea of what the water-spout must be on the great ocean; and the waves dash with fury the base of the mountain, where the priest and his mistress were overwhelmed by an avalanche and where their dying voices are still said to be heard amid the pauses of the nightly wind; I have seen the mountains of La Valais, and the Pays de Vaud; but this country, Victor, pleases me more than all those wonders. The mountains of Switzerland are more majestic and strange, but there is a charm in the banks of this divine river that I never before saw equalled. Look at that castle which overhangs yon precipice; and that also on the island, almost concealed amongst the foliage of those lovely trees; and now that group of labourers coming from among their vines; and that village half hid in the recess of the mountain. Oh, surely the spirit that inhabits and guards this place has a soul more in harmony with man than those who pile the glacier or retire to the inaccessible peaks of the mountains of our own country." Clerval! Beloved friend! Even now it delights me to record your words and to dwell on the praise of which you are so eminently deserving. He was a being formed in the "very poetry of nature." His wild and enthusiastic imagination was chastened by the sensibility of his heart. His soul overflowed with ardent affections, and his friendship was of that devoted and wondrous nature that the world-minded teach us to look for only in the imagination. But even human sympathies were not sufficient to satisfy his eager mind. The scenery of external nature, which others regard only with admiration, he loved with ardour:—

——The sounding cataract
Haunted him like a passion: the tall rock,
The mountain, and the deep and gloomy wood,
Their colours and their forms, were then to him
An appetite; a feeling, and a love,
That had no need of a remoter charm,
By thought supplied, or any interest
Unborrow'd from the eye.
[Wordsworth's "Tintern Abbey".]

And where does he now exist? Is this gentle and lovely being lost forever? Has this mind, so replete with ideas, imaginations fanciful and magnificent, which formed a world, whose existence depended on the life of its creator;—has this mind perished? Does it now only exist in my memory? No, it is not thus; your form so divinely wrought, and beaming with beauty, has decayed, but your spirit still visits and consoles your unhappy friend.

4

Echoes of Goethe
on the Eve of Bismarck
1820 - 1860

The Drachenfels, the classic craggy Rhine cliff immortalized by Byron and pursued by history's first package tourists.

THE HISTORY OF Germany in the mid-nineteenth century turns around the Year of Revolutions, 1848. In the period of comparative European peace leading up to March of that year, the *Vormärz*, the industrial revolution started to take a belated hold, especially in northern Germany and Prussia, leading to a sharp increase in the population and the development of a larger middle class. The intellectual needs of this wealthy new demographic were catered to by late Romantic authors such as Heinrich Heine (b. 1797), a generation at once inspired by the French Revolution and traumatized by the French occupation.

This led to a Romantic, liberal nationalism which viewed a large, modern pan-German state as the only way to safeguard both the rights of ordinary Germans *vis-à-vis* their rulers and the independence of Germany from its powerful neighbour. Hopes for some kind of new democratic order in Germany seemed close to being realized in March 1848 after the social unrest in France spread to Germany: after almost losing control of Berlin to an angry populace, Frederick William IV of Prussia (b. 1795), Germany's most powerful monarch, declared himself ready to accept a constitution and to support the unification of the whole of Germany under it. A popular parliament with delegates from all over what is now Germany as well as Austria and much of modern-day Poland was convened in Frankfurt that spring, but soon proved almost incapable of producing a consensus on the most simple points such as where the borders of a pan-German state should lie. By the time the assembly finally produced a draft constitution in December and called upon the Prussian king to accept and implement its democratic terms, popular sentiment had subsided and governments had regained control and confidence. Frederick William rejected the German crown and cracked down on liberal elements in Prussia; other German monarchs followed suit.

In the years that followed 1848, disappointment in this early failure of democracy, coupled with industrial expansion and a strong economic performance, led to a decline in political agitation. While many of those with idealistic political hopes emigrated, with both Great Britain and the United States of America being popular choices, those who stayed profited from a growing economy and became stakeholders in the status quo. Throughout the 1850s and 1960s, factories were opened and railways laid across the country at breakneck speed.

As the contemporary revolution in transportation was starting to make travel to and around Europe quicker and more affordable, the literary pull of Germany in the English-speaking world had become well established. After the outpouring of Romantic enthusiasm for Germany in the first years of the 1800s, English-speakers travelling there were no longer heading into the great unknown, but following increasingly well-trodden paths.

The Rhine exemplifies the interplay of the cultural and the practical. With the lasting popularity of Byron and the efforts of British Germanophiles, this river had already taken on mythical proportions for the affluent reading classes in the first half of the nineteenth century. By extension, having a knowledge of German language and literature was starting to become a desirable accomplishment, and at the same time Germany became an eminently reachable destination from London, with steamboats shortening the journey and offering something of a package tour, which enticed those who might otherwise have been put off by the still largely unpredictable and uncomfortable nature of international travel.

From Worthy Learners to Merciless Satirists

While little is known about William G. Meredith today, with his *A Tour of the Rhine* (1825) he was at the forefront of a publishing movement as, in the mid-1820s, new steel-plate engraving techniques made illustrations easier to print and led to a flood of picture books produced about the Rhine, satisfying the appetite for images of the river whetted by the Romantics. The first such title was Robert Batty's *Scenery of the Rhine,* and it was followed by swathes of similar material.

Just two years after Meredith's tour, the first regular steamer service started between Cologne and Mainz, much to the delight of British travellers such as William Makepeace Thackeray (b. 1811), who used it in 1830 on a tour up the Rhine which turned into a more extended stay in Germany. At Weimar, like Henry Crabb Robinson almost thirty years before, he made the acquaintance of Goethe; and like those of the previous generation, he made efforts to learn German, a sign of the cultural prestige accruing to the language.

Of course, not all travellers to Germany were interested in its culture. Francis Bond Head (b. 1793), writing *Bubbles from the Brunnens of Nassau* in 1834, amply displayed his philistinism in matters Teutonic with the nonce-plural of the German word *Brunnen,* meaning fountain or source of water. More known up until that point under the name "Galloping Head" for his exploits riding across South America (*Rough Notes Taken During Some Rapid Journeys Across the Pampas and Among the Andes,* 1825), Bond Head was sent to Nassau to "take a cure" in the mineral waters and did such a fine job satirizing medical quackery and the growing hype around German spa towns that his book became a publishing sensation, going through six printed editions in the following years. In later chapters, we will see this satirical view of spa towns and their visitors honed in letters and fiction to a lasting cliché.

Another writer of a more satirical bent who found himself in Germany in the 1830s was Thomas Hood (b. 1799). Also a publisher in his own right (including some of Tennyson's early work), he was forced by financial difficulties—much like the Romantics a generation before—to look to Germany for cheaper living; he ended up staying in Coblenz from 1835 to 1840. Some of his letters to Charles Wentworth Dilkes, editor of the *Atheneum* from 1835, are reproduced here, depicting a tour around Germany in which he, an incorrigible practical joker, fools a maid into believing he is a military prisoner. Returning to Britain in 1840, his time abroad had given him ample material to send up the increasing numbers of British and American tourists in *Up the Rhine*.

Elisabeth Gaskell (b. 1810), travelling to Germany in 1841, was the wife of a minister and, as such, not on the search for a "cheap situation", as it was referred to in the day. Far more importantly, she had a lasting interest in German literature, which had already had an significant influence on her short stories and would go on to provide a multitude of references in her novels. Her letters to Elizabeth Holland skip over the traditional voyage up the Rhine, concentrating far more on an extended stay at Heidelberg and offering detail on everyday upper-middle-class life there at the time.

German literature and culture had taken on an important status not only among the educated classes of Britain, but across the Atlantic too. The first American account of Germany in this anthology is to be found in Herman Melville's (b. 1819) diaries of 1848, published exactly a century later as *Journal of a Visit to London and the Continent*. Having gone to London to sell a manuscript, Melville took advantage of his relative proximity to Europe to do a tour of what he calls, with no small amount of irony, the "storied Rhine". Melville is archetypical of many authors writing about the Rhine in the mid-nineteenth century, caught between his straightforward role as a tourist and his awareness of the slightly ridiculous nature of this role.

In complete contrast to this self-ironizing view stands George Eliot's (b. 1819) earnest description of her journey to Germany in 1855. Partly this is because she—like Gaskell—does not focus at all on the Rhine, treating it as a thoroughfare on her way into the heartlands and avoiding the inevitable contradictions of being highly self-aware on a standard tourist trip. Yet more than anything, it was her typically Victorian worthiness and desire to learn which kept her so focused on her experiences. Eliot fleshed out the passage in her letter about Weimar in an essay, *Three Months in Weimar*, and published further essays based on her trip in 1856 (*The Natural History of German Life*).

The Last Nap of the "Sleepy" Germans

Eliot comes across "sleepy" Weimar and is surprised by the extent to which it has remained untouched by the modern age. Thomas Hood has great success playing a practical joke on a country waitress too uninformed to know that Britain and Prussia are not at war. Meanwhile, Thackeray grows tired of the boorish antics of students at Bonn, while Gaskell—although warned by her hosts of similar problems at Heidelberg—is intrigued by the student festivities and the dances of the peasant girls which, so she claims, are a matter of "instinct" alone.

The picture itself of quaint, if sometimes crude, peasants was not at all new, as the denigrating descriptions of the Romantics have shown; but the new abundance of material about Germany turned this from something travellers remarked upon after arriving in country to a fixed part of what they expected to find. Berthold Auerbach's *Tales of the Black Forest* (*Dorfgeschichten* in Germany), for example, were wildly successful across Europe, especially in Britain, around 1850, anchoring the image of the good-hearted, rustic German peasant in the minds of other writers. It was a picture that was set to change.

✳

William Meredith, *A Tour to the Rhine*

Ems, as a watering place, pleased me much more than Aix or Spa. Two immense palaces form the places of residence of the company. The extensive building in which we lodged, containing 230 rooms and 80 baths, belongs to the King; and the apartments are let at stated prices, affixed over the doors. The ground floor, besides the space occupied by the baths, affords a spacious promenade, arched with stone, and surrounded with stalls for the sale of prints, jewellery, millinery, and various other articles. All the rooms in the upper stories open into an immense corridor, which extends the whole length of the building. The living and wines are supplied by a *restaurateur* at a very reasonable rate. Here those who seek for wild picturesque scenery, will find it in the romantic dells and forests of Nassau, whilst the visitors of a more *allegro* cast will meet a gay and pleasant circle of select society under the same roof with themselves. Immediately opposite the *Grand Hôtel,* and on the banks of the river, are gardens, with bands of music, and booths, where coffee and liqueurs are sold: at the extremity of these is the *redoute.*

A lovely summer's day greatly enhanced the beauty of the scenery beyond Ems, by the side of the Lahn, whose windings the road followed for some miles, till the romantic castle of Nassau came in view. We then crossed at the ferry, and ascended a lofty hill, from the different points of which a variety of rich romantic scenes successively presented themselves. We soon arrived at the village of Holzhausen, where we changed horses. Here a wretched alteration suddenly took place in the country and the weather; the roads were execrable, and hill succeeding hill presented the same combination of barren uncultivated heath, or sombre forest, till with tired horses, and amidst torrents of rain, we entered Schwalbach. A large English family had taken possession of the whole accommodation of the establishment. Milord and his suite seemingly occupied every room in the house, whilst his ponderous carriage had seized possession of the *remise*, and excluded our light *calèche*, till, with some difficulty, we persuaded a surly and smoking German *wagermeister* to suffer them to pass the night together. For ourselves, we obtained beds in an adjoining house, just far enough off to get wet through in reaching it.

Eager to get out of this unhappy place, we were in our carriage early next morning. A drizzling rain fell incessantly, and the road lay over the same succession of wooded hills. At length, after two hours' travelling, we emerged from a thick forest on the brow of an eminence, just as the heavy vapours, rolling away, discovered the rich valley of the Rhine extended before us. The effect was magical; the partial power of the sun rendered the colouring beautifully various. The towers of Mayence were seen at a distance, emerging from the fog, and Wisbaden was close under the foot of the hill. At this latter place we stopped for a short time, and then resumed our journey to Cassel, and over the bridge of boats to Mayence.

Mayence is beautifully situated on the banks of the Rhine; and besides its majestic cathedral, contains several palaces and other noble buildings, many of which are now converted into barracks. Its squares too, and streets, are broad and handsome; but the military form the chief feature of the city. Six thousand Prussians and Austrians were still quartered in the place when we were there, forming one of the *garnisons confédératives* of the Holy Alliance.

(…)

Aug. 19. – Re-crossing the Rhine to Cassel, we followed the direction of the Maine to Frankfort. In our way thither we passed the small town of Hocheimer. The sides of the hill on which it stands are entirely covered with vines, from the grapes of which the famous Hock wine is made. The entrance to Frankfort is very striking: on the site of the ramparts handsome houses have been erected; gardens, with pieces of ornamental water, occupy the place of the moat; and a belt of public walks, with shrubs, flowers and orangeries, encompasses the whole city, except on the side of the river where the principal houses of merchants, ambassadors, or public buildings are situated. Beyond this outer circle are the *Maisons de campagne* of the wealthy citizens, most of whom have also residences within the city. The chief streets are broad, and built with noble houses; and the squares are adorned with elegant fountains. Much business seems to be carried on here, and the merchants form an opulent and highly respectable class. By the politeness of M. Goegel, we were introduced to the reading-room of the

Cassino, where, besides three English papers, the journals of nearly the whole Continent lie on the table.

At Frankfort every one attends the opera: it is held quite a public affair; and although they do not expend so much on it as the Grand Duke at Darmstadt, still the performances are extremely respectable. The house itself is gloomy and shabby, but we understood it was in contemplation to build a new one: the orchestra is good, and very well conducted, and the singers are deservedly admired.

(...)

Sunday, Aug. 29. – We passed a pleasant idle day at Coblentz, promenading about the town, and visiting the different churches. After dinner, about six o'clock, we strolled to some gardens in the neighbouring village of Pfaffendorf. Here we found a respectable assemblage of officers, ladies, and citizens, eating and drinking, whilst dancing was carried on with great spirit in the house: we drank the refreshing beverage, composed of Rhenish wine and Selters water, under the trellice-work of vines, which covered the whole garden. The evening was delicious: the setting sun still struggled with his warmer tints against the moon; but the latter at length gained ascendancy, and shed her sober influence over the rich landscape, whilst her beams danced in the ripples of the Rhine, which rolled at our feet. Lower down, the black outlines of Ehrenbreitstein were seen frowning over the bridge and city of Coblentz.

William Makepeace Thackeray, *Letters*

To Mrs. Carmichael-Smith

Coblentz, July 31st 1830

Cologne as the guide book saith had at one time 365 churches and this the waiter & some gentlemen at the table d'hote was exactly the no of days in the year. It had likewise 1000 virgins who were destroyed by the Romans & whose unfortunate bones have been used to decorate a Church. The town is beastly – the Cathedral unfinished, the weather was hot beyond all bearing - & I was consequently in my own room a great part of the day employing myself between sleeping smoking reading, & eating raw herring & onions.

Yesterday the beauties of the journey began, & I really think the Rhine is almost equal to the Thames. One or two views were of course magnificent – The ladies had got their Byrons to read when they arrived at "the castled crag of Drachenfels" – here is something like unto it (sketch). There was a pretty little girl on board to whom I talked the most delicious sentiment and quoted Shelley and Moore to her great edification and delight. I really did feel rather sentimental, & intended to have made some pathetic verses on her & the Rhine but she came from a boarding school at Boulogne, & that staggered my sentiment; & dinner was ordered & that entirely destroyed it – Last night we arrived here, tomorrow I go on to Francfort – A gentleman of the name of Balfour a fellow passenger is going with me presently to Ems about nine miles from Coblentz.

This is a beautiful place, magnificent old houses, old turrets old bridges &c – I have got one or two sketches: the Moselle & the Rhine here join; the grand fortress of Ehrenbreitstien looks over the town & here you must fill up the description from your imagination – There are some thousand Prussian Soldiers in the town. I walked a mile with a regiment of them this morning at 5. (I went out to sketch) the band is the most beautiful I ever heard far superior to the band of the horse Guards. The men are noble looking fellows in short blue jackets & black crop belts – I have met with some figures among the people here and two who were on board the steamer. The boy with the pipe was exactly like Rapheal & the man would have made a good study for a Buccaneer – We had on board 2 nobles with one of whom I have made acquaintance the Duc de Fitzjames and the old Russian Admiral Tchelchagoff. I have been writing with Seppia as I could get no ink. Good bye Dearest Mother till next week when I will write again.

I wish I could say something better than the stale & formal Remember me to all at home & believe me your affte Son
W. M. Thackeray.

To Mrs. Carmichael-Smith

Godesberg on the Rhine, August 12th 1830
You will see by the direction of this letter that I am not where my last supposed I should be by this time. I am writing now from a village in the neighbourhood of the most beautiful part of the "Father of Rivers" – close to Drachenfels & its six sister Mountains; & not much farther from Nonnenwert. I was induced to come here by meeting at Francfort a Cambridge acquaintance, a German called Schulte – He told me that I would join his party (which consists of My Baynon a tutor of Heses College Oxford & an undergraduate Trotter) he would give me an hours reading in German every day; & engage that I should live at as cheap a rate as at any place in Germany. After we have stayed here for a month he has asked me to stay the same time with him at his Fathers in Westphalia; and I thought this would be the cheapest and pleasantest plan I could pursue. He has given me an introduction to a Gentleman at Dresden, with whom he stayed when there - & he says that for me he thinks it would be an excellent family to stay with.

The place where we are now staying is quiet, & cheap, and excessively beautiful. About three miles off is the town & University of Bonn. We walked in a few days ago, & Schulte met one of his old friends who took us to his room and gave us tea, & afterwards took us to a commerz house where thirty

or forty of the men were assembled to drink smoke & sing – We were rather Lions & treated most civilly – in fact the civility was rather overpowering for with almost every one of these men we had to drink einhalbe – half a tumbler of small sour wine – The men are raw dirty rough looking cubs with little caps & long pipes – from half glasses some bolder spirits proceeded to whole ones & there were half a dozen men who pledged each other in four tumblers a piece. The men I met were all of one club the Rhenanier (I wont answer for spelling) but in the University there are three more – The Prussians, Westphalians and the Burschenschaft. It is the pride of each of these to insult the others, and thereby gain duels, of which they seem extraordinarily fond. On the night I was there, six or seven duels were got up; and are to be fought on Monday in an inn not far from this. Each Club has a president a vice & a sub who are chosen chiefly from their distinction in the duello – I became a great friend of the president of the Rhenaniers inasmuch that he has invited us to a large party of the whole of the club (about 300) which is to take place in a few days – he has got some duels on hand which he has graciously asked us to come & see fought on Monday. The men's singing was I thought excellent, every man has to sing a verse in his turn, I piously & patriotically chanted out God save the King – In the course of the evening they all sung a hymn to the Rhine, upstanding and uncovered – On breaking up I found myself the only strictly sober man in the party although during the evening I had positively imbibed no less than six bottles of the wine – My potations cost me a dollar. 3 shillings – It was after the Port wine and Punch of Cambridge like so much milk and water or vinegar & water for it had an unpleasant effect on my internals; in fact the wine and the dinners have kept me &c &c.
(…)

To Mrs. Carmichael-Smith

Godesberg on the Rhine, August 15th 1830
One of our party is going to England tomorrow, so dearest Mother, I think I can do no harm if I send a few hasty lines home by him.

Since I wrote last, I have been doing little else but reading the German Grammar, a very praiseworthy but not a very pleasant employment – The students of Bonn their duels & their drinking bouts I have cut, for I think they are a wondrous stupid set of fellows – Yesterday morning (and this is by far the most extraordinary event which has happened to me) Yesterday morning I say – I went without my breakfast; & took a mighty long walk to Drachenfels; I was however exceedingly disappointed, for though the view was of course more extended; yet as it only embraced long level tracts of fields, I could have done very well without taking an hours desperate walking up the hill & another hours walk to the hill – Not to mention tearing my boots, & running a nail into my heel.

(…)

My sketchbook & I[1] have almost parted company, for things begin to lose their novelty but I should like to spend a few thousand pounds on the castle of which I have given you a sketch and make a residence of it – Every old Castle and Hill, has a peculiar legend &tradition. I long to read German to understand them or rather I long to understand German to read them.

(…)

To Mrs. Carmichael-Smith

Weimar, September 28th 1830

(…)

Everybody who goes to Cassel sees Wilhelmshöhe; which is I think far superior to Versailles, the water works are very refreshing; there is a new Castle a l'antique with some tolerable pictures, a beautiful Chapel, & a delightful armory. I went in company with a German Student, & a Herr Professor, with whom I afterwards proceeded by diligence to Gotha by way of Eisenach, at Eisenach we stayed two hours, I had time to see Luthers hiding place in the old castle of Worzburg, where while all the world were seeking him he was quietly lodged, translating the Bible & having occasional tiffs with the Author of Evil. They shew you a place in his study where in the height of his wrath he discharged an inkstand at the Devil, who had long tormented him in the shape of blue-bottle fly – In performing this pilgrimage to the Worzburg I lost my dinner & got thoroughly wet through, in this unhappy state I had to proceed to Gotha, under the wracking pains of hunger & rheumatism, which I am sorry to say has been my constant companion since I left Eberfeldt; I have had it in my shoulder & my face for some time I could not use my arms, & afterwards for a considerable period I could not use my teeth!

I slept at Gotha & come on here, & here I trust will end my travels; for though the Society is small it is remarkably good, & tho' court is absurdly ceremonious, I think it will rub off a little of the rust which School & College have given me.

Francis Bond Head, *Bubbles from the Brunnens of Nassau by an Old Man*

About sixty years ago the Stahl and Weinbrunnens were discovered. These springs were found to be quite different from the old one, inasmuch as, instead

---

[1] Thackeray enjoyed making simple pencil or pen-and-ink sketches, and good editions of his letters offer reproductions of them.

of being only sulphureous, they were both strongly impregnated with iron and carbonic acid gas. Instead, therefore, of merely purifying the blood, they boldly undertook to strengthen the human frame; and, in proportion as they attracted notice, so the old original brunnen became neglected. About three years ago a new spring was discovered in the valley above the Weinbrunnen; this did not contain quite so much iron as the Stahl or Weinbrunnen; but possessing other ingredients (among them that of novelty) which were declared to be more salutary, it was patronised by Dr. Fenner, as being preferable to the brimstone as well as other brunnens in the country. It was accordingly called Pauline, after the present Duchess of Nassau, and is now the fashionable brunnen or well of Langen-Schwalbach.

The village doctors, however, disagree on the subject; and Dr. Stritter, a very mild, sensible man, recommends his patients to the strong Stahl brunnen, almost as positively as Dr. Fenner sentences his victims to the Pauline. Which is right and which is wrong, is one of the mysteries of this world; but as the cunning Jews all go to the Stahl brunnen, I strongly suspect that they have some good reason for this departure from the fashion.

As I observed people of all shapes, ages, and constitutions, swallowing the waters of Langen-Schwalbach, I felt that, being absolutely on the brink of the brunnen, I might, at least as an experiment, join this awkward squad – that it would be quite time enough to desert if I should find reason to do so – in short, that by trying the waters I should have a surer proof whether they agreed with me or not, than by listening to the conflicting opinions of all the doctors in the universe. However, not knowing exactly in what quantities to take them, having learnt that Dr. Fenner himself had the greatest number of patients, and that moreover being a one-eyed man he was much the easiest to be found, I walked towards the shay walk near the Allee Saal, resolving eventually to consult him; however, in turning a sharp corner, happening almost to run against a gentleman in black, "cuilumenademptum," I gravely accosted him, and finding, as I did in one moment, that I was right, in the middle of the street I began to explain that he saw before him a wheel which wanted a new tire – a shoe which required a new sole – a worn-out vessel seeking the hand of the tinker; in short, that feeling very old, I merely wanted to become young again.

(...)

During the fashionable season at Langen-Schwalbach, the dinner hour at all the Saals is one o'clock. From about noon scarcely a stranger is to be seen; but a few minutes before the bell strikes one, the town exhibits a picture curious enough, when it is contrasted with the simple costume of the villagers, and the wild-looking country which surrounds them. From all the Hofs and lodging houses, a set of demure, quiet-looking, well-dressed people are suddenly disgorged, who, at a sort of funeral pace, slowly advance towards the Allee Saal, the Goldene Kette, the Kaiser Saal, and one of two other houses, *où l'on dîne*. The ladies are not dressed in bonnets, but in caps, most of which are quiet; the rest being of those indescribable shapes which are to be seen in London or Paris. Whether the stiff stand-up frippery of bright-red ribands was meant to represent a house on fire, or purgatory itself – whether those immense white ornaments were intended for reefs or coral or not – it is out of my department to guess – ladies' caps being riddles only to be explained by themselves.

Thomas Hood, *Letters*

To Charles Wentworth Dilke

752 Alte Graben, Coblenz, 26th Dec., 1836

My dear Dilke,

(…)

You have heard how well I got through my first day's ride – it was a fine morning, and we crossed part of the flat which surrounds Leipzic – what an immense flat it is! An ocean of sand literally stretching beyond the reach of the eye. It seems to have been intended for the grand armies of Europe to decide their differences on. That is to say, if Nature of Providence ever intended to form convenient plains for wholesale butcheries, of which I have some doubt.

However, it is classic ground to the soldier, as several great battles have taken place in the neighbourhood. The next morning, I packed up and started at four, and after rather a long spell got to Brenha, where I found my quarters at a sort of country inn and butcher's shop rolled into one. I only breakfasted at Brenha – spending the rest of my time at a château of Baron B-'s, with De Franck and the Captain – the old Major-domo, the image of a Scotchman, doing the honours. He set down to invite me, and thence foreward I boarded at the château, and only slept and breakfasted at the inn. I had the prettiest girl in the place for my waitress – and told her I was a prisoner of state on parole with the regiment, which interested her in my favour, I suppose: anyhow it brought up the mother – dram bottle in hand – who sat herself down, *tête à tête* at the table, and seemed determined to hear all the rights of it: but I grew very English, and her curiosity could get nothing out of me. At the château we lived like fighting-cocks, and drank a very good wine, made on the estate, as good as much of the Rhenish. (…)

At the inn I had one dinner, one supper, bed twice, and two breakfasts, for ten groschen, or one shilling. But these bye-places are poor, and a little money goes a great way. Here I not only found soap for the first time in Germany, but a place in the *bason* expressly for holding it. The Saxons seemed generally good sort of people. Our next march took us across the Elbe to Wittenberg. A Lieutenant J-, an old crony of De Franck's, met us on the bridge, and insisted on our dining with him, so we got leave, dined at the Casino, and J- showed me the lions of the place.

(…)

Everything about Potsdam smacks of the Great little Frederic, but nothing is more striking than the superabundance of statues. They *swarm*! – there is a whole garrison turned into marble or stone, good, bad, and indifferent. They are as numerous in the garden as the promenaders; there is a Neptune group, for example, without even the apology of a pond. The same at Sans Souci – in fact everywhere. The effect, to my taste, is execrable, or ridiculous. Solitude and stillness seem the proper attributes of a statue. We have no notion of marbles mobbing. I saw, of course, all the apartments and relics of Frederic. The chairs torn by his dogs, his writing-table, &c. The Watteaus on the walls, containing the recurrent *belle* Barberini, pleased me much; he seems to give a nature to courtliness, and a courtliness to nature, that make palace-gardens more like fairy-land, and their inhabitants more like Loves and Graces than I fear they be in reality.

(…)

Thomas Hood, *Up the Rhine*

My dear Gerard, After the postscript of my last letter, you will not be surprised to hear, that a longer stay at Bonn was strongly objected to by my Uncle, who, having "not many days to live," sets a peculiar value on his nights. Like myself, he had been annoyed by the nocturnal rattling and singing, and indeed he declared in the morning that he would as life reside "next door to Vauxhall."

The arrival of the first steam-boat was therefore the signal for our departure; and bidding adieu to Bonn with an emphatic "Peace be with you", we embarked in the Prince William. It had brought a tolerable assortment of tourists from Cologne, and amongst the rest our old acquaintance the Red-faced man. For some reason he fought particularly shy of my Uncle, but with myself he was communicative and complaining as usual. He gave me to understand that he had been prodigiously disgusted by the high Catholic mummeries at Cologne, and still more annoyed by the companionship of the "Yellow-faced Yankee," who of course, to plague him, had taken up his quarters at the same hotel. "Renounce me," said he, "if I could get rid of him – for as we two were the only persons who spoke English in the house, he *would* converse with me, whether I answered or not. Consume his yellow body! He stuck to me like a mustard plaster, and kept drawing my feelings into blisters; however, I've got a good start of him, for he talked of staying a whole week at Cologne." But alas! for the pleasant anticipations of Mr. John Broker! He had barely uttered them, when the turmeric-coloured American appeared running at full speed towards the steam-boat, followed by a leash of porters! "Say I told you so!" exclaimed the petrified citizen – "he'll haunt me up to Schaffhausen, he will, by all that's detestable – yes, there he comes on board!" and even as he spoke, the abhorred personage sprang into the vessel, followed by his three attendants. (...)

The bell now rang, forewarning the passengers and their friends that it was time to separate; whereupon, to the infinite surprise of my Aunt, two remarkably corpulent old gentlemen tumbled into each other's arms, and exchanged such salutes as are only current in England amongst females, or between parties of opposite sexes. To our notions there is something repulsive in this kissing amongst men; but when two weather-beaten veterans, "bearded like the pard", or like Blücher, indulge in these labial courtesies, there is also something ludicrous in the picture. It is, however, a national propensity, like the bowing (...)

And now, Gerard, could I but write scenery as Stanfield paints it, what a rare dioramic sketch you should have of the thick-coming beauties of the abounding river: the Romantic Rolandseck – the religious Nonnenswerth – the Picturesque Drachenfels! But "Views on the Rhine" are little better than shadows even in engravings, and would fare still worse in the black and white of a letter. Can the best japan fluid give a notion of the shifting lights and shades, the variegated tints of the thronging mountains –of the blooming blue of the SiebenGebirge! Besides, there is not a river or a village but has been done in pen and ink ten times over by former tourists. Let it be understood then, once for all, that I shall not attempt to turn prospects into prospectuses, "And do all the gentlemen's seats by the way." I must say a few words, however, on a peculiarity which seems to have escaped the notice of other travellers: the extraordinary transparency of the atmosphere in the vicinity of the Rhine. The rapidity of the current, always racing in the same direction, probably creates a draught which carries off the mists that are so apt to hang about more sluggish streams – or to float lazily to and fro with the ebb and flow of such tide rivers as the Thames: certain it is, that the lovely scenery of the "arrowy Rhine" is viewed through an extremely pure medium. To one like myself, not particularly lynx-sighted, the effect is as if some fairy euphrasy had conferred a supernatural *clairvoyance* on the organs of vision. Trees and shrubs, on the crests of the hills, seem made out, in the artist phrase, to their very twigs; and the whole landscape appears with the same distinctness of detail as if seen through an opera-glass or spectacles. To mention one remarkable instance: some miners were at work on the face of a high precipitous mountain near Unkel; the distance from the steamer was considerable, so that the blows of their sledges and pickaxes were quite unheard; yet there were the little figures, plying their tiny tools, so plainly, so apparently close to the eye, that it was difficult to believe that they were of the common dimensions of the human race. Had those dwarf miners, the Gnomes of German Romance, a material as well as a fabulous existence? Of course not: but I could not help thinking that I saw before me the source whence tradition had derived the Lilliputian mine-hunting elfins of the Wisperthal, who constructed the Devil's Ladder.

Elisabeth Gaskell, *Letters*

Letter 15 to Elizabeth Holland

Monday morning, Knutsford (late 1841)

My dearest Lizzy,

(...)

And now to some account of 'Germany & the Germans', I know it's dull work talking about cathedrals, but I must just say, no human being who has not seen them can conceive of the sublime beauty of the cathedrals in the grand of cities in Flanders. The architects, (so unknown by name to us) must have been the noblest poets, for I never saw such practical poetry – I enjoyed Bruges, Ghent & Antwerp – more than I can tell. While every bit was picturesque the whole was solemn & sublime, appearing so deserted & lonely, as if the world had stood still with them since the 14th century. If ever you go, don't miss these towns on any account. Aix la Chapelle too is another point of grandeur not to be missed. We got to the Rhine at Cologne which smells of the bones of the 3,000 virgins. The Rhine (very sub rosa) was a disappointment. To be sure it rained cats & dogs – but the hills & rocks are round not pointed in their outline – just like Mrs Robberd's engravings – do you remember 'em. We met some charming people, had a splendid day for ascending the Drackenfels, & breakfasting among the vineyards at the top, with a party including some relations of Coleridge[2] – one a son of Judge Coleridge, & all remembering & speaking with affection of the 'old man eloquent'. I should like to tell you of our conversation it was so high-toned & so superior, not that we spoke much, we only listened and admired. You know don't you that Heidelberg is not on the Rhine, about 20 miles from it in a valley far more beautiful, the valley of the Neckar. It's no use trying to describe, & I hate people who attempt it. You must fancy 'an union of all beauties', for Heidelberg, spending scenery, dark pine woods rocks, & the picturesque town, and noble castle to complete it. As for legends the place

---

[2] Given the interest "the old man eloquent" took in German romanticism, there is something very fitting about his being mentioned on the slopes of Drachenfels, the mountain on the Rhine with a ruined castle made so popular in the nineteenth century by Byron's verses in *Childe Harold's Pilgrimage*.

is haunted. There is an Ondine (the name of a genus as well as an individual,) who dwells in the secret spring of the sea green Neckar. The waters of the Neckar as like sea water exactly – rushing & foaming over red sand-stone rocks, which make the most beautiful colouring you can imagine. All this is to relieve my own mind from the oppressive recollection of so much beauty – just the sort of scene of loveliness which made one sigh to look at it. All this has done me the good like the word in 'The Doctor &c', which relieved the author so much. So now to something that will interest you. We were invited to stay at a sister's of Mrs Schabe, Frau von Pickford, englished into Mrs Pickford, though I found you can't slight a German noble more than by dropping the aristocratic *von.*, though nearly every other person is noble. Nothing being required but a patent of nobility to enable any one to become a 'noble lady', & these patents being given on very slight occasions but never purchased. Then the descendents are *vons* for ever – Mrs Pickford is a widow with 3 daughters at home. Emma 29, very good & very plain, sensible unselfish & the refuge of the whole family in any dilemma, Thekla 19, *very* lovely, and one of the most elegant people I ever saw, and Mathilda sixteen – fine looking with pale red hair – the two youngest very full of fun, and all very ladylike. The house is out of Heidelberg, with a splendid view from the windows, gardens & fountains on each side (…) and most tiring walk up the wooded hill behind from which you have *splendid views* (don't be tired of 'splendid views', I can't help it there were so many.) We got there the first evening at tea-time unexpected as to the day, though they were aware of our coming. Mrs P. told us they were all planning to go with Mrs and Miss Howitt to a festival at the Wolf's brunnen about 3 miles off – would we like to go. To be sure we were up to anything – and hardly staid to enquire what & where but flew to put on things and on returning to the drawing found Mrs & Miss H. &every body ready. Our first glimpse at 'Mary' as we called her in joke to each other till I was afraid we should slip it out before her was in the dusk, & I could only see instead of the simple Quaker I had pictured to myself, a lady in a gay-coloured satin, black satin scarf & leghorn bonnet with a plume of drooping white feathers. It was such a funny feeling of astonishment, and miss Howitt was equally unquakerish – so we sallied forth with very dancing spirits along the picturesque road overhung with walnut trees and winding by the side of the Necker, the moon rising over the hill-tops. Presently we left the road & began to follow a rougher path through a pine-wood, very mysterious & dark-looking. We began to hear music – the most lively waltzes and presently came to a splashing fountain, set round with coloured lamps, 20 yards, and another turn and we were in an open space in the dark wood – boarded over, the grass, & about 20 people whirling to the most spirited band I ever heard. About 200 stood by ready to spin off when any one gave up. Most of the men were Heidelberg students, with their pointed beards and mustachios, caps and blouses. The girls were peasant girls, in their picturesque dresses, the dark trees round were hung with lamps. The peasants don't learn dancing, it comes by instinct. A very fashionable waltz step came up while we were at Heidelberg the ecossaise, and the little girls with their empty milk pails went dancing it along the road. To go back to our merry night scene. Mrs P. was afraid the students a most riotous race, might get too boisterous so we did not stay half so long as I should have liked but came home, & a merry supper ended our first evening – we as intimate with the nice Pickford girls as if we had known them for years. I think I must tell you about our sitting-rooms they were so german, 3 opening one out of the other by folding doors as all rooms do in Germany, the Howitts had 6 rooms which were generally all thrown open in this way. No carpets of course on the floors of any rooms, but worsted work chairs cushions & sofas without end – all furniture of walnut-tree wood (so pretty,) and looking glasses in every hole & corner. We breakfasted at ½ past seven – little rolls of exquisite white bread (made with *vinegar*-barn Mrs Housekeeper) butter without salt, & coffee. The Ps took a cup of coffee & two mouthfuls of bread without butter & their breakfast was done. While we used, hungry & ashamed, to keep stealing one roll after another. After breakfast we read, sauntered in the beautiful garden, called on the Howitts, shopped (so amusing) received callers listened to Thekla's magnificent playing – ½ past 12 dinner which was a long affair, first soup, then boiled meat & potatoes (which last we never saw again,) then sausages & pancakes (no bad mixture) then RAW pickled fish & kidney beans or peas stewed in oil, then pudding, then roast meat & salad, then apricot or cherry open flat tart about 1 yd ½ in circumference & no joke such immense things; the desert-cakes, apricots wild strawberries – then coffee – all this spun out till 2 o'clock when we generally went some excursions or at any rate some walk. We never drank tea alone I think. Sometimes some of the students when we had music dancing & all manner of games; sometimes the Howitts – when we all told the most frightening & wild stories we had ever heard, some such fearful ones – all true – then we drank tea out at the Howitts, looking over all the portfolios of splendid engravings, casts &c they had collected (My word! Authorship brings them in a pretty penny) at the Webers – he a Dr of Philosophie – grave German & philosophical, to say nothing of politico-oeconomical evenings at the Schlosser's.

Herman Melville, *Journal of a Tour to London and the Continent*

Sunday, 9th December, 1849

Cologne

Sallied out before breakfast and found my way to the famous cathedral, where the everlasting "crane" stands on the Tower.[3] While inside was accosted by a polite worthy who was very civil pointing out the "curios". He proved a "valet de place." He tormented me home to the Hotel & got a franc out of me. Upon going to the Steamer Office I learned that no boat would leave that morning. So I had to spend the day in Cologne. But it was not altogether unpleasant for me to do. In this antiquated gable-ended old town – full of Middle Age, Charlemagne associations – where Ruebens was born & Mary De Medici died – there is much to interest a pondering man like me. But now to tell how at last I found that I had not put up at the "Hôtel de Cologne," but at the "Hôtel du Rhine" – where my bill for a bed, a tea & a breakfast amounted to some $2, in their unknowable German currency. Having learnt about the Steamer, I went to the veritable Hôtel de Cologne (on the river) & there engaged the services of a *valet de place* to show me the sights of the town for 2 francs. We went to the Cathedral, during service – saw the tomb of the *Three Kings of Cologne* – their skulls. The choir of the church is splendid. The structure itself is one of the most singular in the world. One transept is nearly complete – in new stone, and strangely contrasts with the ruinous condition of the vast unfinished tower on one side. From the Cathedral we went to the Jesuits' Church, where service was being performed. Thence to the Museum & saw some odd old paintings; & one splendid one (a sinking ship, with the Captain at the mast-head – defying his foe) by Scheffer (?). Thence to St. Peter's Church & saw the celebrated *Descent from the Cross* by Ruebens. Paid 2 francs to see the original picture turned round by the Sacristan. Thence home. Went into a book store & purchased some books (Views & Panoramas of the Rhine) & then to the Hotel. At one o'clock dinner was served (Table d'hôte), a regular German dinner & a good one, "I tell you". Innumerable courses - & an apple pudding was served between the courses of meat & poultry. I drank some yellow Rhenish wine which was capital, looking out on the storied Rhine as I dined. After dinner sallied out & roamed about the town – going into churches, buying cigar of pretty cigar girl, & stopping people in the street to light my cigar. I drank in the very vital spirit & soul of old Charlemagne, as I turned the quaint old corners of this quaint old town. Crossed the bridge of boats, & visited the

---

3 Something of a Sagrada Familia, for almost five hundred years Cologne cathedral had the dubious honour of being Europe's largest unfinished structure. Work, which had started in 1248, was stopped in 1473, and was not taken up again until 1842. The cathedral was eventually completed in 1880.

fortifications on the thither side. At dusk stopped at a beer shop - & took a glass of *black ale* in a comical flagon of glass. Then home. And here I am writing up my journal for the last two days. At nine o' clock (3 hours from now) I start for Coblenz – 60 miles from hence. I feel homesick to be sure – being all alone with not a soul to talk to – but then the Rhine is before me, & I must on. The sky is overcast, but it harmonizes with the spirit of the place.

Monday, 10th December, 1849

Coblenz

Embarked last night about 9 ½ P.M. for Coblenz. But before so doing went out after tea to take a final stroll through old Cologne. Upon returning to the hotel, found a large party assembled, filling up all the tables in the Dining Salon. Every man had his bottle of Rhenish, and his cigar. It was a curious scene. I took the tall spires of glasses for castles & towers, and fancied the Rhine flowed between them. I drank a bottle of *Rüdesheimer* (?). When the boat pushed off it was very dark, & I made my way to the 2nd cabin. There I encountered a German who was just from St. Louis in Missouri. I had a talk with him. From 9 ½ P.M. till 5 A.M. I laid down & got up, shivering by turns with the cold. Thrice I went on deck, & found the boat gliding between tall black cliffs & crags. – A grand sight. At last arrived in Coblenz in the dark, & got into a bed at the "*Géant Hoff*" near the quay. At ten o'clock in the morning descended to breakfast, & after than took a *valet de place* & crossed the Bridge of Boats to the famous Quebec fortress Ehrenbreitstein. A magnificent object truly. The view from the summit is superb. Far away winds the Rhine between its castellated mountains. Crossed the river again, & walked about the town, entering the curious old churches, half Gothic, half Italian – and crossed the Moselle at the stone bridge near where Prince Metternich was born. Singular that he was born so near the great fortress of Germany. Still more curious that the finest wine of all the Rhine is grown right under the guns of Ehrenbreitstein. At one o'clock dined at "The Géant" at the table d'hôte. There were some six or eight English present – two or three ladies & many German officers. The dinner was very similar to the dinner at the Hôtel de Cologne yesterday. After dinner walked out to the lower walls & into the country along the battlements. The town is walled entirely. At dinner I drank nothing but Moselle wine – thus keeping the counsel of the "Governor of Coney Island", who maxim it is, "to drink the wine of the country in which you may be travelling." Thus at Cologne on the banks of the Rhine, & looking at the river through the window opposite me – what could I imbibe but Rhenish? And *now*, at Coblenz – at the precise junction of the Moselle – what regale myself with but Moselle? – The wine is bluish – at least *tinged* with blue – and seems a part of the river after which it is called. At dusk I found myself standing in the silence at the point where the two storied old rivers meet. Opposite was the frowning fortress - & some 4000 miles was America & Lizzie. Tomorrow I am *homeward-bound*! Hurrah & three cheers!

George Eliot, *Letters*

George Eliot to Charles Bray

Weimar, 16th August, 1854

Dear Friend,

I hope you want to hear something of me though I confess I do not write to satisfy your wants but my own. It is a necessity to me to know how you all are, and I venture to hope that if I ask you for a letter you send me one.

I have had a month of exquisite enjoyment, and seem to have begun life afresh. I am really strong and well and have recovered the power of learning in spite of age and grey hairs. The first part of our route lay through Belgium. Mr. R. Noel was a very pleasant companion in the steamboat to Antwerp, where he left us for Bonn. From Antwerp we went to Brussels, and by Namur and Liège to Cologne. On the way to Cologne we were joined in our railway carriage by Dr. Brabant, who exerted himself to procure me an interview with Strauss. It was rather melancholy. Strauss looks so strange and cast-down, and my deficient German prevented us from learning more of each other than our exterior which in the case of both would have been better left to the imagination.

We went up the Rhine from Cologne to Mainz, Frankfurt being the main attraction to us for Goethe's sake. A ten hours' railway journey from Frankfurt brought us to Weimar where we have pitched our tent – that is, taken a small lodging, with the intention of staying a month or two. The first sight of Weimar – "the Athens of the North" was a considerable surprise to us. We had expected something stately as your little statue of Goethe and lo! we found a huge village rather than a town – a place so sleepy that it has no gas and its shopkeepers do not think it worth while to put up their names at their doors. But the immense park and plantations with labyrinthine walks are a constant source of new pleasure, and there are charming evening or morning excursions to be made to Belvedere, Tieffurt and Ettersburg, the grand Duke's summer residences.

Above all Liszt is here.[4] He lives with a Russian Princess, who is in fact his wife, and he is a Grand Seigneur in this place, whereas Hofrath or Court Councillor is seldom anything more, as an Englishman would say, than a poor author. Liszt

---

[4] In the 1840s, Europe had been swept by "Lisztomania". The charismatic composer was something of a prototype pop star on the piano, and was known as a kind and charitable personality (he donated significant amounts to the Cologne cathedral fund). In the next chapter, Bagby's *A Weimar Idyll* satirizes the widespread adulation for Liszt, which remained undiminished in his later years.

is extremely kind to us. We have been to a déjêuner at the Altenburg, where he lives, and the Princess has behaved charmingly to us. He is coming to-day to dine with us at the Erbprinz, our usual place for dining, where we have six courses of dishes so imaginative in their conception that my intellect feasts as well as my palate and all for 10 groschen = 1 shilling!

Liszt is the first really inspired man I ever saw. His face might serve as a model for a St. John in its sweetness when he is in repose but seated at the piano he is as grand as one of Michael Angelo's prophets. When I read George Sand's letter to Franz Liszt in her 'Lettres d'un Voyageur,' I little thought that I should ever be seated tête-à-tête with him for an hour, as I was yesterday and telling my ideas and feelings.

Another person who is very kind and agreeable is the Hofrath Schöll, a man thoroughly erudite after the German fashion but without any of the German heaviness. He goes to court, but the other evening at Belvedere he brought his wife and children and took out of his pocket a piece of cake – continental cake – that is, batter pudding baked in a pan with fruit, which he had carried in order to give them a treat after their coffee. I am getting on a little in my German, but am retarded by having work to do which obliges me to read a great deal of French. Liszt and the Princess speak French, but Schöll gives me some practice in German.

(…)

Think always kindly of your sincere and affectionate Friend

Marian Evans.

George Eliot to Charles Bray

Berlin, 12th November, 1854

Dear Friend,

(…)

We reached Berlin last Saturday, or rather a week ago yesterday, and find much to enjoy here. Varnhagen von Ense and Fraulein v. Solmar, old friends of Mr. Lewes's, have received me very kindly, and as they are in the best society of Berlin, this is no slight advantage. Mr. Lewes has not yet had time to call on half his friends, but all whom he has seen appear delighted to meet him again. Fraulein von Solmar has a *salon* which is open every evening but Thursday to persons who have been invited once for all. Varnhagen made a little party for us last Thursday, offers the use of his library, and is altogether cordial. He had corresponded with Carlyle for years before Carlyle came to Germany (in 1852) and was terribly disappointed when he came to know him in the flesh. Varnhagen is a courtier, wears an order round his neck and carries a gold headed cane, so you may image that Carlyle's roughness and petulance were rather shocking to him. Withal this

Varnhagen is a theoretical democrat, and thinks "Past and Present" Carlyle's greatest work, while to his dismay he found that Carlyle talked the fiercest despotism etc. etc.

Last night we went to see "Nathan der Weise." You know, or perhaps you do not know that this play is a sort of dramatic apologue the moral of which is religious tolerance. It thrilled me to think that Lessing dared nearly a hundred years ago to write the grand sentiments and profound thoughts which this play contains for the people's theatre which he dreamed of, but which Germany has never had. In England the words which call down applause here would make the pit rise in horror.

It is amusing to see how very comfortable the Germans are without many of the things England considers the safeguards of society. The Germans eat their Bratwurst and Küchen from house to house in gladness of heart though they have no Episcopal establishment and though they *have* some things which are thought very noxious with us. I think them immensely inferior to us in creative intellect and in the possession of the *means* of life, but they know better how to use the means they have for the end of enjoyment. One sees everywhere in Germany what is the rarest of all things in England – thorough *bien-être,* freedom from gnawing cares and ambitions, contentment in inexpensive pleasures with no suspicion that happiness is a vice which we must not only not indulge in ourselves but as far as possible restrain others from giving way to. There are disadvantages, of course. They don't improve their locks and carriages as we do, and they consider a room furnished when it has a looking glass and an escritoire in it. They put their knives in their mouths, write un-sit-out-able comedies and unreadable books; but they are decidedly happy animals and in spite of Pascal, that is perhaps better than being extremely clever ones – miserable and knowing their misery.

(...)

Best love to all. Forgive all my omissions and commissions and believe ever
Your sincere and affectionate
Marian Evans

"The German" Replaces Germans: The Rise of Jingoism 1860 - 1900

Modern photography meets traditional Black Forest garb. Even as a united, industrial Germany became both admired and feared, its rustic side continued to define cultural clichés.

AFTER OTTO VON BISMARCK became prime minister of Prussia in 1861, he started to reshape the loosely-organized and entirely non-threatening German Confederation into what would become the Second German Empire. Rapid industrialization and wealth creation had turned the liberal pan-German idealism which had been disappointed by the failure of 1848 into a bourgeois, established, pragmatic nationalism happy to sacrifice a democratic agenda for German unification under Prussian military and economic leadership—the much quoted "blood and iron" respectively of Bismarck's 1862 speech to the Prussian parliament.

Denmark in 1863-64, Austria in 1866 and France in 1870-71: Prussia moved swiftly against its neighbours, bringing its new and expansive industrial capacity to bear in a series of lightning wars which, in turn, increased its size and power with every territory it swallowed up. In 1866 the German Confederation was dissolved and in 1871 King William of Prussia (b. 1797) was crowned German Emperor in the Hall of Mirrors at Versailles. For observers at the time, this was an astonishing testament to the frightening potential of a unified, assertive, industrialized Germany at the centre of Europe. Over the next thirty years Prussia consolidated the Second Empire, satisfying dissenters at home with the world's first welfare state and advancing on the international stage to rival Britain and the United States in economic, industrial and military might.

Both despite and due to this newly powerful incarnation of Germany, in the years leading up to the turn of the twentieth century mastery of the German language consolidated its cachet as a sought-after cultural skill in the English-speaking world. The children of the wealthy were often sent to learn it, and the literary achievements of the Romantics had well and truly entered the canon of Western literature. At the same time, however, rampant nationalism was the order of the day, and the changes inside Germany were colliding with those in the English-speaking countries, leading to increasing amounts of prejudice and anxiety. As the brutal and calculating way in which Bismarck united the country showed the potential it had to dominate Europe, Britain was reaching the zenith of its worldwide power and the United States was extending its influence ever wider on its home continent. The interplay of these two factors became evident in a newly jingoistic tone, born both of arrogance towards and fear of Germany as a new world power.

Funny Foreigners—and Funny English-speakers

Nevertheless, at the time of Henry James' (b. 1843) first letters from Germany, in 1860, Germany was still lacking strong political leadership while the United States had almost doubled its territory between 1840 and 1860. It is thus no surprise that James' attitude toward his German hosts was more patronizing than anything, especially given his immaturity at the time. Due to the polished style of his correspondence, it is easy to forget that he was just seventeen in 1860 and had been sent to Germany by his parents to learn the language. In his later letters from another stay in Germany in 1872-73, despite the "enchanted scenery" of the Black Forest, James gives the impression of being distinctly unimpressed by the country and the "flatness of mankind" as represented by the languid spa-town patients around him.

Mark Twain (b. 1835) is thoroughly different in this regard: while capable of making fun of Germany—and especially "the awful German language"—his tone is jovial and he shows a genuine interest in finding out more about the cultural differences between Germany and his homeland. As such, Twain goes very much against the pervasively jingoistic tone of his age. In the 1880 *A Tramp Abroad* he pokes fun at the proverbial laziness of German students, but engages with the reasons behind the slower pace of academic life.

Quite different in his approach to foreign peoples was Thomas Stevens (b. 1854), an Englishman who in 1884 decided to cycle across America. By the time he had finished his 14-week journey, he had become a national celebrity and was commissioned by a magazine to continue his journey around the world, publishing a book of his experiences in 1887. While he may not have been a particularly prejudiced man for his time, his assertions about the features and characteristics of certain "types" today often seem like ill-informed racism, and his general conviction of his superiority as an English-speaking white male drips from every word of his account. Nevertheless, his view of Germany is entertaining, and perhaps one of the last in which Germans are uniformly portrayed as bumbling, cheerful, lazy and servile rather than dangerous and domineering—and this in spite of the mammoth military fortifications he came across in Alsace.

In *Miss Träumerei: A Weimar Idyll* (1895), the now-forgotten American musician and author Albert Morris Bagby is unconcerned with Germans as a whole and more concerned with one single German, Franz Liszt, and one place in Germany, Weimar. His comic novella gently pokes fun at an innocent, earnest, deeply artistic type of young American possessed of an excess of sentiment and wholly too susceptible to the poetic charms of old Europe. It is the culmination of a century of English-speaking interest in Weimar, which, following the enthusiasm of the Romantics, ended up as an impersonation of its old self.

If Bagby is nevertheless generous in his irony, Jerome K. Jerome (b. 1859) is caustic. In his romp through Germany titled *Three Men on the Bummel,* published in 1900, nothing and no-one is safe from his sarcastic wit—neither his wife, his travelling companions, the Germans he comes across nor he himself. This is British jingoism in its most beguiling form: while clearly convinced that God was born an Englishman and that Victorian Britain is the measure of civilized life, Jerome is nevertheless able to mock himself too.

Enchanted Forests and Prussian Soldiers

The extract taken from *Three Men on the Bummel* shows Jerome's ability to view himself and his fellow travellers from the outside, albeit from the perspective of a horse rather than one of the Germans he characterizes. The idea of sentient, thinking, talking animals in Germany often comes to the fore in writing of this time, showing the impact of the folk stories of the Brothers Grimm and of Romantic writers. Twain has an encounter with a distinctly Poe-esque raven in the middle of the same forest where Gaskell (see Chapter 4) once spent an enchanted evening, and Stevens too refers to the fairy-tale aesthetic of the Black Forest.

Throughout the 1800s a body of knowledge and assumptions had been built up about Germany, revolving mainly around enchanted forests, simplistic peasants and decadent spa-towns, which allowed the predominantly professional writers we are dealing with here to call to mind these associations, play with them and either disprove or confirm them.

At the same time new ideas were being spread—not about Germany, but about "Germans", defined very much by the perceived Prussian characteristics of orderliness. In many places Jerome's *Three Men on the Bummel* offers discourses on "the Germans", with many of the same clichés as are alive and well today: the lack of a sense of humour is mentioned, as is the love of *Ordnung* and the unquestioning obedience to authority. Jerome's view is summed up in what may be the most quoted line from the book: "The German citizen is a soldier, and the policeman is his officer." Even if Stevens comments that "the average German would much rather loll around, sipping wine or beer, and smoking cigarettes, than impel a bicycle across a continent" (and what about the average Englishman or American?), the pervading tone of these years is an increase in stereotyping and prejudice, however humorous.

*

Henry James, *Letters*

Bonn, on the Rhine, Prussia
Wednesday, July 18th (1860)

To Thomas Sergeant Perry,

(…)

We came almost directly here, stopping for a couple of days only at Wiesbaden and Frankfort. At the former place of which I suppose you have heard, we drank of course of the hot waters, and witnessed the gambling for which it is famous. Then we sailed up (or down) the Rhine. I am not the first person who has been disappointed in the Rhine and have a better reason that many for such sacreligiousness inasmuch as I had just come from among the mountains of Switzerland whose high privilege it is to make everything else look mean and small.

We are all three of us installed in German families for the learning of the German tongue. Wilky and I together, Willie alone. The gentleman I am with is one Doctor Humpert, Latin and Greek professor at the Gymnasium here. His family is composed of his wife and sister who are to aid him in the task of conversing ceaselessly with us (a task for which they might seem to be but ill qualified as I don't believe that between them they can muster, Germanlike, more than half a dozen teeth.) Also of his son Theodore aged seventeen, of whom I see a little, as he is away at his lessons all day, and of five young Deutschers from six to fourteen years of age. With their company I am favoured only at meals. They are not his sons but are with him for intellectual cultivation, "all the comforts of a home" etc. This is an opportunity for me to see something of German life, in what would be called, I suppose the middle classes. I naturally compare it with the corresponding life at home, and think it truly inferior. The women stop at home all day, doing the housework, drudging, and leading the most homely and I should say joyless lives. I fancy they never look at a book, and all their conversation is about their pots and pans. The sister asked me the other day if we hadn't a king in the United States! The Doctor is a pleasant genial man with very little force of character and more book-learning, that is knowledge of Greek and Sanskrit than anything else. The other day, Sunday last, I think we went all of us, wife, sister and little Deutchers (a nice little party of eleven) to a place called Godeberg within ten minutes of this, by rail, to see a little mound, or mountain they call it, with a ruin on the top. Notwithstanding the stifling heat of the weather, and the dust, we went under a shed on the dusty road and partook of some steaming coffee and boggy loaf-cake, then strolled about and came back to drink some sweetened wine and water.

Bonn am Rhein, Preussen
Sunday, the fifth day of August (1860)

To Thomas Sergeant Perry,

(…)

We both went up and commenced study, which simply consists in translating German into English. I am now working at Schiller's play of *Maria Stuart*, which I like exceedingly, although I do get along so slowly with it. I am convinced that German may take its stand among the difficult languages of the earth. I shall consider myself fortunate if I am able, when I leave Bonn, to translate even the simplest things. I worked on ploddingly until dinner time which is at one o' clock. Shall I tell you what we had for dinner? I took particular note on purpose. Primo, some tepid cabbage-soup, its tepidity being the result of Fraulein Stamm's having poured it out almost a half an hour before we were called to dinner. (Fraulein Stamm is the sister of the Frau Doctorin – she sets the table and waits thereat) secundo – some boiled beef in rags and some excellent and greasy potatoes; terio some Westphalia smoked ham and some black beans. Lastly some stewed cherries and tarts. Voilà. After dinner I went upstairs and set to work again, but had not been long occupied when Willie came in and told us that Mother proposed going to Drachenfels, a mountain on the other side of the Rhine and commanded our attendance. This was cheerfully given. I went with Willie up to mother's lodgings. These are in a huge brick mansion built to imitate a feudal castle, situated immediately on the flat shore of the Rhine, so as that the water, I am told, sweeps in winter round its base. From M.'s sitting room which has a fine big stone balcony overlooking the river there is a lovely view. The Rhine is just here very broad. On its opposite bank are some fertile meadows and green hills called the Seven Mountains. The Drachenfels is one of these. Mother, my Aunt, Willie, Wilky, and Theodor the Doctor's son whom we asked to come with us formed our party. We took the steamboat for a place called Königswinter at the foot of the mountain. On the boat were a lot of students from the University here, who were going down the river to hold what they call a *Commerz* i.e. to go into a room and swill beer and wine with certain formalities and with emulative vigour till an advanced hour in the morning. I saw one of these entertainments in Switzerland and will tell you more about it when I see you. They had already commenced their work with huge ox-horns filled with Rhenish wine, and forced all the ladies on board (the German ones at least) to assist them therein at intervals of about ten minutes.

(…)

Botzen, Austrian Tyrol
September 9th (1872)

Zum Kaiserkrone

To his parents

We have preferred to break the long journey to Innsbruck, over the Brenner at this place, where we find an excellent inn and a little town sufficiently picturesque; but poor Italy already defunct and German in every stick and stone and uglier than ever by contrast. It is a most singular thing – the immediacy with which national differences begin and their universal pervasiveness. There is a sort of cathedral here which is as ugly and graceless and displeasing, as if the lovely churches of Verona were on another planet, instead of just across the Italian frontier. We shall have time, however, I hope, even in our few days in Germany to learn to cease to make invidious comparisons, and to judge things by German principles.

(…)

Homburg, Germany
August 10th (1873)

Dear Mrs. Wister,

(…)

I have been at Homburg a month, having come here, out of sorts, to attempt a "cure" with the waters. I have ceased to drink them – the "cure" not responding to my appeal; but I am staying because I like the place and have a constitutional shrinking from fleeing to ills I know not of. Do you know Homburg at all? It's very pretty – German pretty – and is cool and shady and comfortable generally, and still amusing enough, in spite of the death and burial of the gaming. The Kursaal stands there like a great cavernous tomb ¬– a tomb however in which they have concerts, a reading room and a café.

(…)

Hotel Royal, Baden-Baden
June 23rd (1874)

Dearest father,

(…)

My stopping here, experimentally, was a happy thought, for twenty-four hours observation of this enchanted valley have determined me to abide here for the present. I was deadly sick at the idea of going back to that too too familiar Homburg, and yet I didn't know what else to do. This cuts the knot, as far as I can foresee, effectually. Baden, judged by one walk and one séance last evening on the terrace of the Conversation House, listening to the Band is an absurdly pretty and coquettish little *ville d'eaux* embosomed in a labyrinth of beautiful hills and forest walks. In all this it leaves Homburg quite behind – as also in the facilities for frugal living. (I have just concluded an arrangement to dwell awhile at this extremely comfortable little hotel to the tune of 10 frs. a day) It is inferior to Homburg, I believe, in climate; but after Italy I don't believe I shall find the air oppressive.

Baden-Baden, Germany
July 29th (1874)

Dear Mrs. Wister,

(…)

In truth, I had better have written my letters out and out in Florence, for my spirits have been chilled and my imagination blighted by the dullest weeks of my life, which I am now bringing to their lugubrious term. Were you ever at Baden-Baden, in the good old time of the gaming?[1] With the suppression of this its light has quite gone out and you, even if you are visiting those Quaker relations again about whom you wrote me last summer so charmingly, are not spending days of a greyer hue than those which have been passing over my devoted head, in the shadow of the despoiled Conversation House. Fortunately Baden is enchantingly pretty and I have taken to the woods, like the hunted negro of romance and amused myself with long solitary strolls in the Black Forest. This is really quite fabulously picturesque and has helped to console me for the universal flatness of mankind as represented at Baden. Fortunately, too, I have had a rather absorbing piece of scribbling to do, and the weeks have taken themselves off with a better grace than at one time seemed likely. I scribble in the morning, and walk, as aforesaid, in the verdurous gloom of the Schwarzwald in the afternoon and I sit and listen to the band on the terrace and consume *farce glaces* in the evening. I converse with the waiter and the chambermaid, the trees and the streams, a Russian or two, and a compatriot or two, but with no one who has suggested any ideas worthy of your attention.

Mark Twain, *A Tramp Abroad*

I have never enjoyed a view which had such a serene and satisfying charm about it as this one gives.

The first night we were there, we went to bed and to sleep early; but I awoke at the end of two or three hours, and lay a comfortable while listening to the soothing patter of the rain against the balcony windows. I took it to be rain, but it turned out to be only the murmur of the restless Neckar, tumbling over her dikes and dams far below, in the gorge. I got up and went into the west balcony and saw a wonderful sight. Away down on the level, under the black mass of

---

[1] By the early 1870s, Baden had become the "summer capital of Europe", populated by royals such as the Russian Empress Elisabeth, Frederica Queen of Sweden, and Emperor William of Prussia. Afer gambling was forbidden in Paris—the "winter capital" in the 1830s—high society regularly decamped here to visit the casino, which was closed in 1872 by Prussian parliamentry order.

the Castle, the town lay, stretched along the river, its intricate cobweb of streets jewelled with twinkling lights; there were rows of lights on the bridges; these flung lances of light upon the water, in the black shadows of the arches; and away at the extremity of all this fairy spectacle blinked and glowed a massed multitude of gas jets which seemed to cover acres of ground; it was as if all the diamonds in the world had been spread out there. I did not know before, that a half mile of sextuple railways tracks could be made such an adornment.

One thinks Heidelberg by day – with its surroundings – is the last possibility of the beautiful; but when he sees Heidelberg by night, a fallen Milky Way, with that glittering railway constellation pinned to the border, he requires time to consider upon the verdict.

One never tires of poking about in the dense woods that clothe all these lofty Neckar hills to their tops. The great deeps of a boundless forest have a beguiling and impressive charm in any country; but German legends and fairy tales have given these an added charm. They have peopled that region with gnomes and dwarfs, and all sorts of mysterious and uncanny creatures. At the time I am writing of, I had been reading so much of this literature that sometimes I was not sure but I was beginning to believe in the gnomes and dairies as realities.

One afternoon I got lost in the woods about a mile from the hotels, and presently fell into a train of dreamy thought about animals which talk, and kobolds, and enchanted folk, and the rest of the pleasant legendary stuff; and so, by stimulating my fancy, I finally got to imagining I glimpsed small flitting shapes here and there down the columned aisles o the forest. It was a pine wood, with so thick and soft a carpet of brown needles that one's footfall made no more sound than if he was treading on wool; the tree-trunks were as round and straight and smooth as pillars, and stood close together; they were bare of branches to a point about twenty feet above ground, and from there upward so thick with boughs that not a ray of sunlight could pierce through. The world was bright with sunshine outside, but a deep and mellow twilight reigned in there, and also a silence so profound that I seemed to hear my own breathings.

When I had stood ten minutes, thinking and imagining and getting my spirit in tune with the place, and in the right mood to enjoy the supernatural, a raven suddenly uttered a hoarse croak over my head. It made me start; and then I was angry because I started. I looked up, and the creature was sitting on a limb right over me, looking down at me. I felt something of the same sense of humiliation and injury which one feels when he finds that a human stranger has been clandestinely inspecting him in his privacy and mentally commenting upon him. I eyed the raven and the raven eyed me. Nothing was said during some seconds. Then the bird stepped a little way along his limb to get a better point of observation, lifted his wings, stuck his head far down below his shoulders toward me, and croaked again – a croak with a distinctly insulting expression about it. If he had spoken in English he could not have said any more plainly than he did say in raven, "Well, what do *you* want here?"

(…)

The summer semester was in full tide; consequently the most frequent figure in and about Heidelberg was the student. Most of the students were Germans, of course, but the representatives of foreign lands were very numerous. They hailed from every corner of the globe – for instruction is cheap in Heidelberg, and so is living, too. The Anglo-American Club, composed of British and American students, had twenty-five members, and there was still much material left to draw from.

Nine-tenths of Heidelberg students wore no badges or uniform; the other tenth wore caps of various colors, and belonged to social organizations called "corps". There were five corps, each with a color of its own; there were white caps, blue caps, and red, yellow, and green ones. The famous duel-fighting is confined to the "corps" boys. The "*kneip*" seems to be a specialty of theirs, too. Kneips are held, now and then, to celebrate great occasions, like the election of a beer king, for instance. The solemnity is simple; the five corps assemble at night, and at a signal they all fall loading themselves with beer, out of pint-mugs, as fast as possible, and each man keeps his own count, usually by laying aside a lucifer match for each mug he empties. The election is soon decided. When the candidates can hold no more, a count is instituted and the one who has drank the greatest number of pints is proclaimed king. I was told that the last beer king elected by the corps, or by his own capabilities, emptied his mug seventy-five times. No stomach could hold all that quantity at one time, of course, but there are ways of frequently creating a vacuum, which those who have been much at sea will understand.

One sees so many students abroad at all hours[2], that he presently begins to wonder if they ever have any working hours. Some of them have, some of them haven't. Each can choose for himself whether he will work or play; for German university life is a very free life; it seems to have no restraints. The student does not live in the college buildings, but hires his own lodgings, in any locality he prefers, and he takes his meals when and where he pleases. He goes to bed when it suits him, and does not get up at all unless he wants to. He is not entered at the university for any particular length of time; so he is likely to change about. He passes no examination upon entering college. He merely pays a trifling fee of

---

[2] At serveral points in this work, Twain uses commas in a typically German fashion to separate clauses beginning with that from their introduction: while this method of punctuation is not unknown in English, it is highly unusual and could betray some German influence on his style or writing.

five of ten dollars, receives a card entitling him to the privileges of the university, and that is the end of it. He is now ready for business, or play, as he shall prefer. If he elects to work, he finds a large list of lectures to choose from. He selects the subjects which he will study, and enters his name for these studies; but he can skip attendance.

The result of this system is, that lecture-courses upon specialties of an unusual nature are often delivered to very slim audiences, while those upon more practical and every-day matters of education are delivered to very large ones. I heard of one case where, day after day, the lecturer's audience consisted of three students, and always the same three. But one day two of them remained away. The lecturer began as usual: "Gentlemen," then, without a smile, he corrected himself, saying, "Sir, and went on with his discourse.

Thomas Stevens, *Around the World on a Bicycle*

Crossing the Rhine over a pontoon bridge, I ride along level and, happily, rather less muddy roads, through pleasant suburban villages, near one of which I meet a company of soldiers in undress uniform, strung out carelessly along the road, as though returning from a tramp into the country. As I approach them, pedalling laboriously against a stiff head wind, both myself and the bicycle fairly yellow with clay, both officers and soldiers begin to laugh in a good-natured, bantering sort of manner, and a round dozen of them sing out in chorus "Ah! ah! der Englander." and as I reply, "Yah! yah." in response, and smile as I wheel past them, the laughing and banter go all along the line. The sight of an "Englander" on one of his rambling expeditions of adventure furnishes much amusement to the average German, who, while he cannot help admiring the spirit of enterprise that impels him, fails to comprehend where the enjoyment can possibly come in. The average German would much rather loll around, sipping wine or beer, and smoking cigarettes, than impel a bicycle across a continent. A few miles eastward of the Rhine another grim fortress frowns upon peaceful village and broad, green meads, and off yonder to the right is yet another; sure enough, this Franco-German frontier is one vast military camp[3], with forts, and soldiers, and munitions of war everywhere. When I crossed the Rhine I left Lower Alsace, and am now penetrating the middle Rhine region, where villages are picturesque clusters of gabled cottages – a contrast to the shapeless and ancient-looking stone structures of the French villages. The difference also extends to the inhabitants;

---

[3] Alsace had been conceded by France to Prussia at the close of the 1870-71 war between the two powers. It was immediately subsumed into an entirely new political entity, proclaimed during the last days of the conflict: the Second German Empire.

the peasant women of France, in either real or affected modesty, would usually pretend not to notice anything extraordinary as I wheeled past, but upon looking back they would almost invariably be seen standing and gazing after my receding figure with unmistakable interest; but the women of these Rhine villages burst out into merry peals of laughter.

Rolling over fair roads into the village of Oberkirch, I conclude to remain for the night, and the first thing undertaken is to disburden the bicycle of its covering of clay. The awkward-looking hostler comes around several times and eyes the proceedings with glances of genuine disapproval, doubtless thinking I am cleaning it myself instead of letting him swab it with a besom with the single purpose in view of dodging the inevitable tip. The proprietor can speak a few words of English. He puts his bald head out of the window above, and asks: "Pe you Herr Shtevens?"

"Yah, yah," I reply.

"Do you go mit der veld around?"

"Yah; I goes around mit the world."

"I shoust read about you mit der noospaper."

"Ah, indeed! what newspaper?"

"Die Frankfurter Zeitung. You go around mit der veld." The landlord looks delighted to have for a guest the man who goes "mit der veld around," and spreads the news. During the evening several people of importance and position drop in to take a curious peep at me and my wheel. A dampness about the knees, superinduced by wheeling in rubber leggings, causes me to seek the privilege of the kitchen fire upon arrival. After listening to the incessant chatter of the cook for a few moments, I suddenly dispense with all pantomime, and ask in purest English the privilege of drying my clothing in peace and tranquillity by the kitchen fire. The poor woman hurries out, and soon returns with her highly accomplished master, who, comprehending the situation, forthwith tenders me the loan of his Sunday pantaloons for the evening; which offer I gladly accept, notwithstanding the wide disproportion in their size and mine, the landlord being, horizontally, a very large person. Oberkirch is a pretty village at the entrance to the narrow and charming valley of the River Bench, up which my route leads, into the fir-clad heights of the Black Forest. A few miles farther up the valley I wheel through a small village that nestles amid surroundings the loveliest I have yet seen. Dark, frowning firs intermingled with the lighter green of other vegetation crown the surrounding spurs of the Knibis Mountains; vineyards, small fields of waving rye, and green meadow cover the lower slopes with variegated beauty, at the foot of which huddles the cluster of pretty cottages amid scattered orchards of blossoming fruit-trees. The cheery lute of the herders on the mountains, the carol of birds, and the merry music of dashing mountain-streams fill the fresh morning air with melody. All through this country there are apple-trees, pear-trees, cherry-trees. In the fruit season one can scarce open his mouth out-doors without having the goddess Pomona pop in some delicious morsel. The poplar avenues of France have disappeared, but the road is frequently shaded for miles with fruit-trees. I never before saw a spot so lovely – certainly not in combination with a wellnigh perfect road for wheeling. On through Oppenau and Petersthal my way leads – this latter a place of growing importance as a summer resort, several commodious hotels with swimming-baths, mineral waters, etc., being already prepared to receive the anticipated influx of health and pleasure-seeking guests this coming summer – and then up, up, up among the dark pines leading over the Black Forest Mountains. Mile after mile of steep incline has now been trundled, following the Bench River to its source. Ere long the road I have lately traversed is visible far below, winding and twisting up the mountain-slopes. Groups of swarthy peasant women are carrying on their heads baskets of pine cones to the villages below. At a distance the sight of their bright red dresses among the sombre green of the pines is suggestive of the fairies with which legend has peopled the Black Forest.

The summit is reached at last, and two boundary posts apprise the traveller that on this wooded ridge he passes from Baden into Wurtemberg. The descent for miles is agreeably smooth and gradual; the mountain air blows cool and refreshing, with an odor of the pines; the scenery is Black Forest scenery, and what more could be possibly desired than this happy combination of circumstances. Reaching Freudenstadt about noon, the mountain-climbing, the bracing air, and the pine fragrance cause me to give the good people at the gasthaus an impressive lesson in the effect of cycling on the human appetite. At every town and village I pass through in Wurtemberg the whole juvenile population collects around me in an incredibly short time. The natural impulse of the German small boy appears to be to start running after me, shouting and laughing immoderately, and when passing through some of the larger villages, it is no exaggeration to say that I have had two hundred small Germans, noisy and demonstrative, clattering along behind in their heavy wooden shoes.

Wurtemberg, by this route at least, is a decidedly hilly country, and the roads are far inferior to those of both England and France. There will be, perhaps, three kilometres of trundling up through wooded heights leading out of a small valley, then, after several kilometres over undulating, stony upland roads, a long and not always smooth descent into another small valley, this programme, several times repeated, constituting the journey of the day. The small villages of the peasantry are frequently on the uplands, but the larger towns are invariably in the valleys, sheltered by wooded heights, perched among the crags of the most inaccessible of which are frequently seen the ruins of an old castle. Scores of little boys of eight or ten are breaking stones by the road-side, at which I somewhat marvel, since there is a compulsory school law in Germany; but perhaps to-day is a holiday; or maybe, after school hours, it is customary for these unhappy youngsters to repair to the road-sides and blister their hands with cracking flints. "Hungry as a buzz-saw" I roll into the sleepy old town of Rothenburg at six o'clock, and, repairing to the principal hotel, order supper. Several flunkeys of different degrees of usefulness come in and bow obsequiously from time to time, as I sit around, expecting supper to appear every minute. At seven o'clock the waiter comes in, bows profoundly, and lays the table-cloth; at 7.15 he appears again, this time with a plate, knife, and fork, doing more bowing and scraping as he lays them on the table. Another half-hour rolls by, when, doubtless observing my growing impatience as he happens in at intervals to close a shutter or re-regulate the gas, he produces a small illustrated paper, and, bowing profoundly; lays it before me. I feel very much like making him swallow it, but resigning myself to what appears to be inevitable fate, I wait and wait, and at precisely 8.15 he produces a plate of soup; at 8.30 the kalbscotolet is brought on, and at 8.45 a small plate of mixed biscuits. During the meal I call for another piece of bread, and behold there is a hurrying to and fro, and a resounding of feet scurrying along the stone corridors of the rambling old building, and ten minutes later I receive a small roll. At the opposite end of the long table upon which I am writing some half-dozen ancient and honourable Rothenburgers are having what they doubtless consider a "howling time." Confronting each is a huge tankard of foaming lager, and the one doubtless enjoying himself the most and making the greatest success of exciting the envy and admiration of those around him is a certain ponderous individual who sits from hour to hour in a half comatose condition, barely keeping a large porcelain pipe from going out, and at fifteen-minute intervals taking a telling pull at the lager. Were it not for an occasional blink of the eyelids and the periodical visitation of the tankard to his lips, it would be difficult to tell whether he were awake or sleeping, the act of smoking being barely perceptible to the naked eye.

In the morning I am quite naturally afraid to order anything to eat here for fear of having to wait until mid-day, or thereabouts, before getting it; so, after being the unappreciative recipient of several more bows, more deferential and profound if anything than the bows of yesterday eve, I wheel twelve kilometres to Tubingen for breakfast. It showers occasionally during the forenoon, and after about thirty-five kilometres of hilly country it begins to descend in torrents, compelling me to follow the example of several peasants in seeking the shelter of a thick pine copse. We are soon driven out of it, however, and donning my gossamer rubber suit, I push on to Alberbergen, where I indulge in rye bread and milk, and otherwise while away the hours until three o'clock, when, the rain ceasing, I pull out through the mud for Blaubeuren. Down the beautiful valley of one of the Danube's tributaries I ride on Sunday morning, pedalling to the music of Blaubeuren's church-bells. After waiting until ten o'clock, partly to allow the roads to dry a little, I conclude to wait no longer, and so pull out toward the important and quite beautiful city of Ulm. The character of the country now changes, and with it likewise the characteristics of the people, who verily seem to have stamped upon their features the peculiarities of the region they inhabit. My road eastward of Blaubeuren follows down a narrow, winding valley, beside the rippling head-waters of the Danube, and eighteen kilometres of variable road brings me to the strongly fortified city of Ulm, the place I should have reached yesterday, except for the inclemency of the weather, and where I cross from Wurtemberg into Bavaria. On the uninviting uplands of Central Wurtemberg one looks in vain among the peasant women for a prepossessing countenance or a graceful figure, but along the smiling valleys of Bavaria, the women, though usually with figures disproportionately broad, nevertheless carry themselves with a certain gracefulness; and, while far from the American or English idea of beautiful, are several degrees more so than their relatives of the part of Wurtemberg I have traversed. I stop but a few minutes at Ulm, to test a mug of its lager and inquire the details of the road to Augsburg, yet during that short time I find myself an object of no little curiosity to the citizens, for the fame of my undertaking has pervaded Ulm.

The roads of Bavaria possess the one solitary merit of hardness, otherwise they would be simply abominable, the Bavarian idea of road-making evidently being to spread unlimited quantities of loose stones over the surface. For miles a wheelman is compelled to follow along narrow, wheel-worn tracks, incessantly dodging loose stones, or otherwise to pedal his way cautiously along the edges of the roadway. I am now wheeling through the greatest beer-drinking, sausage-consuming country in the world; hop- gardens are a prominent feature of the landscape, and long links of sausages are dangling in nearly every window. The quantities of these viands I see consumed to-day are something astonishing, though the celebration of the Whitsuntide holidays is probably augmentative of the amount.

Albert Morris Bagby, *Miss Träumerei*

Hidden away in a secluded oblong basin formed by the green hills of Thuringia nestles sleepy little Weimar. Its narrow, crooked streets, ill-paved and lined by plain two and three-story stucco-walled houses, are confined to the old town proper. Their monotonous irregularity is broken by the open, paved market and by the broadening of the way before the mediaeval city church, the theatre and post office, where an occasional bronze statue, public fountain or row of trees gives variety to the dreary stretch of stone and mortar.

Facing the incline a few paces to the left of the market, a proud, many-windowed palace with a great rectangular court and quaint detached tower – the principal landmark for the townsfolk – looms up on the left and lower bank of a brawling little stream dignified by the name of river. An ancient stone-arched bridge leads the approach to the military barracks, pleasure garden and villas on the neighboring hill. Stretching upward from the palace, on both sides of the winding Ilm, the Grand Ducal Park, whose romantic nooks and seductive walks were planned by Duke Carl August and the immortal Goethe, terminates in the hamlet of Ober-Weimar. In the diametrically opposite quarter of the city fields of waving grain, brilliant in the summer with the crimson of the poppy and the deep blue of the cornflower. At the lower extremity of the old town a handsome new museum faces an imposing residence street which climbs the hill to the ornamental Empress Augsuta Place before the railway station at the base of the lofty, forest-crowned Ettersberg. From the upper end of Weimar the magnificent Belvedere Allee, with its long line of stately vials facing the open park, leads to Belvedere, the summer home of the Grand Duke, on the hill a mile-and-a-half distant. Flanking the junction of the Allee with the city street, stand, like the pillars of a huge gateway, companion houses – square, thick-walled and singularly plain.

That on the left is noticeable as the former house of Franz Liszt. His apartments occupied the second, or top, floor. The lower rooms are still inhabited by the family of the court gardener. The royal garden, upon which the sole outer door of the house opens, is hedged from the public gaze by high dense foliage. It is reached by a narrow portal on the Allee at the corner of the residence and by a rustic gate at the end of the drive between long hot-houses, extending from the graveled space about the entry door to the park. An old gabled tool-house with overhanging eaves, a clump of slender towering pines and a high-latticed enclosure for poultry crowd close to the worn stone stoop at the further corner of the edifice, whose prison-like aspect is relieved by a sill full of gay scarlet geraniums in the dormer window under the low rood, and a row of tall exotics partially screening the neatly curtained windows of the ground floor. In this modest home the great Master Liszt received each summer up to the year of his death young pianists whose talents and accomplishments rendered them, to his judgment, worthy of his gratuitous instruction.

One June morning, not a great while previous to the date which deprived the world of this greatest piano-virtuoso of any time, Pauline, his faithful housekeeper and cook, sat, knitting, on the settle before the house. She was a comely, rich-complexioned brunette of forty odd years, with glossy hair, bright eyes and a tall, robust figure. Her feet rested on a low foot-stool; for no sun had appeared by ten o'clock to dry the earth, soaked with a heavy rain in the previous night. As usual, at this hour, all was quiet about the Royal Gardens save the occasional rattling of a carriage over the stony, city approach to the Belvedere Allee, the low cooing of the pigeons on the roof of the tool-house or the shrill cackling from the hennery. The side gate clicked, and a tall spare form, with long flowing hair, strode out from the cluster of bushy pot plants concealing the entrance.

"Good morning, Pauline."

"Good morning, Herr von Ilmstedt," responded the housekeeper in a pleasant voice.

"Has the Master risen?"

"No, he is still sleeping, but he has some important writing on his hand and will receive no one this morning. He gave orders, in case any of the pupils called, to say that there would be a lesson this afternoon."

"Ach, so!" he exclaimed, with habitual celerity. At this familiar rejoinder Pauline drew down the corners of her mouth and professed such ignorance in answer to questions about the Master with which he plied her that he soon called over his shoulder "Adieu!" and disappeared as soon as he came.

"Of course," she muttered contemptuously, listening to his receding footsteps. "I knew he would be the first. Trust me to free this house of such bores! He imitates Herr Doctor in everything. I believe he would wear the coat of an Abbe, too, if he dared. Why, he has even begun to say 'Sapprement' when he is surprised at anything. Ha, ha, ha!"

"How is that, Frau Pauline?"

"Herr Je!" almost shouted the startled matron, jerking her face up to the light to meet a pair of glorious hazel eyes twinkling at her with amusement through a gap in the shrubbery on her right. "Du lieber Himmel!" she ejaculated impressively in further astonishment, at the same time dropping her knitting on the settle and raising in a stupefied fashion slowly to her feet. "Is it you, Miss Muriel?"

"See for yourself, Frau Pauline," laughed the possessor of the handsome eyes, stepping into full view to receive a warm embrace and kiss for either cheek.

Then Pauline, flushing with pleasure, held her off at arm's length, exclaiming, "Mein Gott, how you did frighten me, arriving in that ghostlike fashion; but I am none the less delighted to see you!"

"I slipped in on tiptoe to avoid being seen by Ilmsted. He came up the Allee just as I entered it from the city."

"I sent him off in a hurry," added Pauline, with a mocking grimace; "luckily, too, for now I can hear something of you, while Herr Doctor finishes his nap."

"How is the dear Master?" There was a touch of tenderness and reverence in the inquiry which the speaker's eyes reflected.

"Ach!" began Pauline, with a gesture more eloquent than words: "never in better health; but you will see for yourself presently. Please be seated and tell me everything." Lifting the half-knit stocking form the settle, she placed herself in a listening attitude and resumed work.

"Very well, when you seat yourself," was the response; "you will take cold standing there on the damp earth."

Pauline, flashing a grateful look, murmured "Thanks!" and took the proffered seat on the further end of the settle.

Although long service and responsible position elevated her rank in the household, she never forgot the restrictions imposed by caste, and tempered her familiar treatment of Liszt's divers pupils with proportionate deference. The few who addressed her respectfully as Frau Pauline, however, won her highest regard. Of these Muriel Holme, who she called "Missey," ostensibly intending compliment to her nationality, but secretly as the easiest, most excusable word of endearment, was her prime favorite.

Jerome K. Jerome, *Three Men on the Bummel*

Berlin is a disappointing town; its centre is overcrowded, its outlying parts lifeless, its one famous street, Unter den Linden, an attempt to combine Oxford Street with the Champs Elysée, singularly unimposing, being much too wide for its size; its theatres dainty and charming, where acting is considered of more importance that scenery or dress, where long runs are unknown, successful pieces being played again and again, but never consecutively, so that for a week running you may go to the same Berlin theatre and see a fresh play every night; its opera house unworthy of it; its two music halls, with an unnecessary suggestion of vulgarity and commonness about them, ill-arranged and much too large for comfort. In the Berlin cafés and restaurants, the busy time is from midnight on till three. Yet most of the people who frequent them are up again at seven. Either the Berliner has solved the great problem of modern life: how to do without sleep, or, with Carlyle, he must be looking forward to eternity.

Personally, I know of no other town where such late hours are the vogue, except St Petersburg.[4] But your St Petersburger does not get up early in the morning. At St Petersburg, the music halls, which it is the fashionable thing to attend *after* the theatre – a drive to them taking half an hour in a swift sleigh – do

---

[4] It is interesting that Jerome should alight on the then Russian capital here. As both were new capital cities built in the eighteenth century at great speed by the will of strong monarchs, the St. Petersburg comparison is by no means uncommon in discussions of Berlin (see Wraxall in Chapter 2).

not practically begin till twelve. Through the Neva at four o'clock in the morning you have to literally push your way; and the favourite trains for travellers are those starting about five o' clock in the morning. These trains save the Russian the trouble of getting up early. He wishes his friends 'Good night', and drives down to the station comfortably after supper, without putting the house to any inconvenience.

Potsdam, the Versailles to Berlin, is a beautiful little town, situated among lakes and woods. Here in the shady ways of its quiet, far-reaching park of Sans Souci, it is easy to imagine lean, snuffy Frederick 'bummeling' with a shrill Voltaire.

Acting on my advice, George and Harris consented not to stay long in Berlin, but to push on to Dresden. Most that Berlin has to show can be seen better elsewhere, and we decided to be content with a drive through the town. The hotel porter introduced us to a droshky driver, under whose guidance, so he assured us, we should see everything worth seeing in the shortest possible time. The man himself, who called for us at nine o'clock in the morning, was all that could be desired. He was bright, intelligent, and well-informed; his German was easy to understand and he knew a little English with which to eke it out on occasion. With the man himself there was no fault to be found, but his horse was the most unsympathetic brute I ever sat behind.

He took a dislike to us the moment he saw us. I was the first to come out of the hotel. He turned his head and looked me up and down with a cold, glassy eye, and then he looked across at another horse, a friend of his that was standing facing him. I knew what he said. He had an expressive head, and he made no attempt to disguise his thought. He said:

"Funny things one does come across in the summer time, don't one?"

George followed me out the next moment, and stood behind me. The horse again turned his head and looked. I have never known a horse that could twist himself as this horse did. I have seen a cameloprad do tricks with his neck that compelled one's attention, but this animal was more like the thing one dreams of after a dusty day at Ascot, followed by a dinner with six old chumbs. If I had seen his eyes looking at me from between his hind legs, I doubt if I should have been surprised. He seemed more amused with George, if anything, than with myself. He turned to his friend again.

"Extraordinary, isn't it?" he remarked; "I suppose there must be some place where they grown them"; and then he commenced licking flies off his own left shoulder. I began to wonder whether he had lost his mother when young, and had been brought up by a cat.

George and I climbed in, and sat waiting for Harris. He came a moment later. Myself, I thought he looked rather neat. He wore a white flannel knickerbocker suit, which he had had made specially for bicycling in hot weather; his hat may have been a trifle out of the common, but it did keep the sun off.

The horse gave one look at him, and said "Gott in Himmel!" as plainly as ever horse spoke, and started off down Friedrich Strasse at a brisk walk, leaving Harris and the driver standing on the pavement. His owner called to him to stop, but he took no notice. They ran after us, and overtook us at the corner of the Dorotheen Strasse. I could not catch what the man said to the horse, he spoke quickly and excitedly; but I gathered a few phrases, such as:

"Got to earn my living somehow, haven't I?" "Who asked for your opinion?" "Aye, little you care so long as you can guzzle"

The horse cut the conversation short by turning up the Dorotheen Strasse on his own account. I think what he said was:

"Come on then; don't talk so much. Let's get the job over, and, where possible, let's keep to back streets."

Opposite the Brandenburger Thor our driver hitched the reins to the whip, climbed down, and came around to explain things to us. He pointed out the Thiergarten, and then descanted to us of the Reichstag House. He informed us of its exact height, length, and breadth, after the manner of guides. Then he turned his attention to the Gate. He said it was constructed of sandstone, in imitation of the "Properleer" in Athens.

At this point the horse, which had been occupying its leisure licking its own legs, turned round its head. It did not say anything, it just looked.

The man began again nervously. This time he said it was an imitation of the "Propeyedliar".

Here the horse proceeded up the Linden, and nothing would persuade him not to proceed up the Linden. His owner expostulated with him, but he continued to trot on. From the way he hitched his shoulders as he moved, I somehow felt he was saying:

"They've seen the Gate, haven't they? Very well, that's enough. As for the rest, you don't know what you are talking about, and they wouldn't understand you if you did. You talk German."

It was the same throughout the length of the Linden. The horse consented to stand still sufficiently long to enable us to have a good look at each sight, and to hear the name of it. All explanation and description he cut short by the simply process of moving on.

"What these fellows want," he seemed to say to himself, "is to go home and tell people they have seen these things. If I am doing them an injustice, if they are more intelligent than they look, they can get better information than this old fool of mine is giving them from the guide-book. Who wants to know how high a steeple is? You don't remember it the next five minutes when you are told, and if you do it is because you have nothing else in your head. He just tires me with his talk. Why doesn't he hurry up, and let us all get home to lunch?"

Upon reflection, I am not sure that wall-eyed old brute had not sense on its side. Anyhow, I know there have been occasions, with a guide, when I would have been glad of its interference.

But one is apt to "sin one's mercies", as the Scotch say, and at the time we cursed that horse instead of blessing it.

6
Close Connections and Opposing Policies
1900 - 1920

Views like this over Cologne's Ehrenfeld district came to be common in Germany during its remarkable industrial expansion.

FOR GERMANY, THE decade between 1910 and 1920 was one of zeniths and nadirs, culturally, economically and militarily. Both in terms of internationally important works of literature and in scientific progress, the ante-bellum German Empire had become a monolith: Thomas Mann, Rainer Maria Rilke and Hermann Hesse were read throughout the world, while by its demise in 1918 the German Empire had won more Nobel science prizes than all its rivals put together since its 1871 proclamation. Yet as the November Revolution of 1918 showed, no amount of cultural achievement was enough to prevent brutal, ideologically-motivated bloodletting.

Economically, too, Germany hit a height in the years leading up to the First World War: its population was at over sixty million and its industry outstripped that of every other European nation, leading the world in areas such as steelmaking, chemicals, and pharmaceuticals. Yet by the winter of 1917 there were serious food shortages across the country and the factories that had fired the German economic machine were fast running out both of materials and labourers.

Militarily, Germany had never yet been as imposing as it was in the decade before the First World War. In the summer of 1914 its sea forces were second only to the British Royal Navy, while its army was stronger than that of either France or Russia. What was more, German forces also stood as undefeated in over half a century. By the end of the decade, however, the Empire's expensive and previously impressive navy had scuppered itself in British captivity at Scapa Flow while the army had met its match on the Western Front and its generals been forced to concede defeat—after a loss of around two million young men in the trenches and another half a million civilians to famine and disease.

So in dealing with the first twenty years of the twentieth century, we are following foreign writers into Imperial Germany at its peak. Many of them have learned the language, with knowledge of German culture being more fashionable than it ever had been before—or has been since. As we leave Germany with them in the early 1920s, however, we see a country whose reputation is in tatters and whose future is uncertain.

In this period we see the culmination of many tendencies that have been developing throughout the previous century—some of them almost diametrically opposed. While the danger of German militarism becomes utterly apparent, Germans are still often depicted as polite, even servile and slow-witted, sometimes simple. The pendulum between the two extremes is still just past mid-swing. At the same time, Britain, America and Germany are, thanks to modern technology, growing closer and closer together, as the coincidences on the battlefield during the First World War described in this chapter reveal in an often tragic way. The mesh of links between the countries was, in fact, so thickly-woven before the war that some of the age's greatest writers chose Germany as a setting for their work.

Masterpieces of English Literature about Germany

D. H. Lawrence (b. 1885) is a striking example of the ever-closer ties between the English- and German-speaking worlds before the cataclysm of the Great War, albeit in a rather scandalous fashion: he ran off with the German wife of a modern languages professor from his native Nottingham. The pair spent the three years up to 1914 living abroad, partly in Germany. Lawrence's 1913 short story, *The Prussian Officer*, set in Bavaria, is remarkable for the way it blends the region's mountainous landscape into the psychological state of its characters. Lawrence once wrote that he considered it his best, most powerful short story.

The transatlantic T. S. Eliot (b. 1888) was yet another example of the effect transport and technology was having on connections between Britain, America and Germany, and also of the importance accorded to studying German at the height of the country's influence. Eliot's letters show a man as comfortable and cheerfully ironic on ocean liners as he was at either Harvard, Oxford or—for a brief period in the summer of 1914—Marburg. It is a sign of the extent to which European travel had become *de rigueur* for the elite of the time that Eliot found himself caught unawares in Swabia learning German when the war broke out.

Evelyn Princess Blücher (b. 1876), too, was unprepared for the swiftness with which Europe descended into war. Married to Prince Blücher of the Prussian nobility, this member of the British aristocracy was forced to follow her husband to Berlin at the outbreak of the conflict, from where she kept her diary of 1914 to 1919, later published as *An English Wife in Berlin* in 1920. She charts the ups-and-downs of those years for Germany, as well as her own mixed feelings, and interestingly enough is the only author in this chapter who was not a professional writer of fiction.

As well as Lawrence's short stories, another jewel of early twentieth-century fiction is also set in Germany: Ford Madox Ford's (b. 1873) *The Good Solider* (1915). It is the *non plus ultra* of spa-town writing, that mini-genre we have been following since Francis Bond Head's *Bubbles* of 1834. Ford depicts an antediluvian yet visibly decadent society of European aristocrats, marred by a couple with more than just one skeleton in their closet and narrated by a character so obstinately innocent that he drives readers to despair. Here, the

American-British writer describes a lost age of leisured international mobility before the war, and it is telling that he chose to set this cosmopolitan novel in provincial spa-town Germany.

The loss of Europe's easy *ante-bellum* internationalism is also the theme of Joseph Conrad's (b. 1857) small piece of writing about Germany, to be found in his *Notes on Life and Letters*, published in 1921. In it, Conrad remembers a journey across Germany before the war and sums up the bewilderment of a whole generation of Europeans as they see the reversal of what appeared to be a one-way movement towards integration. His view of Germany, and of the Germans, is coloured both by his Polish heritage and the conflict, and counts as the first text in this selection to shows a clear, specifically anti-German and highly irrational prejudice, as opposed to mere casual jingoism.

One writer who came to feel the change in sentiment with regards to Germany during the First World War was Robert Graves (b. 1895), who in *Goodbye to All That* (1929) remembers the carefree summers he spent with the German side of his family and charts his conscious move away from this background, describing the rise of anti-German prejudice as a result of nationalism and militarism.

Germans: Lucullans against Draconians

For Graves, many of his childhood memories of Bavaria are defined by tastes. The ready availability of fresh fruits and the spicy richness of the food strike him when compared to the bland diet *à la* crustless cucumber sandwiches and lukewarm tea associated with upper-class life in Britain. Blücher, too, sees the importance of good food to Germans, explaining that the *Heimat* they were told they were fighting for was pictured as a place of "fruit trees, ploughed fields". In a passage from 1917 (not quoted here) she talks of how "we are all gaunt and bony now, and have dark shadows around our eyes. Our thoughts are chiefly taken up with wondering what our next meal will be, and dreaming of the good things that once existed." As much as anything, it is Blücher's experience of the famine of 1917-18 that makes her compassionate towards ordinary Germans, whom she sees as victims of the power-mad militarists at the head of the state.

For writers of this period, both before and during the Great War, much of the contradictory view of Germans seems to be expressed in terms of food. The old-fashioned, affable peasant type of German is something of a hobbit, a lover of green countryside, frothy ale and fruit puddings; even the well-to-do relatives of Graves are shown as farmers, while T. S. Eliot's upper-middle-class hosts refuse to allow him to leave the house without alimentary fortification. Meanwhile, the newer, slightly sinister types of German such as the *Kur* doctors of Ford's novel and army officers of Lawrence's tales are ascetics who view food as part of a regime, a matter of discipline. It is this set of incarnations that emerges from the period as the defining stereotype, while the traditional, ruddy and rustic gourmand who so enthused Hume, amused the likes of Stevens and Jerome, and disgusted Coleridge and Shelley seems to disappear with the war.

*

D. H. Lawrence, *The Prussian Officer*

They had marched more than thirty kilometres since dawn, along the white, hot road, where occasional thickets of trees threw a moment of shade, then out into the glare again. On either hand, the valley, wide and shallow, glistered with heat; dark green patches of rye, pale young corn, fallow and meadow and black pine-woods spread in a dull, hot diagram under a glistening sky. But right in front the mountains ranged across, pale blue and very still, the snow gleaming gently out of the deep atmosphere. And towards the mountains, on and on, the regiment marched between the rye-fields and the meadows, between the scraggy fruit-trees set regularly on either side the highroad. The burnished, dark green rye threw off a suffocating heat, the mountains drew gradually nearer and more distinct. While the feet of the soldiers grew hotter, sweat ran through their hair under their helmets, and their knapsacks could burn no more in contact with their shoulders, but seemed instead to give off a cold, prickly sensation.

He walked on and on in silence, staring at the mountains ahead, that rose sheer out of the land, and stood fold behind fold, half earth, half heaven, the heaven, the barrier with slits of soft snow in the pale, bluish peaks.

He could now walk almost without pain. At the start, he had determined not to limp. It had made him sick to take the first steps, and during the first mile or so, he had compressed his breath, and the cold drops of sweat had stood on his forehead, but he had walked it off. What were they after all but bruises! He had looked at them, as he was getting up: deep bruises on the backs of his thighs. And since he had made his first step in the morning, he had been conscious of them, till now he had a tight, hot place in his chest, with suppressing the pain, and holding himself in. There seemed no air when he breathed. But he walked almost lightly.

The captain's hand had trembled in taking his coffee at dawn: his orderly saw it again. And he saw the fine figure of the captain wheeling on horseback at the farm-house ahead, a handsome figure in pale blue uniform with facing of scarlet, and the metal gleaming on the black helmet and the sword scabbard, and dark streaks of sweat coming on the silky bay horse. The orderly felt he was connected with that figure moving so suddenly on horseback: he followed it like a shadow, mute and inevitable and damned by it. And the officer was always aware of the tramp of the company behind, the march of his orderly among the men.

(…)

The soldiers were tramping silently up the glaring hillside. Gradually his head began to revolve slowly, rhythmically. Sometimes it was dark before his eyes, as if he saw this world through a smoked glass, frail shadows and unreal. It gave him a pain in his head to walk.

The air was too scented, it gave no breath. All the lush green-stuff seemed to be issuing its sap, till the air was deathly, sickly with the smell of greenness. There was the perfume of clover, like pure honey and bees. Then there grew a faint acrid tang – they were near the beeches; and then a queer clattering noise, and a suffocating, hideous smell: they were passing a flock of sheep, a shepherd in a black smock, holding his hook. Why should the sheep huddle together under this fierce sun? He felt that the shepherd could not see him, though he could see the shepherd.

At last there was the halt. They stacked rifles in a conical stack, put down their kit in a scattered circle around it, and dispersed a little, sitting on a small knoll high on the hillside. The chatter began. The soldiers were steaming with heat, but were lively. He sat still, seeing the blue mountains rise upon the land, twenty kilometres away. There was a blue fold in the ranges, then out of that, at the foot, the broad bed of the river, stretches of whitey-green water between pinkish-grey shoals among the dark pine-woods. There it was, spread a long way off. And it seemed to come downhill, the river. There was a raft being steered, a mile away. It was a strange country. Nearer, a red-roofed, broad farm with white base and square dots of windows crouched beside the wall of beech-foliage on the wood's edge. There were long strips of rye and clover and pale green corn. And just at his feet, below the knoll, was a darkish bog, where globe flowers stood breathless still on their slim stalks. And some of the pale gold bubbles were burst, and a broken fragment hung in the air. He thought he was going to sleep.

T. S. Eliot, *Letters*

To Eleanor Hinkley

bei Herrn Suptdr. Happich,
Luth. Kirchhof 1, Marburg a. Lahn
26 July 1914

Dear Eleanor

Mit freunlichem (sic) Gruss aus Deutschland! Here I am, safely out of harm's way, settled in the bosom of the family of the Lutheran Pastor, and the church is right across the street. I have just been to church, and felt as good as gold. This will not be an exciting summer, but I think a pleasant one, though I hope you will not circulate any gossip about me and the Pastor's daughter. She is named

Hannah. In the evening, when we gather about the lamp, and the Herr Pfarrer takes a nap and composes his thoughts, and the ladies sew needlework, then the Frau Pfarrer says 'Ach Hannah, spiel uns ein Stuck Beethoven,' and Hannah spiels for 15 minutes. Hannah also sings, and can talk a little French and English (but she hasn't tried it on me). Then we read the paper, and discuss the Balkan Question[1], and the difference in climate between America and Deutschland. Altogether they are aw'f'ly good people, and we all eat a great deal. I feel that I am quite in darkest Germany. I have heard talked not a word of English since my arrival. This is a small town, but as small towns in Germany sometimes are, more a miniature compact city than a small town, as it has very good shops, and a cunning little street car that runs round the town on one track, and little narrow streets. You walk down the middle of the chief business street, and the street is about as wide as a very wide sidewalk, and on the sidewalks just two people can pass squeeze by (two Germans). As the town is very small, and the university numbers 2500, the students are much in evidence. Lately they have been having student fests, and the various clubs parade the streets in the evening carrying paper lanterns of their colours (usually three colours), and as they come winding down the steep narrow streets it makes a pretty sight. The houses are much decorated too; apparently each student hangs a flag of his club colours out of his own window. The students appear a little cub-like and uncouth, but are fearfully polite – I have always considered the Germans the politest people on earth. In fact everyone, servants, railroad employés, and all, are very obliging. From my window I have a beautiful view (there is a little grove – telegraph poles I believe? I am not strong in botany). The house is on the side of this steep hill, and my window looks out over the roofs toward distant hills on the other side of the Lahn valley. The country about is really quite charming, hilly and wooded, with nice walks, not too wild; a woody farming country, such as I like – I don't care for 'sublime' scenery, do you? Only one cannot walk far, or one would miss a meal; for we have five a day. One is either just recovering from a meal or just preparing for one. As I was going out to swim the other day the Frau Superintendant (Superintendant seems to be a sort of rector) suggested that I had better eat some bread and sausage to fortify myself. Really, the food is very good; I had not supposed that I could like German food.

I shan't have anything very exciting to narrate this summer; this is as peaceful a life as one could well find. (…)

---

[1] On the date of this letter, tension in the Balkans between Austro-Hungary and Germany on one side and Serbia and Russia on the other was running at an all-time high following the assassination of Franz Ferdinand, heir to the Austro-Hungarian throne, in Sarajevo on 28 June. Two days after Eliot's letter, on 28 July, Austria-Hungary declared war on Serbia, initiating what would become the First World War.

Evelyn Princess Blücher, *An English Wife in Berlin*

BERLIN, *August* 8, 1914.[2] (…) An officer of our party was to have been married that day to an English girl, who is going to wait for him, he says.

We had many interesting conversations during the journey. The sadness and bitterness of all these Germans leaving England struck me intensely. Here we are, they say, being dragged away from the country that has been our home for years, to fight against our best friends. They all blamed the officials in Berlin, who had, they said, grossly mismanaged the negotiations. It had been an obsession in some of the German officials' minds for years past that Russia meant to attack them. "Well then," said someone of the party, "why not wait until they do it? Why commit suicide to avoid being killed?"

"What chance have we," said someone else, "attacked practically on every side?"

"Is no one friendly to Germany?" asked another.

"Siam is friendly, I am told," was the bitter reply.

As we crossed the frontier, the people began to recognize our train, and we got quite a reception from the village girls along the route. They came and stood outside our windows and sang national war songs and patriotic hymns, and at one or two stations they presented a bouquet to the Ambassadresses.

Passing us in an almost continuous stream on the other way were the trains full of troops, shouting, laughing, singing, and waving their hands, intense joy and excitement depicted on their faces. The Germans are indeed a warlike race. I have, at last, seen them stirred out of their morose dullness, and what I used to think their everlasting heaviness. The thing that impressed us most was the absolute order and expeditiousness of everything and everybody *en route,* especially as soon as we had crossed the border.

Our train journey was slow, but absolutely comfortable, and we reached Berlin safely on the evening of the 8th. It was impossible not to be impressed with the immense enthusiasm prevailing all along the line. No less than 66 troop trains had passed the day before, yet there was no disorder, we were not kept waiting longer than half an hour at one station, and refreshments were handed out to soldiers and civilians everywhere gratis.

BERLIN, *August* 9, 1914. Dazed and stunned as I am by the awful events of

---

[2] Britain entered the hostilities on 4 August, declaring war on Germany after the Empire failed to guarantee Belgian neutrality. It was on this date that the Blüchers had to depart, while T. S. Eliot, an American citizen, was interned by the German government as a non-combatant national and given safe passage out of the country, reaching London in late August.

the last week, I will try and keep some diary of our experiences, jotting them down more or less consecutively as they happen. The thunderstorm which has broken so suddenly over England and Europe has altered the whole tenour of our lives, and whirled us away into an exile which I hope will be but a short one. Everything has come so unexpectedly that I wake up in the morning saying to myself that it was only a bad dream; but the hard reality soon forces itself on my outer view again, and I have to grapple with the situation as well as I can.

Exactly what was the real cause of the war no one seems to know, although it is discussed night and day. One thing grows clearer to me every day: neither the people here nor there wished for war, but here they are now being carried off their legs with patriotism, at seeing so many enemies on every side. It is said in England that Germany provoked the war, and here they emphatically deny it. To me it seems that Europe was thirsting for war, and that the armies and navies were no longer to be restrained. Certainly here, the militarists grew weary of the long lazy peace as they called it, and if the Kaiser had not proclaimed war, he would have been in a precarious position. There are two men at the head of affairs: one is called stupid and the other dangerous. The dangerous one has won the day, and brought the war to hand. Lord Northcliffe seems to be responsible on the other side.

(...)

BERLIN, *April* 1915. Glancing back over the last six months – one of the few things that really impressed themselves on my memory was the sinking of the *Blücher* by the English on January 24.

How well I remember the proud moment when, six months after my marriage, the Emperor sent for me in the middle of a Court ball in Berlin and asked me to launch the new cruiser *Blücher*. How well I remember his words as he smilingly said to me: "I expect you will get into trouble with your English relations if you launch my battleships, now won't you?" His well-known charm of manner attracted me so much, as it does all others. And then, four months after that date, we went to Kiel, and in the presence of Prince Henry of Prussia and the Princess, and General von der Goltz and others, I made my first German speech and broke the champagne bottle, and the *Blücher* floated gracefully into the water.

After the ceremony we went up to the castle for luncheon with Prince and Princess Henry of Prussia (she being sister to the Czarina of Russia and an English princess). We talked England, England, England – she telling us every little anecdote she could think of about her happy days at Windsor with old Queen Victoria, and how she and her sister had so intensely enjoyed rummaging in the old curiosity shops in the town of Windsor, saying laughingly: "We enjoyed mostly getting bargains of old bits of furniture, etc., which we had our suspicions had begun life in the castle itself, and had been 'looted' by servants at different periods, and found their way into these shops."

Among this party for the launching was my sister Freda, who had come out from England with us for it, and since then she is married to Admiral Charlton, who is now at the Admiralty; and, who knows? Maybe he was the very man who controlled this particular episode in the naval warfare!

The *Blücher* had, from the very beginning, ranked as an antiquated man-of-war, and was the slowest unit in the fleet. So it was arranged that she should be chosen to bear the brunt of battle, and stay behind to be sacrificed if necessary, to give the others time to retreat.

The captain of the *Blücher*, when rescued out of the water, was taken to Edinburgh, and on his way there, got into conversation with the English naval officer in command of the guard over them. The German officer had told him that an Englishwoman had launched the *Blücher*, and that her photograph had gone down in the ship. "Yes," answered the English naval officer, "I happen to know all about it, as the lady is my sister-in-law. My name is Throckmorton." It is curious how small the world is.

(…)

BERLIN, *October* 17, 1918. (…) Somebody told me of having seen King Ferdinand at Mannheim, when he was doing his cure, and heard his farewell words, which had been: "Au revoir next year, when I shall be back again for the cure as a private gentleman, no more as king. My friend William will also have abdicated by then; he and I have both outlived our time."

The Emperor – the poor Emperor! "How are the mighty fallen." The Caesar once so omnipotent, with his dream of riding down that magnificent Heer Strasse at the head of a conquering, victorious army, passing through the massed multitudes assembled to greet him, entering Brandenburger Tor, the smiling figure of Victory pointing the way down Unter den Linden! And now this shadow of a king, struggling with destiny to keep his throne but a few days, a few hours, longer.

I have felt bitter enough towards him at times in the past, thinking he could have done more to prevent the unnecessary suffering and cruel methods employed during the war: in particular, the violation of Belgium's neutrality; the sinking of the Lusitania; Miss Cavell's death; the ruthless submarine warfare; the use of poisonous gases; and the senseless air-raids over unfortified towns.

But now that his time has come, one pities him. A deplorable position for a great king to be the object of pity. Why has he let things go so far? Why has he not already abdicated, instead of waiting until he is forced to do so? Every child in the street is saying, "The Kaiser must go." He absolutely seems to cling to his shadow of a throne, and people say, curiously enough, it is the Kaiserin who is advising him and begging him not to go.

Last Sunday he was seen walking through the Tiergarten, a white-haired, broken man. At least he shows physical courage in doing this, as there are, I believe, men enough who would like to shoot him.

It is a pitiful sight to watch the death-throes of a great nation. It reminds me of a great ship slowly sinking before one's eyes, and being swallowed up by the storm-driven waves. I feel intensely for Germany and her brave long-suffering people, who have made such terrific sacrifices and gone through so much woe, only to see their idols shattered and to realize that their sufferings have all been caused by the blundering mistakes and overweening ambition of a class of "supermen".

(…)

BERLIN, *November* 13, 1918. It is late, but I cannot sleep; my nerves are still vibrating with the excitement of the last few days, and brain and heart are filled to overflowing at the thought of the momentous things which are happening in the world. We dined at the L.'s, where, although we were a very cosmopolitan party, we were all more or less affected at the terrible outlook for Germany. A late moon was still shining brightly as we made our way home on foot. The streets are very quiet now, and the few passers-by hurry along, almost afraid of one another, and avoid the shadows, for no one knows who or what may be lurking there. Before every important public building sentries are posted, and in front of the Brandenburger Tor, with its grotesque blue-black shadow of the galloping horses and the car of victory, I can see them pacing up and down.

An atmosphere of exhaustion rather than peace pervades the places where so much tumult and confusion raged but a short time ago. A rising wind is beginning to moan sadly through the Tiergarten, tossing the bare branches of the trees dejectedly, and bringing in its train great masses of dark clouds, which to my excited imagination look like armies in mournful retreat, moving as if in rhythm to the funeral dirge of the melancholy autumn wind.

I never felt so deeply for the German people as I do now, when I see them bravely and persistently trying to redress the wrongs of the war, for which they were in truth never responsible. The greater part of them were men fighting blindly to guard an ideal, the "Heimat," some patch of mother earth, a small cottage half hidden in its sheltering fruit trees, ploughed fields rising on the slope of a hill up to the dark forest of pines, maybe, or a wide stretch of flat countryside where the golden corn-fields sway and wave in the wind as far as the eye can reach.

Ford Madox Ford, *The Good Solider*

This is the saddest story I have ever heard. We had known the Ashburnhams for nine seasons of the town of Nauheim with an extreme intimacy – or, rather, with an acquaintanceship as loose and easy and yet as close as a good glove's with your hand. My wife and I knew Captain and Mrs Ashburnham as well as it was possible to know anybody, and yet, in another sense, we knew nothing at all about them. This is, I believe, a state of things only possible with English people of whom, till today, when I sit down to puzzle out what I know of this sad affair, I knew nothing whatever. Six months ago I had never been to England, and, certainly, I had never sounded the depths of an English heart. I had known the shallows.

I don't mean to say that we were not acquainted with many English people, living, as we perforce lived, in Europe, and being, as we perforce were, leisured Americans, which is as much as to say that we were un-American, we were thrown very much into the society of the nicer English. Paris, you see, was our home. Somewhere between Nice and Bordighera provided yearly winter quarters for us, and Nauheim always received us from July to September. You will gather from this statement that one of us had, as the saying is, a 'heart', and, from the statement that my wife is dead, that she was the sufferer.

Captain Ashburnham also had a heart. But, whereas a yearly month or so at Nauheim tuned him up to exactly the right pitch for the rest of the twelvemonth, the two months or so were only just enough to keep poor Florence alive from year to year. The reason for his heart was, approximately, polo, or too much hard sportsmanship in this youth. The reason for poor Florence's broken years was a storm at sea upon our first crossing to Europe, and the immediate reasons for our imprisonment in that continent were doctor's orders. They said that even the short Channel crossing might well kill the poor thing.

When we all first met, Captain Ashburnham, home on sick leave from an India to which he was never to return, was thirty-three; Mrs Ashburnham – Leonora – was thirty-one. I was thirty-six and poor Florence thirty. Thus today Florence would have been thirty-nine and Captain Ashburnham forty-two; whereas I am forty-five and Leonora forty. You will perceive therefore that our friendship has been a young-middle-aged affair, since we were all of us of quite quiet dispositions, the Ashburnhams being more particularly what in England it is custom to call 'quite good people'.

(…)

Someone has said that the death of a mouse from cancer is the whole sack of Rome by the Goths, and I swear to you that the breaking up of our little four-square coterie was such another unthinkable event. Supposing that you should come upon us sitting together at one of the little tables in the front of the club house, let us say, at Homburg, taking tea of an afternoon and watching the miniature golf, you would have said that, as human affairs go, we were an extraordinarily safe castle. We were, if you will, one of those tall ships with the white sails upon a blue sea, one of those things that seem the proudest and the safest of all the beautiful and safe things that God has permitted the mind of men to frame. Where better could one take refuge? Where better?

Permanence? Stability? I can't believe it's gone. I can't believe that the long, tranquil life, which was just stepping a minuet, vanished in four crashing days at the end of nine years and six weeks. Upon my word, yes, our intimacy was like a minuet, simply because on every possible circumstance we knew where to go, where to sit, which table we unanimously should choose; and we could rise and go, all four together, without a signal from any one of us, always to the music of the *Kur* orchestra, always in the temperate sunshine, or, if it rained, in discreet shelters. No indeed, it can't be gone. You can't kill a *minuet de la cour.* You may shut up the music book, close the harpsichord; in the cupboard and presses the rats may destroy the white satin favours. The mob may sack Versailles; the Trianon may fall, but surely the minuet – the minuet itself is dancing itself away into the furthest stars, even as our minuet of the Hessian bathing places must be stepping itself still.[3] Isn't there any heaven where old beautiful dances, old beautiful intimacies prolong themselves? Isn't there any Nirvana pervaded by the faint thrilling of instruments that have fallen into the dust of wormwood but that yet had frail, tremulous, and everlasting souls?

No, by God, it is false! It wasn't a minuet that we stepped; it was a prison, a prison full of screaming hysterics, tied down so that they might not outsound the rolling of our carriage wheels as we went along the shaded avenues of the Taunus Wald.

(…)

It was a very hot summer, in August 1904; and Florence had already been taking the baths for a month. I don't know how it feels to be a patient at one of those places. I never was a patient anywhere. I daresay the patients get a home feeling and some sort of anchorage in the spot. They seem to like the bath attendants, with their cheerful faces, their air of authority, their white linen. But, for myself, to be at Nauheim gave me a sense – what shall I say? – a sense

---

[3] It is interesting to note the extent to which German provinces, as well as cities, often had their own names and derivatives in current English usage into the twentieth century: the Palatinate, for example, or Thuringia and its adjective Thuringian, most of which have fallen out use and would seem somewhat affected today—with the notable exceptions of Saxony and Bavaria. This example, "Hessian" as the adjectival form of Hesse, seems to have dropped away too.

almost of nakedness – the nakedness that one feels on the seashore or in any great open space. I had no attachments, no accumulations. In one's own home it is as if little, innate sympathies draw one to particular chairs that seem to enfold one in an embrace, or take one along particular streets that seem friendly when others may be hostile. And, believe me, that feeling is a very important part of life. I know it well, that have been for so long a wanderer upon the face of public resorts. And one is too polished up. Heaven knows I was never an untidy man. But the feeling that I had when, whilst poor Florence was taking her morning bath, I stood upon the carefully swept steps of the *Englischer Hof,* looking at the carefully arranged trees in tubs upon the carefully calculated gaiety, at the carefully calculated hour, the tall trees of the public gardens, going up to the right; the reddish stones of the baths – or were they white half-timber chalets? Upon my word I have forgotten, I who was there so often. That will give you the measure of how much I was in the landscape. I could find my way blindfolded into the hot rooms, to the douche rooms, to the fountain in the centre of the quadrangle where the rusty water gushes out. Yes, I could find my way blindfolded. I know the exact distances. From the Hotel Regina you took one hundred and eighty-seven paces, then, turning sharp, lefthanded, four hundred and twenty took you straight down to the fountain. From the *Englischer Hof,* starting on the sidewalk, it was ninety-seven paces and the same four hundred and twenty, but turning lefthanded this time.

And now you have to understand that, having nothing in the world to do – but nothing whatever! I fell into the habit of counting my footsteps. I would walk with Florence to the baths. And, of course, she entertained me with her conversation. It was, as I have said, wonderful what she could make conversation out of. She walked very lightly, and her hair was very nicely done, and she dressed beautifully and very expensively. Of course she had money of her own, but I shouldn't have minded. As yet you know I can't remember a single one of her dresses. Or I can remember just one, a very simple one of blue figured silk – a Chinese pattern – very full in the skirts and broadening out over the shoulders. And her hair was copper-colored, and the heels of her shoes were exceedingly high, so that she tripped upon the points of her toes. And when she came to the door of the bathing place, and when it opened to receive her, she would look back at me with a little coquettish smile, so that her cheek appeared to be caressing her shoulder.

I seem to remember that, with that dress, she wore an immensely broad leghorn hat – the Chapeau de Paille of Rubens, only very white. The hat would be tied with a lightly knotted scarf of the same stuff as her dress. She knew how to give value to her blue eyes. And round her neck would be some simple pink, coral beads. And her complexion had a perfect clearness, a perfect smoothness...

Yes, that is how I most exactly remember her, in that dress, in that hat, looking over her shoulder at me so that the eyes flashed very blue – dark pebble blue…

And, what the devil! For whose benefit did she do it? For that of the bath attendant? of the passers-by? I don't know. Anyhow, it can't have been for me, for never, in all the years of her life, never on any possible occasion, or in any other place did she so smile to me, mockingly, invitingly. Ah, she was a riddle; but then, all women are riddles. And it occurs to me that some way back I began a sentence that I have never finished… It was about the feeling that I had when I stood on the steps of my hotel every morning before starting out to fetch Florence back from the bath. Natty. precise, well-brushed, conscious of being rather small amongst the long English, the lank Americans, the rotund Germans, and the obese Russian Jewesses, I should stand there, tapping a cigarette in the outside of my case, surveying for a moment the world in the sunlight. But a day was to come when I was never to do it again alone. You can imagine, therefore, what the coming of the Ashburnhams meant to me.

I have forgotten the aspect of many things, but I shall never forget the aspect of the dining-room of the Hotel Excelsior on that evening – and on so many other evenings. Whole castles have vanished from my memory, whole cities that I have never visited again, but that white room, festooned with paper-mâché fruits and flowers; the tall windows; the many tables; the black screen round the door with three golden cranes flying upward on each panel; the palm-tree in the centre of the room; the swish of the waiter's feet; the cold expensive elegance; the mien of the diners as they came in every evening – their air of earnestness as if they must go through a meal prescribed by the *Kur* authorities and their air of sobriety as if they must seek not by any means to enjoy their meals – those things I shall not easily forget.

Joseph Conrad, *Notes on Life and Letters*

The first days of the third week in July, while the telegraph wires hummed with words of enormous import which were to fill blue-books, yellow-books, white-books, and rouse the wonder of mankind, passed for us in light-hearted preparation for the journey. What was it but just a rush through Germany to get across as quick as possible.

It is the part of the earth's solid surface of which I know the least. In all my life I had been across it only twice. I may well say of "vidi tantum;" and the very little I saw was through the window of a railway carriage at express speed. Those journeys of mine had been more like pilgrimages when one hurries on towards the goal for the satisfaction of a deeper need than curiosity. In this last instance, too, I was so incurious that I would have liked to fall asleep on the shores of

England and open my eyes, if it were possible, only on the other side of the Silesian frontier.

Yet, in truth, as many others have done, I had "sensed it" – that promised land of steel, of chemical dyes, of method, of efficiency; that race planted in the middle of Europe assuming the grotesque vanity of Europeans amongst effete Asiatics or barbarous niggers; and with a consciousness of superiority freeing their hands from all moral bounds, anxious to take up, if I may express myself so, the "perfect man's burden." Meantime in a clearing of the Teutonic forest their sages were rearing a Tree of Cynical Wisdom, a sort of Upas tree whose shade may be seen lying now over the prostrate body of Belgium. It must be said that they laboured openly enough, watering it from the most authentic sources of all madness, and watching with their be-spectacled eyes the slow ripening of the glorious blood-red fruit. The sincerest words of peace, word of menace, and I verily believe words of abasement even, if there had been a voice vile enough to utter them, would have been wasted on their ecstasy. For when the fruit ripens on a branch, it must fall. There is nothing on earth that can prevent it.

For reasons which at first seemed to me somewhat obscure one of my companions whose wishes are law decided that our travels should begin in an unusual way by the crossing of the North Sea. We should proceed from Harwich to Hamburg.

It was really a surprisingly small dinghy and it ran to and fro like a water-insect fussing noisily down there with immense self-importance. Within hail of us the hull of the Elbe Lightship floated all dark and silent under its enormous, round, service lantern; a faithful black shadow watching the broad estuary full of lights.

Such was my first view of the Elbe approaches under the wings of peace, ready for flight away from the luckless shores of Europe. Our visual impressions remain with us so persistently that I find it extremely difficult to hold fast to the rational belief that now everything is dark over there, that the Elbe Lightship has been towed away from its port of duty, the triumphant beam of Heligoland extinguished, and the pilot ship laid up, or turned to warlike uses for lack of its proper work to do. And obviously it must be so. Any trickle of oversea trade that passes yet that way must be creeping along cautiously, with the unlighted, war-blighted, black coast close on one, and sudden death close on the other hand.

For, all the space we steamed through on that Sunday evening must be now one great mine field, sown thickly with the seeds of hate; while submarines steal out to sea, over the very spot, perhaps, where the insect dinghy put a pilot on board of us with so much fussy importance.

(…)

On this journey of ours which for me was essentially not a progress but a retracing of footsteps on the road of life, I had no beacons to look out for in Germany. I had never lingered in that land which, as a whole, is so singularly barren of memorable manifestations of generous sympathies and magnanimous impulses. An ineradicable, invincible provincialism of envy and vanity, clings to the forms of its thought like a frowsy garment. Even while very young I turned my eyes away from it instinctively as from a threatening phantom. I believe children and dogs have in their innocence, special powers of perception as far as spectral apparitions and coming misfortunes are concerned.

Robert Graves, *Goodbye to All That*

My mother took us abroad to stay at my grandfather's house in Germany five times between my second and twelfth year. Then he died, and we never went again. He owned a big old manor house at Deisenhofen, ten miles from Munich; by name 'Laufzorn', which means 'Begone, anger!' Our summers there were easily the best things of my early childhood. Pine forests and hot sun, red deer, black and red squirrels, acres of blueberries and wild strawberries, nine or ten different kinds of edible mushrooms which we went into the forest to pick, and unfamiliar flowers in the fields – Munich lies high, and outcrops of Alpine flowers in the fields occur here and there; a farm with all the usual animals except sheep; drives through the countryside in a brake behind my grandfather's greys; and bathing in the Isar under a waterfall. The Isar was bright green, and said to be the fastest river of Europe. We used to visit the uncles who kept a peacock farm a few miles away; and a grand-uncle, Johannes von Ranke, the ethnologist, who lived on the lakeshore of Tegernsee, where everyone had buttercup-blonde hair; and occasionally my Aunt Agnes, Freifrau Baronin von Aufsess of Aufsess Castle, some hours away by train, high up in the Bavarian Alps.

Aufsess, built in the ninth century, stood so remote that it had never been sacked, but remained Aufsess property ever since. To the original building, a keep with only a ladder-entrance half-way up, a medieval castle had been added. Its treasures of plate and armour were amazing. My Uncle Siegfried showed us children the chapel: its walls hung with enamelled shields of each Aufsess baron, impaled with the arms of the noble family into which he had married. He pointed to a stone in the floor which pulled up by a ring, and said: 'That is the family vault where all Aufsess go when they die. I'll be down there one day.' He scowled comically. (But he got killed in the war as an officer of the Imperial German Staff and, I believe, they never found his body.)
(…)
Laufzorn, which my grandfather had bought and restored from a ruinous condition, could not compare in tradition with Aufsess, though it had for a

time been a shooting lodge of the Bavarian kings. Still, two ghosts went with the place; the farm labourers used to see them frequently. (…) The bottom storey formed part of the farm. A carriage-drive ran right through it, with a wide, covered courtyard in the centre, where cattle were once driven to safety in times of baronial feud. On one side of the drive lay the estate steward's quarters, on the other the farm servants' inn and kitchen, in the middle storey lived my grandfather and his family. The top storey was a store for corn, apples, and other farm produce; and up here my cousin Wilhelm – later shot down in an air battle by a schoolfellow of mine – used to lie for hours picking off mice with an air-gun.

Bavarian food had a richness and spiciness that we always missed on our return to England. We liked the rye bread, the dark pine-honey, the huge ice-cream puddings made with fresh raspberry juice and the help of the snow stored during the winter in an ice-house, my grandfather's venison, the honey-cakes, the pastries, and particularly the sauces made with different kinds of mushrooms. Also the pretzels, the carrots cooked in sugar, and summer pudding of cranberries and blueberries. In the orchard, close to the house, we could eat as many apples, pears and greengages as we liked. There were also rows of blackcurrant and gooseberry bushes in the garden. The estate, despite the recency of my grandfather's tenure, his liberalism, and his experience in modern agricultural methods, remained feudalistic. The poor, sweaty, savage-looking farm servants, who talked a dialect we could not understand[4], frightened us. They ranked lower even than the servants at home; as for the colony of Italians, settled about half a mile from the house, whom my grandfather had imported for cheap labour for his brick factory – we associated them in our minds with 'the gipsies of the wood' of the song.
(…)

The headmaster of Rokeby school who caned me for forgetting my gymnastic shoes loved German culture, and impressed this feeling on the school, so that it stood to my credit that I could speak German and had visited Germany. At my other preparatory schools this German connexion seemed something at least excusable, and perhaps even interesting. Only at Charterhouse did it rank as a social offence. My history from the age of fourteen, when I began to think for myself, is a forced rejection of the German in me.

---

[4] Dialect is a feature of German which has remained strong to this day. The language has become standardized to a far lesser extent and at a far slower pace than French or English, which linguists tend to attribute to its pluricentrality, i.e. the range of equivalently powerful regional centres, as opposed to a tone-setting capital such as Paris or London. Along with their Austrian and Swiss cousins, Bavarian dialects remain some of the strongest and most impenetrable to other speakers.

7

From 1920s Bohemia
to 1930s Germania
1925 - 1935

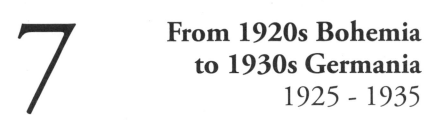

Images of the stacks of these comically high-value notes required for even the simplest of purchases came to symbolize Germany's economic malaise in the 1920s.

THE WEIMAR REPUBLIC had been born out of chaos in 1919 and was dogged by events both within and without Germany from that moment on. The harsh terms of the Treaty of Versailles, which came into effect in 1920, saw it listing from the very start, struggling economically and suffering from foreign occupation, which made it easy prey for disgruntled generals and political extremists. It is unsurprising that the first recorded example of the use of the German word "putsch" in English is from the
s of London on 14 November 1919.

The early twenties were set to the rhythm of hyperinflation, which reached its crescendo in the autumn of 1923 when, as a temporary new version of the Mark was introduced to stabilize the situation, the exchange rate was set as one trillion to one. The currency reform worked, however: the economy started to grow immediately and, after an agreement with foreign banks in 1924, Germany was able to meet its reparation obligations; the French then withdrew from the punitive occupation of the Rhineland and suddenly the putsching malcontents such as the newly-founded Nazi Party were left punching at thin air.

For Weimar Germany, the Roaring Twenties had begun. Pent-up demand both domestically and in export markets saw its industry, which still enjoyed a notable technological advance, producing flat out, while the chaos of the previous years had broken down the old cultural hierarchy: Expressionism, Bauhaus architecture, legendarily raunchy cabaret—Germany, and especially Berlin, was almost unrecognizable by the Wall Street Crash of 1929.

What the ensuing Great Depression revealed was that the favourable economic climate of the late 1920s had masked a growing and widespread reactionary alienation from the chic urban Germany of flappers, jazz musicians and film stars. In the run-up to the 1932 elections, the Nazis deftly linked the desperation produced by swingeing cuts in state expenditure and mass unemployment with a more general cultural malaise and nostalgia for the days when Germany was still in the strict, paternalistic hands of the Hohenzollern emperors. The old caricature image of Germans so popular abroad became a potent symbol of a better past for an unsettled populace and on 30 January 1933 President Hindenburg (b. 1847), a sternly moustachioed former Prussian general, made Adolf Hitler (b. 1889) chancellor of Germany. Within the year, Germany's first truly democratic state had been entirely replaced by what would become its most notorious dictatorship.

Patrick Leigh Fermor asked in the introduction to *A Time of Gifts* when "officers with Iron Crosses and fencing slashes, monocles and staccato laughs

(...) reciting the Hymn of Hate among the sausages and the beer-mugs (...) replace(d) the early nineteenth-century stereotype of picturesque principalities exclusively populated—except for Prussia—by philosophers and composers and bandsmen and peasants and students drinking and singing in harmony?" His guess was the Franco-Prussian War, and it is indeed here that the pendulum started swinging; Evelyn Princess Blücher's account of the German atrocities during the First World War (see previous chapter) showed precisely when the militaristic finally eclipsed the bucolic as the Teutonic stereotype of choice.

Leigh Fermor continues: "More recently, *All Quiet on the Western Front* had appeared; tales of night life in Berlin came soon after... There was not much else until the Nazis came into power." The truth in this statement is borne out by the fact that in previous generations literary heavyweights such as Henry James and T. S. Eliot were found trying to learn German by applying themselves to hefty tomes of Schiller; in the late 1920s writers in Germany were more likely to pick up what German they had in Berlin nightclubs or, later, from sinister interviews with the Gestapo.

The Weimar Republic: From Zenith to Nadir

The first extract in this chapter dates from around 1929, although it was reworked and not published until 1988, making it symptomatic of writing about Germany in this period. Here Stephen Spender (b. 1909) describes his experiences of what he calls in the retrospective introduction "that strange Indian Summer—the Weimar Republic. For many of my friends and for myself, Germany seemed a paradise where there was no censorship and young Germans enjoyed extraordinary freedom in their lives." In *The Temple*, Spender's narrator Paul portrays the hedonistic body-cult of well-to-do young Germans, showing how blissfully ignorant they were of the up-swell in intolerance rising beneath them.

If Spender's focus is on those with the time and money to make the most of the Weimar years, his friend Christopher Isherwood (b. 1904) comes across the losers of the 1920s. As opposed to the comparative wealth of Spender's Hamburg and Cologne, the city portrayed in *Goodbye to Berlin* (published in 1939) is stricken with poverty. Set in 1932-33, it shows how the economic turmoil of the 1920s had created the perfect environment for young Bohemians as inflation had wiped out savings, forcing people to rent out rooms in their homes and driving down prices. It also created a tacit acceptance of prostitution as the desperate sold their bodies to tourists whose hard currency was worth more than the unreliable Reichsmark. If the decadence of interwar Berlin is legendary in the English-speaking world, this is in no small part due to the flair of Isherwood's writing and his runaway success with *Cabaret*.

Gerald Hamilton (b. 1888) describes the atmosphere of Berlin in 1933 in the far more prosaic terms of a memoirist. In *Mr. Norris and I*, published in 1956, he replies to his depiction in *Mr. Norris Changes Trains*, Isherwood's other novelette of early 1930s Berlin, and gives a brief but fascinating insight into what made Berlin so attractive to well-off British free-thinkers in the twilight years of the Weimar Republic.

On paper, Patrick Leigh Fermor (b. 1915) too would have been the perfect candidate to join Spender and Isherwood's German expatriate set: highly educated but lacking in motivation and qualification, an upper-middle-class-to-aristocratic background, a clear dislike of the stuffy intolerance of post-Edwardian Britain. Yet Fermor's experience of 1933 Germany is just one part of a longer, more elemental, almost mythical journey on foot across a continent. In *A Time of Gifts*, written in 1977, the author was as intrigued by the atmosphere of foreboding in 1933 Germany as he was fascinated by the country's history, the ancient legends of the Rhine and the forests.

Also arriving in Germany in 1933 was Martha Dodd (b. 1908), daughter of the American ambassador to Berlin. At first alarmingly susceptible to the Nazi movement, in her 1939 *My Years in Germany* (titled *Through Embassy Eyes* in the US), Dodd charts her sometimes exasperatingly slow realization that Hitler's regime was a dangerous dictatorship. Her writing had a clear political aim in trying to steer the United States away from isolationism, and she uses her own initial naïve blindness to the horrors of Nazism as a tool in this endeavour.

Another young woman bowled over by the Nazi dictatorship was Unity Mitford (b. 1914). Her infatuation with the Nazi regime—and above all with Hitler—went far deeper, however. Although two of the aristocratic Mitford sisters also flirted with fascism, creating a national scandal in the United Kingdom in the 1930s and beyond, Unity's particular adoration for Hitler was clearly of a different, psychologically unhinged character. She was repatriated to Britain on Hitler's personal orders in 1940 after having shot herself on the outbreak of the Second World War. Her letters, published along with those of her five sisters in 2007, constitute by far the strangest written description of Germany in this collection.

Delayed Publication

Given the effect these letters would have had on the already damaged reputation of the Mitford family, it is understandable that they were not published until so recently. Stephen Spender delayed the publication of his novel—by and large written shortly after his visits to Germany—until the late 1980s, in no small part due to the openly sexual depictions. The next longest delay in publication was that of Patrick Leigh Fermor's account, which, like Spender's, was reworked but largely based on existing material. Hamilton, meanwhile, only wrote about 1930s Berlin two decades later, and the two freshest accounts, those of Isherwood and Dodd, were both published in 1939.

In this respect, we are dealing with an entirely retrospective set of writing, and given the importance of the year 1933, which only became entirely clear subsequently, the extracts coalesce to a large extent around it. Due to the delayed publication of all the writing in this chapter, the usual chronological order based on the year of release has been abandoned; instead, the moment at which the accounts are set has been used to structure the extracts.

*

Stephen Spender, *The Temple*

They crossed a wide bridge over the Rhine. Whilst they were on the bridge, they had to walk single file along the pavement, there were so many people there, and so much traffic on the road. They could not talk. Paul observed Joachim closely. He was dressed in the pseudo-English Hamburg style, which looked rather foreign in Cologne. He wore grey flannel trousers and a jacket of a light blue colour. Striding along, Joachim stood tall and straight, his head erect. He held the little case containing his bathing things and his camera lightly in his left hand in a manner nonchalantly self-aware. The sun beat down on his tanned skin. He stared round him almost defiantly and always with that air of entertaining and being entertained. People turned to look back at him.

On the far side of the bridge they followed a broad path which left the road and went through a garden past the long modern building for international exhibitions. Everything seemed clean and new and polished like gun-metal on this side of the Rhine. The Exhibition Building[1], with its long lines of low walls and symmetrical windows, stretching far away from each side of its central tower, looked diminished, microscopic almost under the immense glare of the afternoon.

"Isn't it wonderful?" said Joachim, grinning at Paul. He put up his face toward the sun, and lifted up an arm to shield his eyes. "It is so bright," he said. "I can hardly look at it." Then he let his hand drop against the concrete parapet in front of the river. He drew it quickly away again. "Oh, it is so hot! You can scarcely touch it! Let us go and swim at once."

They soon reached the *Schwimmbad*. After they had undressed, they walked

---

[1] Nowadays, no German city is complete without its *Messe*, or exhibition halls. The modern German predilection for putting on large expos is based on a long tradition of German cities functioning as meeting-places for trade and industries, most notably Leipzig's and Frankfurt's role as age-old centres for printing and publishing.

slowly down to the water. Paul lagged behind. Joachim said: "Why can't you keep up? Is it so awfully difficult?"

The current of the Rhine at Cologne being very strong, when Paul got into the water he was immediately swept off his feet. Joachim said, grinning: "What is the matter with you, Paul? You don't seem to be able to stand on your feet at all." But he said it teasingly and he laughed.

Paul struggled to his feet, and then walked further out, whilst the stream tugged at his legs as if they were being pulled by cables.

"Try and swim against the current now!"

Paul swam as hard as he could but he was carried backwards by the stream.

"Swim! Swim!" Joachim shouted, laughing. "I'll race you!" He threw himself down into the water beside Paul and appeared to be advancing rapidly. But when Paul looked at the shore he saw it was gliding forwards, not backward. Even Joachim could not quite hold his own against the current.

Paul abandoned any attempt to conquer the Rhine. He swam downstream, enjoying the incredibly swift motion of the water carrying him. Joachim, after diving under the floating wooden platforms which surrounded the bathing place, moved far out into the centre of the river. When a string of barges came downstream he climbed up the side of one of them and then dived off its deck the other side. Being liable to cramp, and not able to swim well, Paul was grateful that Joachim had gone away. He no longer had to behave athletically. He began to enjoy himself, floating on his back and thinking about poetry. (…)

Paul walked away towards the place where people were doing gymnastic exercises.

He watched the writhing figure of the mostly middle-aged members of the German youth movement. As he looked at them – men, women, boys, shrimp-pink, yellow or mahogany – they struck him as ludicrous, even the beautiful ones, and some were beautiful. After being in Germany for just over two months, he found himself beginning to tire of the self-conscious insistence of the Germans on their bodies. They worshipped the body, as though it were a temple. (…)

Christopher Isherwood, *Goodbye to Berlin*

The inhabitants of this street know me by sight already. At the grocer's people no longer turn their heads on hearing my English accent as I order a pound of butter. At the street corner, after dark, the three whores no longer whisper throatily: "Komm, Süsser!" as I pass.

The three whores are all plainly over fifty years old. They do not attempt to conceal their age. They are not noticeably rouged or powdered. They wear baggy old fur coats and longish skirts and matronly hats. I happened to mention them to Bobby and he explained to me that there is a recognized demand for the comfortable type of woman. Many middle-aged men prefer them to girls. They even attract boys in their 'teens. A boy, explained Bobby, feels shy with a girl of his own age but not with a woman old enough to be his mother. Like most barmen, Bobby is a great expert on all sexual questions.

The other evening, I went to call on him during business hours.

It was still very early, about nine o'clock, when I arrived at the Troika. The place was much larger and grander than I had expected. A commissionaire braided like an archduke regarded my hatless head with suspicion until I spoke to him in English. A smart cloak-room girl insisted on taking my overcoat, which hides the worst stains on my baggy flannel trousers. A page-boy, seated on the counter, didn't rise to open the inner door. Bobby, to my relief, was at his place behind a blue and silver bar. I made towards him as towards an old friend. He greeted me most amiably:

"Good evening, Mr Isherwood. Very glad to see you here."

I ordered a beer and settled myself on a stool in the corner. With my back to the wall, I could survey the whole room.

"How's business?" I asked.

Bobby's care-worn, powdered, night-dweller's face became grave. He inclined his head towards me, over the bar, with confidential flattering seriousness.

"Not much good, Mr Isherwood. The kind of public we have nowadays… you wouldn't believe it! Why, a year ago, we'd have turned them away at the door. They order a beer and think they've got the right to sit here the whole evening."

Bobby spoke with extreme bitterness. I began to feel uncomfortable.

"What'll you drink?" I asked guiltily gulping down my beer; and added, lest there should be any misunderstanding: "I'd like a whisky and soda."

Bobby said he'd have one, too.

The room was nearly empty. I looked the few guests over, trying to see them through Bobby's disillusioned eyes. There were three attractive well-dressed girls sitting at the bar: the one nearest to me was particularly elegant, she had quite a cosmopolitan air. But during a lull in the conversation, I caught fragments of her talk with the other barman. She spoke broad Berlin dialect. She was tired and bored; her mouth dropped. A young man approached her and joined in the discussion; a handsome broad-shouldered boy in a well-cut dinner-jacket, who might well have been an English public-school prefect on holiday.

"*Nee, nee,*" I heard him say. "*Bei mir nicht!*"[2] He grinned and made a curt,

---

[2] An intriguingly oblique fragment of German on the basis of which the reader can only guess at the content of the conversation; bei mir nicht can mean anything from "not in my case" to "you won't get away with that around me".

brutal gesture of the streets.

Over in the corner sat a page-boy, talking to the little old lavatory attendant in his white jacket. The boy said something, laughed and broke off suddenly into a huge yawn. The three magicians on their platform were chatting, evidently unwilling to begin until they had an audience worth playing to. At one of the tables, I thought I saw a genuine guest, a stout man with a moustache. After a moment, however, I caught his eye, he made a little bow and I knew that he must be the manager.

The door opened. Two men and two women came in. The women were elderly, had thick legs, cropped hair, and costly evening-gowns. The men were lethargic, pale, probably Dutch. Here, unmistakeably, was Money. In an instant, the Troika was transformed. The manager, the cigarette-boy, and the lavatory attendant rose simultaneously to their feet. The lavatory attendant disappeared. The manager said something in a furious undertone to the cigarette boy, who also disappeared. He then advanced, bowing and smiling, to the guest's table and shook hands with the two men. The cigarette-boy reappeared with his tray, followed by a waiter who hurried forward with a wine-list.

Gerald Hamilton, *Mr. Norris and I*

This period of my life was on the whole a very happy one. Bohemia in Berlin was outwardly the same as Bohemia anywhere else, but it was more agreeably mixed and international than in London. It was at this time that I first met Christopher Isherwood, a poor and struggling writer, and I am sure neither he nor I dreamed that he would reach the prominence he occupies to-day. The famous *pension* referred to in "Mr. Norris" was visited by me almost daily. I first met the original of "Sally Bowles" at that *pension*. She asked me to come in the next morning for a talk, but arriving punctually at the time I was invited, I was told she was not yet up. However, hearing I was there, she called out gaily, "It's alright, come and talk to me while I have my bath, darling." I knew I was in Berlin's Bohemia at last. (…)

During the last years of the decrepit Weimar Republic, Berlin outvied Paris with its night life. But though it was supposed to be gay, there was a sordid element about it which was very noticeable. There were alleged to be no less than 132 homosexual cafés registered as such with the tolerant police. Some of them were used only by ladies as a rendezvous for their Lesbian friends. Others were exclusively for *Transvestiten*, men and boys who like to dress up as women. The rest were patronized by the usual kind of homosexuals who hoped to meet their destiny at such places. There were weekly homosexual papers, such as the famous *Freundschaft* which published the most fantastic advertisements I have ever seen in print. Then again there were some cafés which specialized in a particular attraction, such as having a genuine hermaphrodite on the premises. The height of decadence was reached on the so-called *strich* or avenue, where prostitutes offered themselves for sale. There were girls in men's clothes, often holding a whip, boys in girl's clothes, and the usual supply of men and women offering themselves to either sex in return for ample payment.

(...)

On the 30th January, 1933, Adolf Hitler became Chancellor of the German Empire. Until the very eve of that historic date nobody in Berlin believed that the old President would succumb to the intrigues of the *camarilla* consisting of Papen, Hindenburg's son, and Meissner. I lived at that time at the house of an attaché of the Argentine Embassy as a paying guest, having had to give up my own apartment some months previously. I felt, however, that although no harm would come to me as the guest of a well-known diplomat, nevertheless this new Germany was no place for me. Indeed, very soon after the Nazis came into power, I received a *vorladung* from the political police, who questioned me closely about my former activities.

The Nazi party in Germany seemed to me then the very incarnation of those ideas against which I had struggled for so many years. It represented to me warfare, hatred, intolerance, cruelty, and bloodshed. When I showed the official who questioned me, not without some pride, a letter of thanks signed by the first President of the German Republic, Ebert, for the work I had done in saving German children after the Blockade, he glanced at it and merely remarked, "*Das ist für uns gar keine Empfehlung*" ("That is for us no recommendation."). So I decided to leave Germany before it was too late, and it was with a sigh of relief that I crossed for the last time the German-Belgian frontier. After that, Germany rapidly became a caricature of itself.

Patrick Leigh Fermor, *A Time of Gifts*

How exhilarating to be away from the plain! With every minute that passed the mountains climbed with greater resolution. Bridges linked the little towns from bank to bank and the water scurried round the piers on either side as we threaded upstream. Shuttered for the winter, hotels rose above the town roofs and piers for passenger steamers jutted into the stream. Unfabled as yet, Bad Godesberg slipped past. Castles crumbled on pinnacles. They loomed on their spikes like the turrets of the Green Knight before Sir Gawain; and one of them —so my unfolding river map told me – might have been built by Roland. Charlemagne was associated with the next. Standing among tall trees, the palaces of electors and princes and pleasure-loving archbishops reflected the sunlight from many windows. The castle of the Princes of Wied moved out of the wings, floated to the centre and then drifted slowly off-stage again. Was this where the short-reigned Mpret of Albania grew up? Were any of these castles, I wondered, abodes of those romantic-sounding noblemen, Rheingrafen and Wildgrafen – Rhine-Counts or Counts of the Forest, or the Wilderness or of Deer? If I had had to be German, I thought, I wouldn't have minded being a Wildgrave; or a Rheingrave... A shout from the cabin broke into these thoughts: Uli handed up a tin plate of delicious baked beans garnished with some more frightful Speck, which was quickly hidden and sent to join the Rheingold when no one was looking.

On the concertina-folds of my map these annotated shores resembled a historical traffic-block. We were chugging along Caesar's *limes* with the Franks. 'Caesar threw a bridge across the Rhine...' Yes, but where? Later emperors moved the frontier eastward into the mountains far beyond the left bank, where, so they said, the Hercynian forest, home of unicorns, was too dense for a cohort to deploy, let alone a legion. (Look what happened to the legions of Quintilius Varus a hundred miles north-east! Those were vague regions, utterly unlike the shores of the brilliant Rhine: the Frigund of German myth, a thicket that still continued after sixty days of travel and the haunt, when the unicorns trotted away into fable, of wolves and elks and reindeers and the aurochs. The Dark Ages, when they reached them, found no lights to extinguish, for none had ever shone there.)

(...)

Coblenz is on a slant. Every street tilted and I was always looking across towers and chimney-pots and down on the two corridors of mountain that conducted the streams to their meeting. It was a buoyant place under a clear sky, everything in the air whispered that the plains were far behind and the sunlight sent a flicker and a flash of reflections glancing up from the snow; and two more invisible lines had been crossed and important ones: the accent had changed and wine cellars had taken the place of beer-halls. Instead of those grey mastodontic mugs, wine-glasses glittered on the oak. (It was under a vista of old casks in a Weinstube that I settled with my diary till bedtime.) The plain bowls of these wine-glasses were poised on slender glass stalks, or on diminishing pagodas of little globes, and both kinds of stern were coloured: a deep green for Mosel and, for Rhenish, a brown smoky gold that was almost amber. When horny hands lifted them, each flashed forth its coloured message in the lamplight. It is impossible, drinking by the glass in those charmingly named inns and wine-cellars, not to drink too much. Deceptively and treacherously, those innocent-looking goblets hold nearly half a bottle and simply by sipping one could explore the two great rivers below and the Danube and all Swabia, and Franconia too by proxy, and the vales of Imhof and the faraway slopes of Würzburg: journeying in time from year to year, with draughts as cool as a deep well, limpidly varying from dark gold to pale silver and smelling of glades and meadows and flowers. Gothic inscriptions still flaunted across the walls, but they were harmless here, and free of the gloom imposed by those boisterous and pace-forcing black-letter hortations in the beer-halls of the north. And the style was better: less emphatic, more lucid and laconic; and both consoling and profound in content; or so it seemed as the hours passed. *Glaub, was wahr ist,* enjoined a message across an antlered wall, *Lieb, was rar ist; Trink, was klar ist.*[3] I only realized as I stumbled to bed how pliantly I had obeyed.

It was the shortest day of the year and signs of the season were becoming hourly more marked. Every other person in the streets was heading for home with a tall and newly felled fir-sapling across his shoulder, and it was under a mesh of Christmas decorations that I was sucked into the Liebfrauenkirche next day. The romanesque nave was packed and an anthem of great choral splendour rose from the gothic, choir stalls, while the cauliflowering incense followed the plainsong across the slopes of the sunbeams. A Dominican in horn-rimmed spectacles delivered a vigorous sermon. A number of Brownshirts – I'd forgotten all about them for the moment – was scattered among the congregation, with eyes lowered and their caps in their hands. They looked rather odd. They should have been out in the forest, dancing round Odin and Thor, or Loki perhaps.

Martha Dodd, *My Years in Germany*

We had a slow sail up the Elbe and finally docked at Hamburg. Germany was here at last, with all of its profound meaning, the new future only guessed at and begun, to which my father gave all the idealism of his deeply emotional and disciplined life, with which he expected to co-operate and [from] which he hoped to benefit. I was moved by the eagerness, which he unconsciously expressed in returning in one of the highest positions our country can offer to its citizens, to the country he had so well loved, understood, and defended. For us, his children, here was a new adventure breaking into our middle youth, not sought after, not really fully appreciated; it was not an end or a beginning for us—or so we thought—but an episode occurring in the security of circumstance and love. It was not recklessness for us; it was our parents' gift of an experience which could open or close or mean nothing in our lives. We greeted Germany with excited

---

[3] *Glaub, was wahr ist/Lieb, was rar ist/Trink, was klar ist*—a command typical of the German wine-making territories meaning "Believe that which is true/Love that which is rare/Drink that which is clear."

hearts, taking the future in our stride with the uncapturable nonchalance of youth, ready for anything or for nothing.

We must have presented one of the most amazing spectacles in the history of diplomatic arrivals, though, of course, we were completely unconscious of it at the time. My father had misread a telegram sent by the counsellor of the Embassy. He thought that the tickets to Berlin, the private car, etc., had all been arranged, so we didn't bother about arranging for them on board, and in the confusion of disembarking forgot to get our necessary cards. Until the last moment he was busy with interviewers and newspapermen. One of the journalists was a correspondent of a Jewish newspaper in Hamburg. He wrote an article saying that my father had been sent over to solve the Jewish problem. Later we heard about it, and realized how badly garbled the account was. The German papers were very polite to us, but took the occasion to point out that this was the way of Jews.

My brother had planned to drive our Chevrolet to Berlin, but had done nothing about the red tape of getting it off the ship, with the permits and licences, and so on, that it involved.

The Counsellor, the adviser to the Ambassador and next in rank to him, a gentleman of the most extreme Protocol (we hadn't yet heard this word) school, with grey-white hair and moustache which looked curled, elegant dress, gloves, stick and proper hat, a complexion of flaming hue, clipped, polite, and definitely condescending accent, was so horrified at our informality that his rage almost— not quite—transcended the bounds allowed by his rigid code of behaviour. We had no pretentious car, we had no chauffeur; valets, secretaries, and personal maids were ominously missing—in fact, we looked like simple ordinary human beings the like of which he had not permitted himself to mingle with for perhaps most of his adult life.

Finally, everything was put in order, my brother driving the modest car and the rest of us going by a regular train to Berlin (we should have at least taken the "Flying Hamburger," the fastest and most expensive special).[4] My father sat in one compartment talking over the political developments of Germany with the Counsellor, who was attempting in the most polished manner he could summon, to hint that my father was no longer a simple professor, but a great diplomat, and his habits and ways of life should be altered accordingly. But the honest and subtle, gentle and slightly nervous scholar was to remain as firm in his integrity of character as if there had been no change in his environment or position. I didn't realize how futile all admonitions were, and I am sure my

---

[4] The German diesel service between Hamburg and Berlin was for a period the fastest scheduled train in the world, covering 177 miles in just 138 minutes.

father was as supremely indifferent to them then as he was to be later when great pressure from all sources was applied to effect the desired transformation.

My mother and I were in another compartment, she uneasy and heavy of heart at the thought of the duties and change in life-patterns confronting her; and I sound asleep on her shoulder, both of us shrouded in expensive flowers.

The train stopped suddenly and I had just time enough to rub my eyes, jam on my hat and step onto the platform, a little dazed and very embarrassed. Before me was a large gathering of excited people; newspapermen crowding around us, and the ever-watchful Counsellor attempting to keep them away; Foreign Office representatives, other diplomats, and many Americans, come to look over the strange Ambassador and his family. The flashlights were a steady stream of blinding light and somehow or other I found myself grinning stupidly into the camera with bunches of orchids and other flowers up to my ears. My father took the newspapermen aside and gave them a prepared statement of greeting and we were hustled away.

I was put into a car with a young man who, I soon learned, was our Protocol secretary. I finally got the definition. He was pointing out the sights of Berlin to me. We drove around the Reichstag building, which he duly named. I exclaimed: "Oh, I thought it was burned down! It looks all right to me. Tell me what happened." He leaned over to me, after several such natural but indiscreet questions, and said, "Shssh! Young lady, you must learn to be seen and not heard. You mustn't say so much and ask so many questions. This isn't America and you can't say all the things you think." I was astonished, but subdued for the time being. This was my first contact with the reality of Germany under a dictatorship and it took me a long time to take his advice seriously. Long habits of life are hard to change overnight.

(…)

Saturday, June 30th[5], was as beautiful and warm a day as we had yet had in Germany. I determined to spend the day on the beach, imitating the German habit of acquiring a sunburn as early as possible in the season. I had a date with a friend of mine, a young secretary in a foreign embassy. In less than a week, I planned to go to Russia and, since I had heard the heat was unbearable, I was getting in training as well.

We took down the top of the Ford roadster and drove to Gross Glienicke,

---

[5] The weekend night of 30 June-1 July 1934 was soon to become known as the "Night of the Long Knives". After Hitler became Chancellor in early 1933, a series of laws followed which effectively abolished the Weimar Republic, outlawing regional assemblies, political parties and unions, which might still challenge Nazi power. During the Night of the Long Knives Hitler turned pre-emptively on potential rivals within the Nazi Party such as Röhm, head of the paramilitary SA, as well as remaining anti-Nazis including his immediate predecessor as Chancellor, Kurt von Schleicher.

a lovely and fairly private lake near Wansee. I baked in the sun the whole day, retiring to the shade only for cooling drinks and sandwiches. It was a beautiful serene blue day, the lake shimmering and glittering in front of us, and the sun spreading its fire over us. It was a silent and soft day – we didn't even have the energy or desire to talk politics or discuss the new tension in the atmosphere. At six o'clock we decided we had had enough sun and we drove slowly and quietly back to Berlin, our heads giddy and our bodies burning from the sun.

We passed through lanes of acacia tress, their beautiful white clustered blossoms, like bunches of rich ivory-tinted grapes, falling heavily forward and down, their scent like ripe grapes in the sun-laden air. Then there would be lanes of green coolness as we sped by luxuriant dark trees, then a stretch of sun-warmed sharp pine odour, almost like dry pungent dust in the nostrils.

We were not thinking of yesterday, or tomorrow, of the Nazis or of politics. Men and women were speeding by us both ways on bicycles, with small children in little wagons on the side, or in baskets on the front; a swift throb of a motorcycle mounted with strange goggled figures from another world, women carrying flowers, sturdy men walking with knapsacks by their sides. It was a homely, hot, and friendly day – I had my skirts pulled up to the edge of my bathing suit underneath, to get the last touch of the sun and the sudden cooling breezes which came when we had a long road of swiftness before us. I was happy, pleased with my day and my companion, full of sympathy for the earnest, simply kindly German people, so obviously taking a hard-earned walk or rest, enjoying themselves and their countryside so intensely.

It was six o'clock when we drove into Berlin. I pulled down my skirt and sat up straight and proper as befits a diplomat's daughter. The atmosphere had changed, fewer people were on the streets, many of them in curious static groups. Soon we noticed there was an unusual number of police standing around. As we drove nearer and nearer to the heart of the city, we saw heavy army trucks, machine guns, many soldiers, S.S. men, and especially large numbers of the green uniformed Goering police – and no S.A. men. The familiar Brown Shirt was significantly absent. As we came closer to home, we realized something very serious was happening. More truckloads of arms and soldiers on the edges of the streets and in the parks, some streets blocked off, guards and police everywhere. Hardly a person dressed in civilian clothes could be seen as we neared Tiergarten Strasse, and traffic seemed to have stopped. We had a diplomatic number so we were allowed free passage. Across from our house entrance was another sinister lining of trucks, soldiers, and the paraphernalia of war. Standarten Strasse, only a few blocks from our entrance, was roped off, and a cordon of police thrown around it. This was the street whose name had been changed to honour the distinguished Roehm, favourite of Hitler.

My companion was alarmed by this time. He let me off at the head of the lane that led to our Embassy and sped away to his own. I flew towards the house in the broiling sun. Breaking suddenly into our darkened house, the cool air striking me in the face, I turned a little dizzy, my eyes blinded for a moment from the lack of light. I stumbled up the first flight of stairs. When I got halfway up I saw the shadowy figure of my brother at the head of the steps. He called out nervously, "Martha, is that you? Where have you been? We were worried about you. Von Schleicher has been shot. We don't know what is happening. There is martial law in Berlin."

Unity Mitford, *Letters*

Unity to Diana

Königinstrasse 121, Munich
Sunday, 1 July 1934

Darling Nard,
(...)
The excitement here over the Röhm affair is terrific, everyone is horrified. No-one knew about it until last night. I heard rumours after dinner & immediately went into the town, where there were printed accounts of it stuck up in the chief squares. I couldn't believe it at first. I went to the Brown House, but the street was guarded by SS men so I couldn't get near. I waited in a huge crowd in a square near for two hours, they were all waiting to see Hitler & Goebbels come away from the Brown House. While we stood there several huge columns of SS, SA & Stahlhelm marched past us to the Brown House, & huge lorries full of sandbags with SS or Reichswehr sitting on top, & there were SS men dashing about the whole time on motorbikes & cars. It was all very exciting. Then word was passed round that Hitler & Goebbels had left by a back entrance & were already flying to Berlin, so I came home. Today no-one can talk of anything else, & there is a rumour that Schleicher & his wife, Röhm, & Heines have all killed themselves. I wonder if it is true. I am so *terribly* sorry for the Führer – you know Röhm was eldest comrade & friend, the only one that called him 'du' in public. How anyone could do what Röhm did I don't know. It must have been so dreadful for Hitler when he arrested Röhm himself & tore off his decorations. Then he went to arrest Heines & found him in bed with a boy. Did that get into the English papers? *Poor* Hitler. The whole thing is so dreadful. I must now go into the town & find out what has happened since last night.
    With best love to you & the Kits & Nan from
    Bobo

Kaulbachstrasse 49, Munich
19 September 1935

Darling Nard,

I'm afraid you must have had an *awful* journey. Even I, travelling only as far as here, was frozen when I arrived; and when I woke up yesterday morning and heard the wind whistling I thought of your poor crossing.

Well now I have a lot to tell you. Yesterday about 12, on my way to the hairdresser, I was walking up the Ludwigstrasse & just going to cross one of the side streets & there was a large Merc in it waiting to be able to cross the Ludwigstrasse & to my astonishment in front sat the Führer. I stood for about ½ a minute saluting about 5 feet from him, but he didn't see me. When I got to the hairdresser I felt quite faint & my knees were giving, you know how one does when one sees him unexpectedly. But I was so pleased, because it was the first time I had seen him like that, quite by chance, in the street. Hardly any of the people recognised him.

I went to the Osteria, & found Erich & Heemstra & Micky there[6], I made them sit in the garden & I sat alone inside. He came about 2.30, & smiled wonderfully as he shook hands, but then I waited & waited & no-one came. I was in despair, I thought he wasn't going to ask me. Rosa came & told me she had heard he wasn't in a good mood, so then I thought he certainly wouldn't invite me. However at last, at about 3, Brückner came & asked me to go to him. I feel sure the Führer had pain, which I know he sometimes does have. For one thing he didn't stand up when I came to the table, which he *always* does. Also the skin around the outside corners of his eyes was yellow. And then he couldn't seem to keep still, he moved backwards & forwards the whole time, with his hands on his knees, you know how he does. I was so unhappy about it, it is so terrible to think of him being in pain. However he was in the most divine mood imaginable, I think he was almost sweeter yesterday than I have ever known him. We talked a lot about the Parteitag, he was terribly pleased at the way it had all gone off. He said he felt terribly flat now that it's all over, & that it was so depressing driving away from Nürnberg, a few people in the street for about 100 yards & then no-one. I explained to him why that was, that they all thought he was going to the Flughafen and I think that cheered him up, but he was sad that the people had waited so long & hadn't seen him. He told me where we had sat at both the Congresses, and said he had seen me at the opera, but of course that was you. He put his hand on my shoulder twice & on my arm once. I told him

---

6 Heemstra refers to Ella van Heemstra, the mother of Audrey Hepburn. Like Michael Burn (see Chapter 8), van Heemstra and her husband flirted with Nazism. During the Second World War she would send Burn care parcels during his incarceration in Colditz, a favour he returned in the immediate aftermath, thus saving the life of the sickly young Audrey.

about having to go to Paris, & he was sorry for me, but then he said 'But in Paris you will see real Life, and then Munich will seem like a rocky island to you'. (He said the word 'island' in English.) I said no, Munich will always be my Paradise. (…)

V Best love, German greetings & Heil Hitler!

Bobo

8 Writing through the Nazi Stranglehold 1935 - 1939

Propaganda was as all-encompassing as censorship and the grip of the police state in Nazi Germany.

WITH NAZI POWER thoroughly consolidated at home, Hitler and his government turned their eyes abroad. In early 1935 the Saarland, placed under League of Nations supervision for fifteen years following the Treaty of Versailles, voted to reincorporate itself into Germany. Emboldened, Hitler announced in March that the strength of the German army would be increased to 500,000 and that the Luftwaffe would be founded, before pressuring the British into allowing Germany to build a new fleet—in contravention of the Versailles treaty.

Having essentially torn up the 1919 agreement, Hitler saw little need to respect its remaining provisions, reoccupying the demilitarized Rhineland in early 1936 before more or less openly supporting the fascists in the Spanish Civil War that summer. In March 1938 Austria was swallowed up into the Reich, becoming part of a united German state for the first time in its history and correcting what many pan-German nationalists on both sides of the border saw as a historical mistake.

The idea of uniting all "people of German blood" under one German state set in motion a logic of its own. The Sudetenland area of the Czech Republic was next on the list, as were several parts of Poland with German minorities. In autumn 1938 the Munich Agreement was signed with Britain and France allowing Hitler the Sudetenland in exchange for a guarantee of Czechoslovakian independence; it was derogated less than six months later as German troops occupied Prague. The strategy of appeasement with which Britain and France had tried to maintain peace in Europe had clearly run its course, and over the summer of 1939 preparations for the partition of Poland were made in secret between Germany and the Soviet Union. On 1 September 1939 Germany invaded Poland, precipitating the Second World War in Europe.

While this expansionist policy was set in motion abroad, Nazi control inside Germany tightened unceasingly. For people of Jewish heritage, rank discrimination turned into pro-active persecution in the wake of the Night of Broken Glass, or *Kristallnacht* in November 1938; laws were enacted the following month preventing Jewish people from working and impounding their savings. Meanwhile, a flood of other legislation entered German law perverting the very notion of law itself. Just after the beginning of the Second World War, the "act against elements damaging to the health of the people"—*Verordnung gegen Volksschädlinge*, which essentially gave judges free rein to use the death penalty—removed the last vestiges of a constitutional state with recourse to justice. The fingers of the Gestapo and their network of informants tightened around dissident elements, making criticism of the regime a dangerous matter, even in private.

Not unexpectedly, writers in this period were almost universally appalled by the extremes of Nazi rule. Although none of them was directly subject to violence, all were conscious of spies, censors and of the danger of expressing criticism of the regime on paper. The appetite for news about Germany at this time, and for history of it afterwards, means that journalists' work was particularly plentiful and is well preserved, a trend which continued through the Second World War. Works of imaginative fiction set in Germany, meanwhile, fell away entirely, and descriptions were less about cities and countryside than about people and events.

Diaries and Columns

Passing through Germany in May 1935 en route to Italy with her Jewish husband Leonard, Virginia Woolf (b. 1882) wrote two diary entries about her experiences there. In a disturbingly comic episode, the Woolfs ended up driving through a village in advance of what later turned out to be Hermann Göring's motorcade, with Mitzi, their pet dog, proving to be very popular indeed with the assembled crowd.

Samuel Beckett (b. 1906) too kept a diary of his time in Germany from late 1936 to 1937. As large portions of it are illegible, quoting from it at length is difficult, and there are some omissions in the short passage reproduced here. Beckett seems not to have been immediately struck by the repressive nature of the Nazi regime, as the early entry following his journey over the North Sea shows. Later in the diaries, however, he makes frequent and derogatory comments about the leading Nazis and arranges to see the work of underground artists.

North Carolina's most famous writer, Thomas Wolfe (b. 1900), often talked of Germany as his spiritual home and spent a lot of time there as an adult. He wrote the short story, *I Have a Thing to Tell You*, shortly after witnessing a Jewish railway passenger being arrested trying to leave Germany in late summer 1936. He knew full well that its critical tone would lead to him being barred from returning to his favourite country and to his books being banned there.

A third traveller to Germany in 1936 was the African-American sociologist W. E. B. Dubois (b. 1868), who had been invited there on a research stipend. He wrote a regular column, "A Forum of Fact and Opinion", for the *Pittsburgh Courier,* a weekly newspaper for African-Americans, and used it to describe his experiences in Germany. As someone regularly on the receiving end of racial discrimination in the United States, his is a singularly remarkable perspective on Nazi Germany and its campaign against the Jewish population.

Richard Hillary (b. 1919), meanwhile, went to Germany in 1938, a visit he recalled for his 1942 book *The Last Enemy;* the Oxford-educated Spitfire pilot wrote it after having been shot down in the Battle of Britain and having had to bail out of a second burning aircraft just one week later. Hillary describes a rowing event his university eight attended in which they pulled off an unexpected win, much to the bewilderment and dismay of the opposing German crew.

This chapter closes as the Second World War begins in earnest, in early September 1939. William Shirer (b. 1904), who would later become world-famous with his *The Rise and Fall of the Third Reich*, worked as a foreign correspondent in Berlin from 1934 to 1940. Leaving Germany due to tightening censorship in December 1940, Shirer used his own private journal as a basis for *Berlin Diary*, published in 1941. Academic analysis has shown that in reworking the text he made slight, but not unimportant, changes to some parts of it in order to make his stance more clearly condemnatory of the Third Reich—but there is no reason to doubt the authenticity and first-hand nature of the diary as a whole.

Germanophiles in the Shadow of Censorship

Even before fleeing—and smuggling out his diary—in 1940, Shirer had had to submit his reports to German censors. This was a time in which written material critical of Nazism could be dangerous to its author if found with him or her in Germany, and as such Woolf waited until she crossed into Austria before really recording her feelings about Germany, while Dubois took material critical of the Reich over the border before sending it to be published in Pittsburgh. Everywhere in these texts the fear of raids, searches and interrogations pervades. Only Hillary's book, written from the comparative safety of the British Isles, seems to have much by way of flair, of a free choice of words about it.

Despite the ugliness of German society in the late 1930s, many of the authors had or developed an attachment to Germany. Wolfe finally saw that he had to distance himself after witnessing the dangers of the police state first-hand, but did so with a heavy heart: "I've written a wonderful piece—after it gets published I won't be able to go back to the place where I'm liked best and have more friends than anywhere in the world," he wrote to a friend shortly after leaving Germany.

Beckett, regardless of his frequent jokes about the dictatorship and fun at the expense of its bureaucratic neologisms ("Devisenbewirtschaftungsstelle. Jawol!"), remained in Germany for almost a year and filled his diaries with German words. Clearly he had a fascination that went deeper than the contemporary unsavoury political climate, as did Dubois, who seems to have spent much of his time in Germany immersed in opera. Even Richard Hillary, writing during the Second World War in a politically anti-German climate and having been shot down twice by the Luftwaffe, still quoted both Schiller and Goethe in the first twenty pages of *The Last Enemy* and made a clear distinction between German culture and the Nazi ideology which had debased it. Even at five minutes to Germany's darkest hour, certain aspects of its culture seemed to still stand for something among English language writers.

*

Virginia Woolf, *Diary*

Thursday 9 May

Sitting in the sun outside the German Customs. A car with the swastika on the back window just passed through the barrier into Germany. L. is in the customs. I am nibbling at *Aaron's Rod.*[1] Ought I to go in & see what is happening? A fine dry windy morning. The Dutch customs took 10 seconds. This has taken 10 minutes already. The windows are barred. Here they came out & the grim man laughed at Mitz. But L. said that when a peasant came in & stood with his hat on the man said This office is like a Church & made him move it. Heil Hitler said the little thin boy opening his bag, perhaps with an apple in it, at the barrier. We become obsequious – delighted that is when the officers smile at Mitzi – the first stoop in our back.

That a work of art means that one part gets strength from another part.

At Ulken: home reached late after being turned aside to make way for the Minister President.

By the Rhine, sitting at the window, looking out on the river. The waiter has been talking. He has been in America: democratic; talks as if he were host. Like a little supple monkey. "Let me see now, you like good coffee. What have we nice?" & so on. Also the manager – was in the City Road – wanted to go back & keep a German hostel in Bedford Place. We were chased across the river by Hitler (or Goering) had to pass through ranks of children with red flags. They cheered Mitzi. I raised my hand. People gathering in the sunshine – rather forced like school sports. Banners stretched across the street "The Jew is our enemy" "There is no place for Jews in –". So we whizzed along until we got out of range of the docile hysterical crowd. Our obsequiousness gradually turning to anger. Nerves rather frayed. A sense of stupid mass feeling masked by good temper. So we came here, Unkel, an old country house, with curved banister, shallow steps, a black grated stair door, & courtyard. A number of little eyes in the roof, rabbits & doves in outhouses. The innkeeper is playing cards with his wife. They

---

[1] What a coincidence that Woolf should be reading a novel by D. H. Lawrence (see Chapter 6) as she crosses the border into Germany.

all want to go away – back to Islington, back to Washington – Oh so lovely, said the waiter, who wants to go on talking.

Sunday 12 May
Innsbruck

L. says I may now tell the truth, but I have forgotten 2 days of truth, & my pen is weeping ink. Let me see. We went on from the old country house Inn, which ran their charges up high, & drove down the Rhine, & tried to see it as an engaged couple in 1840 – no good. An ugly, pretentious country – operatic scenery. High, but insignificant hills, bristling with black & green fir trees, with correct towers & ruins – a river that runs with coal barges like Oxford Street, traffic on the cobbled roads: & then a wall had fallen, & we were made to cross over to the right side again. And so to – to where? I begin to forget. The dullest day of them all. But we got to (...) Heidelberg, which is – yes – a very distinguished University town, on the Neckar. The dons & their daughters were having a musical evening. I saw them tripping out to each other's houses with pale blue Beethoven quartets under their arms. Something like the Verralls & the Darwins in old Cambridge – the same dress, & nice intelligent faces. Great rhododendrons blooming. Still hot & blue. And the river like sliding plate glass. And next day to Augsburg – a dull town, but with a bath. A room with a bath. The country steadily improves – becomes shaped & spaced. From Augsburg to Innsbruck where I sit in the empty room – the hotel suites quite empty, & the town quiet as the grave, & and very stately. What did we see today? Great snow hills, with black rifts in them. Torrents. Lakes; one copper green. And it rained for the first time & was cold in the mountains. Fancy living with dirty snow at the door in May! Lovely, but utilitarian, pine woods. Black troops herded together. The Hitler feeling relaxed, though every village had a painted sign "Die Juden sind hier unwunscht". But this seemed to put up by authority. Changed into Austria at last; & we are now almost out of earshot.

Samuel Beckett, *German Diaries*
2/10/36, Hamburg, Lloyd Hotel

Not till nearly 11 last night passports and money declaration. Had not realised that I could not bring out more foreign money than I brought in. As this is only £1 & 2 dollars odd, getting out is not going to be easy. Declaration valid only till Jan 1. If I want longer (-), I must go to a Devisenbewirtschaftungsstelle. Jawol! Up at 5, not off till after. Bus to Hauptbahnhof. Collapsed in here opposite. Shave, bath, whisky (2nd bottle, 1st having gone last night when bar found shut after Cuxhaven. Went to Brieflager & Paketlager, nothing in either. Wandered around by Binnenalster, Lombardbrücke, Jungfernstieg. Adolf Hitler Platz (was Rathausmarkt)[2] and section bounded by Alsterdamm, Glockengießerwall, Steintorwall (where hotel is) & Mönckebergstrasse. Lunch in restaurant attached to hotel. Then after a short time off again, by Asterwall, the long way to Rödingsmarkt with overhead railway. (…) Schwansteinweg, Englische Planke, Neuer Steinweg, Millerntor (which I had intended to reach from Alsterwall via Graskeller, Ellentorbrücke, Alter Steinweg, Fronnemarkt). Then on to Eimsbüttlerstrasse, Kielerstrasse, Wilhelminestrasse, to a (-) at corner of Reeperbahn. Then on to Reeperbahn, through the Sandwisch to Cuxhaven Allee across Seewantenstrasse to Landungsbrücke (-). Then Tram to Hauptbahnhof. Laid out. Finished whisky. Dined at a foul hole, 1.50 for Graupensuppe, Ragoût, Cheese & beer. Then a cup of coffee in another foul hole (all beside hotel, too (-)).

Drank Pschorrbräu at lunch. Not alas from the Kasseler Ratskeller. Tried Fremdenverkehrsverein in Hbf. for a family. They had nothing but Pensionen and advised me to look in Fremdenblatt (-). Nothing but Pensionen there either. So it looks as though it must be a pension, which I dread.

The two Alsters are lovely (-). Reeperbahn extraordinary, long boulevard (-) with Kinos, bars, cafés, dancings, etc. along both sides. It would want to be night.

Thomas Wolfe, *I Have a Thing to Tell You*

"Oh, yes," he said wearily. "I have slept an hour. I came back home. My girl was asleep – I did not want to wake her up. So I laid down upon the couch. I did not efen take off my clothes. I was afraid I would be coming too late to see you at the station. And that," he said peering at me most earnestly again, "would be too dret-ful!"

"Why don't you go back home and sleep today after the train goes? I don't think you'll be able to do much at the office, feeling as you do. Wouldn't it be better if you took the day off and caught up on your sleep?"

"Well, then," said Hartmann abruptly, yet rather indifferently, "I will tell you something. It does not matter. It really does not matter. I will take something –

---

[2] Most prominent examples of the rampant Nazi tendency toward renaming streets and squares were reversed after the war: the central Rathausmarkt in Hamburg was returned to its original appellation immediately following the demise of the regime. Yet official street name reminders of hundreds of lesser-known Nazi figures are still an issue for many local councils even today. In recent years, the debate has extended to cover streets and squares named after figures such as Hindenburg, who although not a convinced Nazi, was nonetheless responsible for giving Hitler the chancellery.

some coffee or something" – he shrugged his shoulders – "it will not be too bad. But, Gott!" again the desperately gleeful laugh, "how I shall sleep tonight! After that I shall try to know my girl again."

"I hope so, Franz. I'm afraid she hasn't seen much of you the last month or so."

"Well, then," said Hartmann, as before, "I will tell you something – it does not matter. It really does not matter. She is a good girl – she knows about these things – you like her, yes? – you think she is nice?"

"Yes, I think she is very nice."

"Well, then," said Hartmann, "I may tell you: she is very nice. We get along together very well. I hope they will let me keep her," he said quietly.

"They? Who do you mean by 'they', Franz?"

"Oh," he said, wearily, "these people – these stupid people – that you know about."

"But, good Lord, Franz! Surely they have not yet forbidden that, have they? Why you can step right out on the Kurfürstendamm and get a dozen girls before you've walked a block!"

"Oh," said Hartmann, "you mean the little whores. Yes, you may still go to the little whores. That is quite alright. You see, my dear shap" – here Hartmann's small face puckered in a look of impish malice and he began to speak in that tone of exaggerated and mincing refinement that characterized some of his more vicious utterances – "I will now tell you something: Under the Dritte Reich we are all so happy, everything is so fine and healthy that it is perfectly God damn dret-ful," he sneered. "You may go to the little whores in the Kurfürstendamm. But you cannot have a girl. If you have a girl you must marry her and – may I tell you?" he said frankly – "I cannot marry. I do not make enough money. It would *quite* impossible!" he said decisively. "And may I tell you this?" he continued, pacing nervously up and down the room, taking rapid puffs at his cigarette. "If you have a girl, then you must have two rooms. And that is also quite impossible! I have not efen money enough to afford two rooms."

"You mean, if you are living with a girl you are compelled by law to have two rooms?"

"It is the law, yes," said Hartmann, nodding with the air of finality with which a German states established custom. "You must. If you are living with a girl, she must have a room. Then you can say," he went on seriously "you are not living with each other. You may sleep together every night. But then, you see, you will be good. You will not do some things against the Party… Gott!" he cried, and lifting his impish face, he laughed again. "It is all quite dret-ful."

"But it they find, Franz, that you're living with her in a single room?"

"Well, then," he said quietly, "I may tell you that she will have to go." And then, wearily, with the tone of indifference that had become so marked in one short year: "It does not matter. I do not care. I pay no attention to these stupid people. I have my work. I have my girl. If they let me keep them that is all that matters."

But now that porter had come in and was busy adjusting the straps of the leather trunk. I packed my briefcase with the letters, books and manuscript that had accumulated and gave it to the man. He dragged the baggage out into the hall and told us he would wait for us below.

(...)

The hour had come: along the station platform there was a flurry of excitement in the crowd, a light flashed, the porters moved along the quay. I turned and looked up the tracks. The train was sweeping down on us. It bore down swiftly, sweeping in around the edges of the Zoölogic Gardens, the huge snout of the locomotive looming bluntly, the fenders touched with trimmings of bright green. The great machine steamed hotly past and halted. The dull line of the coaches was broken vividly in the middle with the glittering red of the Mitropa dining car.

We swung into action. My porter, heaving up my heavy leather case, clambered quickly up the steps and found a seat for me. There was a blur of voices all around, an excited tumult of farewell. Hartmann shook hands hard and fast, his small and bitter face was contorted as if he were weeping, as indeed he was. With a sudden shock of recognition I saw how close together were his laughter and his grief. I heard his curiously vibrant, deep and tragic voice saying, "Good-bye, good-bye, dear Paul, *auf wiedershen.*"

Then I climbed up into the train. The guard slammed the door. Even as I made my way down the narrow corridor toward my compartment the train started, was in motion. These forms, these faces and these lives all slid away.

Hartman kept walking forward, waving his hat, his face still contorted with that strange grimace that was half bitter mirth, half sorrow. Then the train swept out around the curve. And he was lost.

We gathered speed. The streets and buildings of the West slipped past me – those solid ugly streets, those great solid ugly buildings of the Victorian German style, that yet, with all the pleasant green of trees, the window-boxes bright with red geraniums, the air of order, substance and comfort, had always been as familiar and as pleasant to me as the quiet streets and houses of the little town. Already we were sweeping through Charlottenburg. We passed the station without halting and on the platforms, with the old and poignant feeling of loss and of regret, I saw the people waiting for the Stadtbahn train. Upon its elevated track the great train swept on smoothly toward the West, gathering in momentum slowly. We passed the Funkturm. Almost before I knew it we were running through the western outskirts of the city, out toward the open country. We passed an aviation field. I saw the hangars and a flock of shining planes. Even as I looked a great silver-bodied plane moved out, taxied along and gathered speed, lifted its tail end, as we vanished, broke slowly from the earth.

And now the city was behind us. Those familiar faces, forms and voices of just six minutes past were now remote from me as dreams, imprisoned there as in another world, a world hived of four million lives, of hope and fear and hatred, anguish and despair, of love, of cruelty and devotion, that was called Berlin.

And now the land was stroking past, the level land of Brandenburg, the lonely flatland of the north that I had always heard to be so ugly and that I had found so strange, so haunting and so beautiful. The dark solitude of the forest was around us now, the loneliness of the *kiefern* trees, tall, slender, towering and straight as sailing masts, bearing upon their tops the burden of their needled and eternal green. Their naked poles shone with that lovely gold-bronze color that is itself like the material distillation of a magic light. And all between was magic too. The forest dusk was gold-brown, also, with this magic light, the earth gold-brown and barren, the trees themselves alone and separate, a pole-like forest filled with haunting light.

And then, the light would open and the wood be gone. And we were sweeping through the level cultivated earth, tilled thriftily to the very edge of the track. And I could see the clusters of farm buildings, the red-tiled roofs, the cross-quarterings of barns and houses. Then we would find the magic of the woods again.

W. E. B. Dubois, *Forum of Fact and Opinion (Pittsburgh Courier)*

Berlin is settling down to normalcy after the Olympian Games.[3] The decorations had mostly disappeared from the streets by September 1. The crowds on the streets seemed ordinary, and the cafés on Unter den Linden half empty. Probably the number of foreigners who visited the games was large, but scarcely as many as were expected. On the other hand, Germany poured into Berlin in overwhelming numbers. As a specimen of organization the games were superbly done; as a gesture toward international peace and good will, their value cannot be over-estimated in a world which sees a Spanish civil war of terrible cruelty, the steady re-arming of the leading nations, and a world atmosphere of suspicion and distrust.

---

3 Dubois was in Germany for the famous 1936 Berlin Games, so skilfully co-opted by the Nazis for propaganda purposes and yet made all the more memorable by the victories of athletes who utterly contradicted the Nazi ideal of Aryan supermen: most famously, Jesse Owens.

(...)

The contrast between North and South Germany is broad. Munich isn't a world city. It has retained its individuality. It is a city of the theater, of music, of marvelous old buildings, and of beer. Americans who have tasted strong beer made for long keeping, wide distribution, and exportation have no idea of the delicacy and satisfying quality of the best German beer. It is always astonishing, especially in South Germany, to see how much time is spent in the beer hall: and yet one is still tempted now, as in other days, to say that it is hard to see how ordinary, educated human beings could spend their time better. Certainly in America the movies, the cabarets, and the card parties would not provide an enticing substitute. The beer halls are large and well aired. The music, when there is music, is good. The proportion of alcohol in the best beer is very small, and the social intercourse with friends and of strangers with each other gives a public courtesy which one cannot find in the American attempt to be at once exclusive and public.

I have written already a word here and there about minor aspects of the German scene. I am sure my friends have understood my hesitations and reticence; it simply wasn't safe to attempt anything further. Even my mail when Mrs. DuBois sent me a minor receipt to sign, was opened to see if money was being smuggled in.

But now I have ended my sojourn – or at least shall have long before this is published: and to insure its reaching *The Courier* on time I am taking it to a foreign land to mail.

This does not mean that I have not enjoyed my five and more months in Germany. I have. I have been treated with uniform courtesy and consideration. It would be impossible for me to have spent a similarly long time in any part of the United States, without some, if not frequent cases of personal insult or discrimination. I cannot record a single instance here.

It is always difficult to characterize a whole nation. One cannot really know 67 million people, much less indict them. I have simply looked on. I have used my eyes and, to a lesser extent, my ears. I have talked with some people, but not widely, nor inquisitively.

Chiefly I have traveled. I have been in all parts of Germany: in Prussia, including Mecklenburg, Brandenburg, Hanover and Schlesien[4]; I have seen the

---

[4] Germany here is as malleable a concept as ever: Schlesien, usually known in English as Silesia, was considered very much part of Germany and had remained under rule from Berlin even after the Versailles conference. Today, the region based around Wroclaw and Cracow is part of Poland. Dubois, meanwhile, clearly still counts Alsace and Austria as part of Germany, despite the former having been re-ceded to France in 1919 and the latter still being an independent country in 1936.

Hansa cities of the northwest and East Prussia; I have looked on the North Sea and the Alps, and traveled through Saxony, Thuringia, Westphalia, Wurttemburg and Bavaria. I have seen the waters of the Rhine, Elbe, Weser, Oder and Danube. I have seen all the great German cities: Berlin, Hamburg, Luebeck, Bremen, both Frankfurts, Cologne, Mayence, Stuttgart, Breslau, and Munich, not to mention Vienna and Strassburg. I have seen Germany; and not in the mists of a tourist's rush, but in a slow and thoughtful leisure. I have read German newspapers of all sorts and places; I have read books, listened to lectures, gone to operas, plays and movies, and watched a nation at work and at play. I have talked with a half dozen officials.

Germany in overwhelming majority stands behind Adolf Hitler today. Germany has food and housing, and is, on the whole, contented and prosperous. Unemployment in four years has been reduced from seven to two millions or less. The whole nation is dotted with new homes for the common people, new roads, new public buildings and new public works of all kinds. Food is good, pure and cheap. Public order is perfect, and there is almost no visible crime. And yet, in direct and contradictory paradox to all this, Germany is silent, nervous, suppressed; it speaks in whispers; there is no public opinion, no opposition, no discussion of anything; there are waves of enthusiasm, but never any protest of the slightest degree. Last winter 12 million were in want of food and clothes, and this winter not less than 9 million, perhaps 10. There is a campaign of prejudice carried on openly, continuously and determinedly against all non-Nordic races, but specifically against the Jews, which surpasses in vindictive cruelty and public insult anything I have ever seen; and I have seen much. Here is the paradox and contradiction. It is so complicated that one cannot express it without seeming to convict one's self of deliberate misstatement. And the testimony of the casual, non-German-speaking visitor to the Olympic Games is worse than valueless in any direction.

When a group or nation acts incomprehensively, the answer lies in a background of fact, unknown or imperfectly comprehended by the onlooker. So it is in this case. Germany has lived through four horrors in living history that no people can experience and remain entirely normal. These are: War; the Treaty of Versailles; Inflation; Depression, and Revolution. Save the few who were actually in the trenches of the A. E. F., our generation in America has no adequate notion of war. There is a war monument in Hamburg which is the most eloquent and ghastly memory I have ever seen. It is a square, straight shaft of gray granite, and it says simply: "40,000 sons of this city gave their lives for you in 1914-18." Forty thousand dead youth from a single German city! Then came a treaty of peace which was no less devilish in its concealed ingenuity.

When an American Negro says "I have met no discrimination on account of race," it is well for those of us who know to apply considerable doses of salt. For our people, in self-defense, have adopted a well-known protective mechanism: under given circumstances, we carefully ascertain where we are wanted or endured, and where we are insulted or debarred. Then we go only where we can, and of course suffer no discrimination. When, therefore, I say I have not suffered from race prejudice in Germany, this calls for explanation.

There is race prejudice in Germany, and a regular planned propaganda to increase it and make it characteristic of the Third Reich. But it is not instinctive prejudice, except in the case of the Jews, and not altogether there. I mean that German prejudice is not the result of long belief, backed by child teaching and outward insignia like color or hair. It is a reasoned prejudice, or an economic fear. Consequently, in the case of Negroes, it does not show itself readily. My friend used to say that she liked Paris because she could start out without wondering where she would get lunch. So in Berlin or elsewhere in Germany.; I can go to any hotel which I can afford; I can dine where I please and have the head-waiter bow me welcome; I can go to any theater and find the strange lady next to me bow pleasantly or pass a conventional word if necessary; I can join a sightseeing tour without comment, etc. In fine, I have complete civic freedom and public courtesy. Of course, if my appearance is pronounced, I shall be an object of curiosity and even excited attention: a black man in a small German city would be a matter of crowds and staring that might be very annoying, but he would not be insulted nor guyed; nor, least of all, would he be refused such accommodation or courtesy as he demanded.

On the other hand, in social lines, there are limits: I have been invited to dinner in German homes and eaten with German women and men in good restaurants. On the other hand, no German woman of good standing would marry a Negro under ordinary circumstances, nor could she do so legally. It is a question if she could legally marry a Japanese. In public dance halls and in the half-world Negroes must be welcomed with care and secretly; police spies would quickly suppress any open commerce.

In the case of the Jews, one meets something different, which an American Negro does not readily understand. Prejudice against Jews in Germany comes nearer being instinctive that color prejudice. For many centuries Germans have disliked Jews. But the reasons have varied, and are not at all analogous to white dislike of blacks in America. (…)

Richard Hillary, *The Last Enemy*

We wrote to the German and Hungarian Governments expressing the hope that we might be allowed to row in their respective countries. They replied that they would be delighted, sent us the times of their regattas (which we very well knew), and expressed the wish that they might be allowed to pay our expenses. We wrote back with appropriate surprise and gratification, and having collected eight others, on July 3, 1938, we set forth.

Half of us went by car and half by train, but we contrived somehow to arrive in Bad Ems together, two days before the race. We were to row for General Göring's Prize Fours. They had originally been the Kaiser Fours, and the gallant General had taken them over.

We left our things at the hotel where we were to stay and took a look at the town which, with its mass of green trees rising in a sheer sweep on either side of the river, made an enchanting picture. Down at the boathouse we had our first encounter with Popeye. He was the local coach and had been a sergeant-major in the last war. With his squat muscled body, his toothless mouth sucking a pipe, the inevitable cap over one eye, his identity was beyond dispute. Popeye was to prove our one invaluable ally. He was very proud of his English though we never discovered where he learned it. After expressing a horrified surprise that we had not brought our own boat, he was full of ideas for helping us.

"Mr. Waldron," he said, "I fix you right up tomorrow this afternoon. You see, I get a boat."

The next day saw the arrival of several very serious-looking crews and a host of supporters, but no boat. Again we went to Popeye.

"Ah gentlemen," he said. "My wife, she drunk since two years but tomorrow she come."

We hoped he meant the boat. Fortunately, he did, and while leaky and low in the water, it was still a boat and we were mighty relieved to see it. By this time we were regarded with contemptuous amusement by the elegantly turned-out German crews. They came with car-loads of supporters and set, determined faces. Shortly before the race we walked down to the changing-rooms to get ready. All five German crews were lying flat on their backs on mattresses, great brown stupid-looking giants, taking deep breaths. It was all very impressive. I was getting out of my shirt when one of them came up and spoke to me, or rather harangued me, for I had no chance to say anything. He had been watching us, he said, and could only come to the conclusion that we were thoroughly representative of a decadent race. No German crew would dream of appearing so lackadaisical if rowing in England: they would train and they would win. Losing this race might not appear very important to us, but I could rest assured that the German people would not fail to notice and learn from our defeat.

I suggested that it might be advisable to wait until after the race before shooting his mouth off, but he was not listening. It was Popeye who finally silenced him by announcing that we would win. This caused a roar of laughter and everyone was happy again. As Popeye was our one and only supporter, we taught him to shout "You got to go, boys, you got to go." He assured us that we would hear him.

Looking back, this race was really a surprisingly accurate pointer to the course of the war. We were quite untrained, lacked any form of organisation and were really quite hopelessly casual. We even arrived late at the start, where all five German crews were lined up, eager to go. (...) Beside us there was a flurry of oars and all five German crews were several lengths up the river. We got off to a very shaky start and I can't ever remember hearing the gun fired. (...) "You got to go, boys, you got to go. All my dough she is on you." I looked up to see Popeye hanging from a branch on the side of the river, his anxious face almost touching the water. When Frank took one hand off his oar and waved to him, I really thought the little man was going to fall in. As we came up to the bridge that was the half-way mark we must have been five lengths behind; but it was at that moment that somebody spat on us. It was a tactical error. Sammy Stockton, who was stroking the boat, took us up the next half of the course as though pursued by all the fiends in hell and we won the race by two-fifths of a second. General Goering had to surrender his cup and we took it back with us to England.

William Shirer, *Berlin Diary: The Journal of a Foreign Correspondent*

Berlin, September 27, (1938)
A motorized division rolled through the city's streets just at dusk this evening in the direction of the Czech frontier. I went out to the corner of the Linden where the column was turning down the Wilhelmstrasse, expecting to see a tremendous demonstration. I pictured the scenes I had read of in 1914 when the cheering throngs on this same street tossed flowers at the marching soldiers, and the girls ran up and kissed them. The hour was undoubtedly chosen today to catch the hundreds of thousands of Berliners pouring out of their offices at the end of the day's work. But they ducked into the subways, refused to look on and the handful that did stood at the curb in utter silence unable to find a word of cheer for the flower of their youth going away to the glorious war. It has been the most striking demonstration against war I've ever seen. Hitler himself reported furious. I had not been standing long at the corner when a policeman came up the Wilhelmstrasse from the direction of the Chancellery and shouted to the few of us standing at the curb that the Führer was on his balcony reviewing the troops. Few moved. I went down to have a look. Hitler stood there, and there weren't two hundred people in the street or the great square of the Wilhelmsplatz. Hitler looked grim, then angry, and soon went inside, leaving his troops to parade by

unreviewed. What I've seen tonight almost rekindles a little faith in the German people. They are dead set against war.

Berlin, September 1, later (1939)
It's a "counterattack"! At dawn this morning Hitler moved against Poland. It's a flagrant, inexcusable, unprovoked act of aggression. But Hitler and the High Command call it a "counterattack". A grey morning with overhanging clouds. The people in the street were apathetic when I drove to the Rundfunk for my first broadcast at eight fifteen a.m. Across from the Adllon the morning shift of workers was busy on the new I. G. Farben building just as if nothing had happened. None of the men bought the Extras which the newsboys were shouting. Along the east-west axis the Luftwaffe were mounting five big anti-aircraft guns to protect Hitler when he addresses the Reichstag at ten a.m. Jordan and I had to remain at the radio to handle Hitler's speech for America. Throughout the speech, I thought as I listened, ran a curious strain, as though Hitler himself were dazed at the fix he had got himself into and felt a little desperate about it. Somehow he did not carry conviction and there was much less cheering in the Reichstag than on previous, less important occasions. Jordan must have reacted the same way: As we waited to translate the speech for America, he whispered: "Sounds like his swan song." It really did. He sounded discouraged when he told the Reichstag that Italy would not be coming into the war because "we are unwilling to call in outside help for this struggle. We will fulfil this task by ourselves." And yet Paragraph 3 of the Axis military alliance calls for immediate, automatic Italian support with "all its military resources on land, at sea, and in the air." What about that? He sounded desperate when, referring to Molotov's speech of yesterday at the Russian ratification of the Nazi-Soviet accord, he said: "I can only underline every word of Foreign Commissar Molotov's speech."

Tomorrow Britain and France probably will come in and you have your second World War. The British and French tonight sent an ultimatum[5] to Hitler to withdraw his troops from Poland or their ambassadors will ask for their passports. Presumably they will get their passports.

Later. Two thirty a.m. – Almost through our first black-out. The city is completely darkened. It takes a little getting used to. You grope around the pitch-black streets and pretty soon your eyes get used to it. You can make out the whitewashed

---

[5] Both Britain and France were pledged to defend Poland. After the ultimatum they had issued expired the following day on 2 September, the two allies declared war on Nazi Germany on 3 September 1939. What ensued was an eight-month period known as the Phoney War in which there was no large-scale military action between the Allies and Nazi Germany until Hitler's Blitzkrieg in the Low Countries in spring 1940.

curbstones. We had our first air-raid alarm at seven p.m. I was at the radio just beginning my script for broadcast at eight fifteen. The lights went out, and all the German employees grabbed their gasmasks and, not a little frightened, rushed for the shelter. No one offered me a mask, but the wardens insisted that I go to the cellar. In the darkness and confusion I escaped outside and went down to the studios, where I found a small room in which a candle was burning on the table. There I scribbled out my notes. No planes came over. But with the English and French in, it may be different tomorrow. I shall then be in the by no means pleasant predicament of hoping they bomb the hell out of this town without getting me. The ugly shrill of the sirens, the rushing to a cellar with your gas-mask (if you have one), the utter darkness of the night – how will human nerves stand for that long?

One curious thing about Berlin on this first night of the war: the cafés, restaurants, and beer-halls were packed. The people just a bit apprehensive after the air-raid, I felt. Finished broadcasting at one thirty a.m., stumbled a half-mile down the Kaiserdamm in the dark, and finally found a taxi. But another pedestrian appeared out of the dark and jumped in first. We finally shared it, he very drunk and the driver drunker, both cursing the darkness and the war.

The isolation from the outside world that you feel on a night like this is increased by a new decree issued tonight prohibiting the listening to foreign broadcasts. Who's afraid of the truth? And no wonder. Curious that not a single Polish bomber got through tonight. But will it be the same with the British and the French?

9

From the Darkest Hour
to *Stunde Null*
1940 - 1950

By early 1945, large swathes of German city-centres were in ruins, as this view of Cologne exemplifies.

AT THE END of 1941 German troops had Europe entirely in their hands, from Tromsø in northern Norway to Athens, from Biarritz near the Spanish border to the gates of Moscow. Germany itself had been expanded into the "Greater German Reich", which—with the exception of the Netherlands—covered every part of Europe which had been referred to as Germany during the course of history (and therefore at some point during the course of this anthology). Bohemia, Moravia (today the Czech and Slovak Republics, respectively), Silesia and Prussia (today in Poland), all of Austria: the great pan-German dream of uniting all German-speakers in a single nation state had been realized.

In coming true, the dream proved itself to have been a delusion. Despite the previous claims of German nationalists both inside and outside Germany, it turned out that the Eastern territories were not full of clearly definable "ethnic Germans" longing for liberty from "Slav" discrimination and *Lebensraum*. The ill-founded assumptions behind this chauvinism became painfully clear following the defeat of 1945. Silesia and Prussia, for generations considered politically German, were suddenly Poland by virtue of the fact that Poles were actually in the majority, and German-speaking families were either forced out or went of their own accord. The territory of post-1945 Germany was reduced to areas to which no other country had laid claim; everything else, from Alsace to Courland, was assigned to whichever non-German population group was also present there. The remainder, divided into four zones of occupation, had a nominal population of around sixty million and took on at least another ten million Germans fleeing from where they were no longer welcome. Meanwhile millions more left the Russian zone for the three occupied by the Western Allies.

Refugees clogging up a battered infrastructure, cities reduced to rubble, the countryside ravaged by a lack of manpower and one of the coldest winters in the twentieth century: it is hard to overstate the scale of the destruction and suffering in Germany in 1945-46, compounded by the utter moral bankruptcy of the nation as a whole. Never before has one country disgraced itself and debased its own language and culture to such an extent in so short a time. Colonialism, slavery, genocide: the Germans were not the first to perpetrate crimes based on racist ideology, but they were the first to do it with such conviction, with so much collusion from so many, and with the means of a highly developed industrial and technological apparatus. The extent to which the whole heritage of the Germans was perverted and rendered unusable by the Nazis was also unparalleled, as was their grip on every level of society and their use of the means of a dictatorial police state.

Indeed, given the political situation of Germany in the 1940s, it is at a first glance surprising how few gaps in English-language writing about it there are— and how few there were at the time. On reflection, the seemingly surprising wealth of material is easily explained: with America only entering into the Second World War in December 1941, American news correspondents were in Berlin for longer than their British or Commonwealth counterparts.

Beyond that, the law of averages would suggest that some English-speakers were likely to find themselves on the wrong side of the divide stranded in Germany, and that those who became prisoners of war would have some experience of Germany, too. As of 1945, the military advance into and subsequent occupation of Germany placed hundreds of thousands of Allied personnel in a country whose stories would often be told far later. Overall the writers in this chapter break down into those who escaped Germany (journalists), those who were trapped there (civilians, prisoners of war) and, finally those who were deployed there (soldiers and writers).

Journalists, Civilians, Combatants

The most exciting escape from Germany was made by *New York Times* foreign correspondent Howard K. Smith (b. 1914) in December 1941. He managed to catch the last train out of Germany into neutral Switzerland before Germany declared war on the United States, and as such named his 1942 memoir *The Last Train*. The extract here is of material about German civilian morale in 1940, skilfully illustrated using the appearance of Berlin's Unter den Linden boulevard.

The extract from Harry Flannery's (b. 1900) depiction of wartime Germany, titled *Assignment to Berlin*, continues through the winter into 1941. He was the replacement for William Shirer (see Chapter 8) who, fed up with censorship, left Berlin in late 1940. Flannery, like Smith, published his book about Germany speedily in 1942, illustrating the considerable public demand for up-to-date writing about what was now undoubtedly the enemy.

From journalists who escaped Nazi Germany to those who were trapped there, we join Michael "Micky" Burn (b. 1912) in 1943 in a fictional version of Colditz Castle. Captured during the ill-fated St. Nazaire raid of 1942, Burn spent the remainder of the war in German prisoner of war camps, where, between planning escapes, he gave lectures on socialism to inmates and wrote a novel, *Yes, Farwell,* which blends and shapes his experiences of captivity to form a narrative. Burn, who had flirted with Nazism before the war (and once lunched with Unity Mitford in Munich before meeting Hitler with her at Nuremburg— see Chapter 6), depicts his narrator's journey to communism, making this, the only work even approaching imaginative fiction set in Germany in these years, fittingly enough, something of a typical *Bildungsroman*.

Although not strictly a prisoner, Christabel Bielenberg, née Burton (b. 1909), was trapped in Germany in the 1940s. Having married a German lawyer in 1934 and taken German citizenship, she found herself living the life of an ordinary German during the Second World War. Her unique memoir *The Past is Myself*, published in 1968, covers her life between 1932 and 1945. In the extract below she travels to Berlin at Christmas 1944 to try and rescue her husband, who was close to the circle involved in the von Stauffenberg bomb plot, from the Ravensbrück concentration camp. Bielenberg's writing is not only clear, precise and utterly engaging, but also balanced and charitable.

Evelyn Waugh (b. 1903), visiting Nuremberg to report for an American magazine on the trials in 1946, was understandably in a far less generous mood. In the two entries from his diaries, not published until 1995, we see him picking around the ruins of the old town and watching Nazi war criminals squirm, all with slight ironic detachment. As did many of those accompanying Allied forces into Germany, Waugh became instantly aware of difference between the level of comfort he was experiencing at official functions and the dire situation of the general population.

This was a contrast which also frequently struck Michael Howard (b. 1925), a young British officer assigned to the T-Force, a regiment responsible for dismantling German industrial equipment which might be of use to Britain and procuring the expertise of German technicians and scientists by way of reparations. In 2010 Howard released his letters home, written in 1946, with a retrospective commentary under the title *Otherwise Occupied*. Twenty-one years old at the time, his was an astonishing tale showing just how the Second World War reshaped the lives of a generation, and how quickly relationships of all kinds between English and German speakers were rekindled in the most strenuous of circumstances.

Rabid Nazis and Reluctant Soldiers

Those looking for staunch post-war antipathy will not even find it in the letters of Ernest Hemingway, embedded with US troops as a war correspondent during the first advance into German territory in September 1944. Despite expressing his pleasure at "following tank tracks through the woods and flushing them finally" and "seeing the artillery catch them when they had to take to the roads", by December 1946 he was already writing to Ernst Rowohlt (characterized as Franz by Tom Wolfe, see previous Chapter) in conciliatory tones: "You certainly had a hell of a war and I am delighted that you were not one of the numerous Krauts that we killed in Schnee Eifel or Hurtgen Forest. Do not think that this is the language of the oppressive victor as you certainly killed many more of our boys at both of these places than we killed of you. (Glad we never killed each other)."

When it comes to the fortunes of war, Hemingway takes an undogmatic attitude—as do most of the other writers here—despite the horrific nature of German war crimes and even after the revelations about the Holocaust. The difficult questions about who voted for the Nazis and why, about who helped them carry out their crimes and with what motivation, about how many slipped back into post-war society unpunished, seem to have been put on hold in the 1940s, only to come back with a vengeance in later years.

*

Howard K. Smith, *Last Train from Berlin*

The graph of German morale is not a graceful, snaky thing which slithers upwards in long rises and downwards in slow calm declines like the graph of almost any people living in peace. It is a low, jagged line which leaps spasmodically upwards in one instant and collapses into sharp depressions in the next. The reason for its abrupt contours is the unmitigated fear of this war which afflicts the German people, and their gullible readiness to believe anything, however fantastic, which indicates and early end to it. (…)

The graph has never been on a high plane, even in peacetime. From my days of travelling constantly back and forth between England and Germany, I am convinced that, however effective Hitler's nerve-war was against England, really the first victims of the war of nerves were Hitler's own people. The British were worried, extremely worried at the time of Munich: I know because I was there and I was worried too. But when I went to Germany a short while later, the signs of strain there were far greater than any I, personally, had seen in England. A dear friend of mine form Munich told me she fainted from the strain and could not get the family doctor to come because he was visiting two other people who had collapsed from strain. At the pension I usually stayed in when I was in Cologne, I found, after Munich, the manager had given up his lease and moved outside town, because he feared living too near the railway station. The general reaction was, I think, best summed up by a German student I knew in Munich who had studied in America. When I asked him how it felt being a young German in Hitler's Reich, he said: "It's like being married to a daring young man on a flying trapeze. There's never a dull moment, but it's disastrous to your nerves." (…)

The opening of the campaign in France (…) brought a decided reaction: a severe drop. One of the most dangerous features of the German consciousness is to think in parallels to the World War. The mention of names of places bloodily fought over in the last war invariably conjures up images of a similar outcome. The news of the crossing of the Belgian border on May 10 did this. In a pension on the Kurfürstendamm where I lived at that time (…) an ageing Prussian, came to my room as soon as he had read the headlines on his paper. He sat down and looked worriedly and intently at me.

"It's begun," he said. I acknowledged it had.

"Now it will really get started," he said, peering again at his folded newspaper.

"We didn't want this war. We really didn't." Tears welled in those hard, old eyes as he proceeded to ague the oft-repeated German case. This was typical of the World War generation: no faith in German strength, believing more fully than any Englishman or Frenchman in German inferiority, praying for mercy to the only foreigner within reach. It was a pathetic little show, but it was hard to for me to work up sympathy. Those who cower first also become the haughtiest and most overbearing when triumph comes.

(…)

About a month later, an extraordinary thing happened. The graph reached its all-time high. It was the only occasion in the better part of six years I have spent in Germany that I saw real, uninhibited enthusiasm, with Germans weeping and laughing from pure, spontaneous joy. It has never happened before and it has never happened since. A division of Berlin infantry had returned from France. It was to march from the East-West axis through the Brandenburg gate of victory down Unter den Linden. Then the whole division was to be demobilized. This was, at last, a real, tangible sign of victory and the end of the war Germans detested and feared. Sons, husbands and fathers, sun-tanned and healthy after long military training, happy as kids after the great triumph, were returning home to their families to stay. The buildings on Unter den Linden were veiled in great red and white pennants forty yards long and ten feet broad. The thoroughfare, and all the streets running into it were jammed with cheering thousands. The soldiers marched past the reviewing stand on Pariser Platz[1] before the American and (ironically) French embassy buildings, where Goebbels and the commander of the local garrison received their salute and returned it. (…)

The triumphal reviewing stands remained intact on Pariser Platz, mounted

---

[1] Pariser Platz, the square between the Brandenburg Gate and the start of the Unter den Linden boulevard, was home to not only to the American and French embassies but also the prestigious Hotel Adlon, frequented by American news correspondents such as Shirer, Flannery, and Smith himself. Following the war, it found itself on the front line between East and West Berlin, a deserted, flattened no-man's-land; since the Reunification, both embassies have returned to this address, while the Hotel Adlon has reopened—all in new buildings inspired by the original architecture.

by the eagle of the German army, for another month. Obviously more divisions were coming home to be demobilized. Then, from the centre of the stands, the army eagle was removed, and the golden, stylized spread eagle of the Luftwaffe, the air force, was set up in its place. Obviously, there would be a few irresistible blows at England, another victory, and the Berlin Luftwaffe units would be brought home to march in the path of the infantry through the Victory Gate, to freedom from war duty. England would quickly see the sense of the Fuehrer's promise of peace and his desire to "spare the Empire," and the whole thing would be over.

It is no mere newspaperman's creation that Germany, the People and the Leaders, expected Britain to talk peace at this time. From a highly reliable source, I learned at the time that the Propaganda Ministry issued contracts to decorating firms to line the main streets of German cities with Victory Pillars for the triumphal march homeward of all German troops. The source is the director of one of the firms which received a contract and whose firm actually began working on the street decorations in July, 1940. Also, from trustworthy sources, I heard Hitler called to Berlin one of his leading architects to build a new, special Triumphal Arch outside Berlin. The arch was to be slightly bigger that the *Arc de Triomphe* in Paris.

What happened to those hopes is history. Churchill was not having any that season. The gilt on the wings of the stylized eagle tarnished in the first snows of winter, and late one evening when I was walking up Unter den Linden, I stopped to watch a squad of workers knocking the planks of the triumphal stands apart and carting away these tissues of hope, in trucks, They worked swiftly, and next morning Pariser Platz was clean and open again. Morale sank steeply after that. (…)

Harry Flannery, *Assignment to Berlin*

The Nazis showed United States motion-picture films of the raids on London. These were included in the regular *Wochenchau* [sic], the German news weekly. This part of the film began with the pictures of Nazi ground men loading ponderous bombs, ten feet long and so heavy they had to be pulled by a tractor and six men and were hoisted into place on the planes by steel cords on special cranes. The Nazi planes were then shown in the clouds. The outlines of the Thames appeared below. The bombs were released from their racks. Mountains of earth were thrown high in the sky. Clouds of smoke arose. Then came the United States pictures of London ruins. At one point King George and Queen Elizabeth looked upon the devastation. No accompanying voice identified them, and I do not believe the German audience knew who they were. At any rate there was no reaction in the audience.

The attitude of that German audience was, as a whole, revealing. The bombing of London ended with a large close-up of Winston Churchill, upon which a voice in German cried: "Winston Churchill, the cause of it all!" Almost any other audience, especially in a country at war, would have hissed the leader of the enemy, probably cried out in angry vengeance, at least mumbled, but the Germans sat silent and still.

One other part of that same film was also interesting. It showed a contingent of the Japanese army marching by. An American audience, seeing a scene of its allies, would have cheered, but the Germans again did little more than make inaudible remarks and cough nervously. I suppose that was principally because the Germans, as some had remarked to me, thought it at least inconsistent that they, presented as the superior people, white, blond, and Aryan, who were admonished to preserve the purity of their race, should have the little brown men as their principal allies. That was partly the reason for the lack of reaction to this part of the news weekly, but the attitude was one of the many incidents that were to demonstrate to me that the Germans were not enthusiastic about the war, or about anything much since it had come, that they accepted it as a grim serious business for which they could offer no cheers except when inspired by one of their orator leaders of when commanded by cheer-leaders.

Except for the outbursts from the Nazi orators, over the radio and in the press, and except for the reports of feverish diplomatic activity and rumours of troop movements, we in Berlin hardly knew a war was on during the early part of 1941. There were no air raids to disturb our rest, and the conflict seemed far away.

Snow that had fallen in November remained on the ground as the new year arrived, with snow flurries every few days. One Sunday, before dinner with Joe Harsch (a fellow journalist) on the Budapesterstrasse, we walked along the wooded paths of the Tiergarten watching the strolling soldiers with booted girls on their arms, families striding briskly by, children coasting without benefit of sled down slippery mounds of snow, skaters on the ponds, and wild ducks still waddling about the ice on the streams and swimming in the open places made by barges.

Crowds milled up and down Unter den Linden, stopped to look in the store windows, and slowly wandered on their way. Almost every Sunday there were men and women on the streets rattling their little red boxes in collections for Winter Relief – a fund for the needy in a country where, with no unemployed, it did not seem logical that there should be anyone who required State aid. It was whispered that most of the money was used to pay the costs of the war. In any case, the Winter Relief collections were made for three days a week beginning Friday about every other week.

As I walked down Unter den Linden on this Sunday, German bands played on the island spaces between the two roadways, and figures in character, including comic cows and horses, danced to the music. Even hot wieners were offered for sale, if you surrendered fifty grams of meat marks to the women attending the temporary booths. People dressed in old-time costumes rode by in carriages and stopped at street corners to collect. Along the Linden, as I went by, the collectors were tall men dressed in tall hats and tight-fitting black clothes, carrying brooms to represent the German good-luck character, the chimney-sweep.

To add variety to the occasions, each collection was in charge of a different group. One week it would be the police, another the army, the labour front, the Red Cross, or the Hitler Youth. The tags also were changed so that you might get tiny flowers one week, miniature books on the war, another small tanks, anti-aircraft guns, flamethrowers and other weapons on still another, and, on the day of the police, little traffic signs. I remember that the pins on January 19 were curious little figures of picturesque Berlin types, the quaint flower women of the Potsdamerplatz[2], the milkmen who went by in the old days ringing their bells, the *Dienstmänner* in their long white aprons, and such individuals as Erich Carow, characterful tavern-keeper in Berlin's north end. One time you were tagged with signs of the zodiac, with the idea being that you would choose one for your birth-date. Usually I tried to dodge the tags, but I did get one on this occasion. I found that it was intended for one of twins. The tags on another day were small glass badges on which were relief heads of Germany's prominent men: Hitler, von Hindenburg, Bismarck, Goethe, Schiller, and others. As a publicity manoeuvre, the Nazis turned out less of the Hitler head so that they became more scarce and brought a higher premium – as much as two hundred marks. In my script that day I managed, despite the censors, to say that the Germans were offering high prices for the head of Hitler.

(…)

For the first time since I had been in the Reich, I was able to find a seat in a train going to Hamburg. The German people were not travelling toward bomb targets. As I made this journey, I tried to discover the fabled fake Berlin. Two Americans and a number of Germans had asserted that they had seen it north

---

[2] Potsdamer Platz, another important Berlin square later divided by the Wall. Its reconstruction in the 1990s became symbolic not only of the Reunification itself, but also of the modern forces of globalization and commercialization and their effect on the city of Berlin: many who had hoped for a more historically-sensitive plan for Potsdamer Platz were indignant at finished cluster of somewhat uninspiring corporate buildings such as the "Sony Centre".

of Berlin on the route to Hamburg, but it eluded me. The idea was fantastic, but possible. After all, the Germans, who spent long months and vast sums for camouflage, could have built what would look like Berlin in a blackout. If the night were dark enough, planes flying at great heights could see little of the lakes and rivers. There was reason to believe there was a false city since the British reported twice in the autumn of 1941 that they had flown over Berlin when I knew they had not. Perhaps they were over the phantom capital.

Fake Berlin or not, the Nazis worked hard in the summer and autumn of 1941 to make it more difficult to hit objectives in the real city. The most pretentious undertaking was along the East-West Axis. That five-mile-long street, so wide that five cars could pass abreast on either side of the centre island, was a guiding arrow to the heart of the capital for the men in the clouds. As it passed through the Brandenburg Gate, the Reichstag, the Kroll Opera House, and a railway station, the Lehrter Bahnhof, were off to the left; the Wilhelmstrasse with the Chancellery, the Foreign Office and the Propaganda Ministry, and the two railway stations, the Potsdamer and Anhalter Bahnhof, were to the right, and the old palaces and the Friedrichstrasse Bahnhof almost straight ahead. West of the Brandenburg Gate, for more than two miles the Tiergarten lay on each side of the Axis. In this section workmen erected steel poles fifteen feet high, stretched over them wire netting covered with green shreds of cloth, and here and there placed rows of the tops of pine and other trees. Traffic could continue under the netting, but the Axis, as far as bombers were concerned, had been blended into the Tiergarten. The other three miles of the Axis had not been covered when I left, but it was likely that the Nazis would blot it from bombing eyes by erecting covered scaffolding to represent buildings.

That had been done elsewhere. A lake, the Litzensee, which shone as a guide to aviators, had been covered in that fashion. It was interesting to note that the wild ducks which had swum on the Litzensee in other days were still there under the fake buildings. Deutschland Halle and other prominent landmarks in that region were covered with netting so that they appeared as parks with paths running through them. To further the illusion, open spaces, as in the Adolf Hitler Platz, and a park near the Axis, were filled with pseudo-structures.

Hamburg was also camouflaged. The railway station into which I came had become a park to planes overhead, and other buildings in the vicinity also were either blotted from view of given new outlines. As I came into the centre of the city, I saw even more ambitious changes. It happens that there are two lakes in the centre, the Binnen Alster and the Aussen Alster. The former small body of water was covered with scaffold buildings, with but a narrow water lane retained for necessary traffic. To make the air picture more deceptive, the outlines of the Binnen Alster were reproduced in a part of the larger Aussen Alster, and the bridge that runs between the two was represented in a new position. Later, as I took the boat down the Elbe into the harbour, I looked casually on what appeared to be a hilly island, with rocks and trees, and paid little attention until, when almost past, I saw the end of a factory jutting from the uncompleted part of what, at a few hundred yards, was a convincing deserted bit of land.

Michael Burn, *Yes, Farewell*

Alan sat in the window alcove, waiting or the sentries to be relieved. The little town hung far below, a cluster of grey roofs and steep provincial streets crowded as if he could father them up into his hand. A river, fifty yards across, which would soon be flooding the outlying fields, slipped between the houses, and the road bridge over it was the pivot of the view. The river was like lips, and the fields that arched away behind and beyond were like high cheekbones; honey-coloured fields melting into horizons of dark forests, and the river fading into the blue dust of hills. Four kilometres away a spire rose, and near it the turrets of another castle. Europe enveloped them, immense and turbulent, expanding beyond the forest and tilled fields; Europe with her towers and genius and self-destruction, the castle with its living dead.

The view was not majestic, not beautiful, but because the prisoners yearned for freedom, to them it seemed beautiful. Really it was plain like a plain face and reminded Alan of the military landscapes on which he used to plot targets as a recruit. Half right a church spire. Central foreground to central background, a secondary road. Half-left, factory chimneys and a weir. The factory was half the town. It had sucked in a sprawl of dignified outhouses which had once been the castle's stables. The weathercock still had princely arms gilded on it, and a great gate and court-yard showed where the carriages must have driven in and out. A narrow sluice, diverted from the river, ran through the town alongside the factory, and the roaring of the mill wheel came to the prisoners with a thudding intensity, day and night.

Far away and far below. The Germans went about their unknown errands in the streets, crossing the bridge, fishing in the river, looking up at the castle with blurred faces, like rubbed shillings. Most of the women wore mourning. The men were either very old or very young. They were all proud of the castle. The prisoners might have been their private property; and the prisoners looked down on the town, and it grew into them. They would never forget it.

Alan was curious about one house. It was like his home, small, square, white and one-storeyed, built on the artificial island between the river and the sluice, at the sharp corner of a grass peninsula. It had the aloofness of a country house, yet it was obviously connected with the factory and he imagined that it belonged to the owner or the manager. He pictured the anxieties, ambitions and lives of the people who lived in it. It put him in touch with the simple existence from which he was cut off. He imagined them, sometimes he saw them, at meals, dressing and undressing in their own bed-rooms, going to work in the morning, making plans in order to carry them out the next day and not in some far off future. He spied on their movements and guessed at their relationship to one another. A tottering old frau occasionally forced herself along the short drive to the white gate and back. She always wore black and at times a much younger woman supported her. A third generation, a boy and a girl, played on the lawn in summer, shouting and making gestures at the castle windows.

He watched now. No car was to be seen anywhere. All seemed to have gone back centuries. He often had this impression about Germany and the Germans. They had been so modern in war, that other countries had been left behind, and yet here in the heart of their own country everything seemed to be so unmodern, almost primitive. They had gone ahead of themselves, were trying to live beyond their means. An aged carriage, like the carriage of Napoleon captured at Waterloo, was being hosed in the old stable-yard. Oxen drew ribbed carts across the bridge. Suddenly a young officer appeared, running full-tilt, from the direction of the station, where a puff of smoke dragged above the houses. He raced up the front steps, and soon the two women came out with him. The children were dancing round in excitement. They stared for a moment at the castle. He was very smart and wore the ridiculous little sword carried by German officers in their Sunday best. They went through a private entrance into the factory yards, and men working there stopped to shake hands and have a chat.

These people, thought Alan, are not surprised or horrified at wars. War is part of this climate. In Frederick's time these fields were ravaged year after year. Napoleon's soldiers may have been billeted in this white house, their horses may have been stabled here. The old woman probably remembered Bismarck and the days when Germany was a rising nation; she would remember, vividly, 1914, and the Kaiser, and Versailles, and the Russian revolution. She and the people who lived here were near these things. They were accustomed to meteors and avalanches and sudden victories and long ordeals, and now their country, like an Australian family, after two generations was going back to shirtsleeves. The fortune would hold out another year, perhaps. The young officer had returned from fighting the Russians in the east of the British and Americans in the south. The children were still being told that Germany was a heroic nation battling against the hosts of spiritual annihilation, and on official holidays they waved swastikas. They would grow up to something different. He asked himself what would become of them, and of the factory and the house, in a little while, when the British or the Russians or the Americans or all three arrived there, as arrive they would. It would be something new, people said in speeches, but it was hard to break the spell of the past and this territory, Europe, had been like a magnet to armour. Who would take iron out of the mountain? Who would end these wars?

Christabel Bielenberg, *The Past is Myself*

The programme of music was interrupted to tell us that a few planes were over West Germany. The soldier looked up and said: 'They don't even leave us alone on Christmas Eve, the –s.' He seemed to be addressing no one in particular, but the girl behind the counter surprised me by answering: 'Well, Christmas Eve isn't Christmas for them, is it?'

'No, I don't think it is,' I said.

'Going far?' She moved her elbows along the counter. 'Don't mind him,' she added in a low voice, 'he's going to the Russian front, his leave was up today of all days, poor chap- Wife and three kids at home. Ach so, you are going to Berlin? I'm glad I'm not you. It must be an awful place.' She looked thoughtfully at the radio.

'I wish they would stop this war, don't you?' 'I don't know,' I said cautiously, 'perhaps they have a wonder weapon, after all, which is going to change everything. What do you think?'

'I don't know either,' she answered, 'but I never have trusted those Berliners – too blooming smart altogether.'

'Yes, but it's not only the Berliners who are running the war.'

'Maybe not, but the Government is there, isn't it?'

Our conversation was interrupted by the crackling of the loud-speaker over the door – '*Achtung, Achtung*, the Berlin Express is drawing into Platform 4.' I gathered up my belongings and paid for my cup of soup, or perhaps it had been coffee – there wasn't much difference in the taste these days. The dreadful picture of Hitler seemed to be eyeing me as I pushed towards the door; I decided he looked as if he had acute indigestion.

The express steamed in with its engine and carriages caked with snow. The carriages at the end of the train seemed to be unheated, for the windows were white with hoarfrost. Some of the tem, too, were broken so I wandered to the front and climbed into the first carriage behind the locomotive. The only disadvantage of being in the front half of the train was the danger from the 'Jabo[3]' point of view. Some of the Allied pilots had brought engine-busting to a fine art. A whining dive, a burst of fire, and the punctured steam kettle drew slowly to a forced stop, the steam whistling out through the bullet holes. Others

---

3 "Jabo" is short for "Jäger-Bomber", or "fighter bomber" aircraft.

could make several bosh shots and the passengers in the front carriages then had to jump for it, darting backwards and forwards across the rails and crouching for protection behind the train. However, I reckoned I was safe for the night anyway; I was tired, the carriage was warm, and I was asleep in my corner before the train left the station.

In Stuttgart there seemed to have been a raid, and several houses were still burning. Whilst I had slept, the carriage had filled, and the corridor, too, seemed packed with soldiers. Ours was probably the only heated carriage on the train. The fug was stupefying. I pushed off down the corridor to the lavatory, only to find two soldiers asleep against the basin. One of the soldiers in the corridor shouted 'Hey, Franz, *eine Dame*,' a lady, and the two boys turned their backs without seeming to waken. When I got back to my compartment my place had been taken by a woman who must have come in from the corridor. She looked completely exhausted and was already half asleep. I was feeling very fresh again and I realized that, compared with the others, I was brown and abominably healthy looking. So I decided to sit down in the corridor. One of the group of soldiers were playing *Skat*, chalking up the score on the panel of the door, and further up a chirpy Berliner was sitting on his rolled up great coat, regaling all and sundry in his unmistakable dialect, with a riotous description of his part in the retreat through France. 'Run – run,' he was saying, 'I have never run so fast in my life,' he turned to me, his face wreathed in smiles. 'Sit down, Fräulein – no, wait till I pat up the cushions and dust the sofa.' He jumped to his feet; every bit of his uniform, from his scruffy little cap to his clumsy boots, seemed too big for him. German army clothes are not just off the peg, but look as if they came off any old peg; only the officers are inclined to dress up like peacocks.

'You've never seen an army on the run, I bet – well it's the funniest sight on God's earth. Once an army gets running, nothing can stop it. First we threw away our drinking bottles, then our helmets, belts and ammunition – finally our rifles. Then we just bolted!' He burst out laughing. 'I can see them now, chasing us, just as we popped over one hill they got to the top of the one before. Americans, mind you, a fairly easy lot, every time we shouted "*Scheisse*", they stopped and sent for air cover. They get sore feet like poor Jup here – hey, Jup' he nudged a cherubic-looking figure who was sitting astride his gunny sack, perspiring gentling and leaning against the door. 'But we made it, didn't we old friend?' Jup smiled down good-naturedly and nodded; he seemed half-asleep.

It was obvious that the little Berliner was the wit of the party, and that he was probably laying it on a bit thick for my benefit.

'Where are you off to now?' I asked, feeling rather bewildered. 'I haven't a clue,' came the answer, 'we have to report in Magdeburg. But one thing I can tell you, Fräulein, I'm not trying for an Iron Cross; and I'm going to see I don't get a wooden one either. I've got this far and when the war is over I'm going to be back in Berlin with my missus, running my vegetable stall.' His voice had changed and I looked at him quickly. He looked back at me with an expression of sudden defiance on his otherwise nondescript face. A spark of what I thought to be complete understanding flashed between us. I knew what he meant, that little Berliner. We were both being kicked around, surely we were, caught up in a ruthless uncontrollable machine, but by God it wouldn't get us – not if we could help it.

I remembered that I had a bottle of Kirsch[4] in my rucksack. It had been meant as a present for Arnold, but this seemed the moment. I climbed back into the carriage and came back with it under my arm – a whole litre. I had traded it for a silver tea-pot on a rather foolhardy expedition to the Rhine one day. At the sight of it, our little group miraculously increased in number, even the *Skat* game seemed to peter out. Someone produced a pen-knife and dug out the cork and handed me back the bottle with a bow. '*Zum Wohl, Gnädigste.*'

'Here's to next Christmas,' I said '– at home,' and I spluttered a bit after the first gulp. It was good strong Kirsch all right, straight from the farm home-brewed and far stronger than any ordinary branded variety. As the bottle did the rounds, they wiped it on their sleeves and murmured '*Heimat – Weihnachten,*' and after Jup had had his turn he fumbled in his pocket and brought out a mouth organ. He banded it on his knee and pursed his lips, and the first reed-like notes of that most haunting of all German soldier-songs vibrated hesitantly at first, and then seemed to gather volume and strength above the rumbling of the train. '*In der Heimat, in der Heimat, da gibt's ein Wiedersehen.*'

We hummed it gently, each of us lost in our separate worlds. Peter in Ravensbrück, the Black Forest, England – where were my brothers? – my sister in Canada? A fair boy in the background slipped naturally into alto harmony. 'In the homeland, in the homeland, there we shall meet again.'

I was sorry to lose my friends at Magdeburg. We had talked through the rest of the night and into the morning and emptied the bottle of Kirsch. At one time Jup, who had been a waiter in Munich, had turned to me and told me confidentially that one could see that a lady was present by the way that boys were watching their language. As their every second word seemed to me to start with F, I wondered rather fuzzily what it would have been like had I not been there.

They could have been a cross section of any army, anywhere, that little group

---

[4] "Kirsch", which means cherry, is a common abbreviation of "Kirschwasser", a clear, colourless cherry brandy for which the Black Forest is renowned—and a key ingredient in a good Black Forest Gateau.

of soldiers. Blown about the whims of higher authority, to the East, to the West, and now back again to the East. They had not particular hates, no resentments, no particular ambition, except to stay alive and get back to their families – although some of them had no idea where their families were. Heini, the little Berliner, could easily have been a London cockney, with his *Galgenhumor*[5], as the Germans call it; a tough cynical, chirpy, unabashed sense of humour which seems to thrive only in big cities.

As he left, he squared his small shoulders, clicked his heels, raised he right arm and said: "Well, whoever still wants to listen, *Heil Hilter,* etc, etc.' In one absurd gesture he somehow managed to caricature the whole rotten business.

Evelyn Waugh, *Diary*

Nuremberg, Sunday 31 March 1946

Up at dawn. A car with two seedy barristers in the back impatient at 5.30. An uncomfortable troop carrier. Arrived at Nuremberg at 12 our time, 1 theirs. An hour's delay at the airport. No luncheon by the time we reached the Grand Hotel. After this grim start everything went smoothly. Nuremberg consists of a large luxury hotel run by the American army and a large luxury courthouse, everything else a waste of corpse-scented rubble with a handful of middle-aged, middle-class Germans in Homburg hats picking their way through the demolition – typical modern functional magnificence designed for mass parades, now full of German Jews in American uniforms photographing one another in the act of giving the Nazi salute from Hitler's rostrum. About eighty per cent of the Americans in Nuremberg seemed to be Jews, for they alone speak German. A walk with Baedeker in the old town trying to identify the ruins. Then, sharp at 6.30, the social life began. Mervyn called for me, led me to a cocktail party in a corner of the hotel where we drank fresh young German champagne among various, mainly English, officials of the court. We drove far into suburbs to a villa where he lives with three colleagues and dined. I was surprised by their zeal and *esprit de corps*. In England we talk of the trials as an injudicious travesty. Here they believe their work to be valuable and know it to be arduous. Close acquaintants with their beliefs has aroused animosity to the Germans such as I have not heard expressed for five years. We talked of P. G. Wodehouse. They wished to bring him to trial.

I found I had been categorized VIP – Very Important Person. It seemed odd to be asked 'Are you a VIP' and to answer without embarrassment, 'Yes'. The title conferred certain substantial advantages, such as a private bath and a select dining-room in the courthouse.

---

[5] Literally "gallows humour".

Monday 1 April-Tuesday 2 April 1946

To the courts. A huge building with corridors full of offices. The court, a hall in the style of William II renaissance, furnished with functional lighting and furniture. From the front row of the gallery, in great comfort, we saw the prisoners brought in and the court assemble. Only Kaltenbrunner looked an obvious criminal. When the court opened one put on earphones and, with a dial by the chair, switched at will to English, French, German or Russian. A faint continuous chatter rose from the glass cage where the interpreters sit. Interpretation was almost simultaneous with the speeches, and one had the curious illusion of seeing two men bullyragging and seeming to hear their own voices in the piping American accents of the girl interpreter. Interest varied greatly with the skill and personality of the interpreter.

First the defence called evidence, against Russian protests, to demonstrate that the Ribbentrop-Molotov pact had an attached secret protocol with the partition of Poland defined on the map. Then Sir David Maxwell-Fyfe began his cross-examination of Ribbentrop. Ribbentrop was like a seedy schoolmaster being ragged, who knows he doesn't know the lesson, knows that the boys know, knows he has done the sum wrong on the blackboard, knows he has nothing to hope for at the school, but still hopes he can hold out to end of term to get a 'character' for another post. He lied instinctively and without apparent motive. Maxwell-Fyfe built the case with great artistry. A luncheon interval during which VIPs and lesser visitors were segregated. The court rose at 5. I went to see the room where a French Jew keeps lampshades of human skin, shrunken heads, soap said to be made of corpses and so forth. A dinner party that evening at the hotel. Host 'Khaki' Roberts, dancing and 'brains trust'. The reigning beauty was Miss Glover, Maimie's old secretary.

Next day I went with Dame Laura Knight to see the pictures she is painting of the prisoners in the dock with a background of corpses and burning buildings. The papers on a table had by chance taken the form of a cross and she was in doubt whether to leave them so. 'You don't think it *illustration* do you?', she kept asking. I tried to explain that I liked 'illustration', but the poor old girl had plainly had her tastes warped by Roger Fry. The trial that day was dull, becoming very dull in the afternoon when there was a long technical dispute about documents and cumulative evidence. Air Marshall Elliott turned up and heard only this part of the trial. I had great luck in the day of my arrival. At least half the proceedings are tedious to the unprofessional hearer.

GERMANY: BEYOND THE ENCHANTED FOREST

Michael Howard, *Otherwise Occupied*

Lt. M. Howard R.B., 1 Bucks, B.A.O.R.
          5th April 1946

Darling Mama,

This is as much to practise my typing as to tell you anything, but there are a few odd items of news that I can deal with. Firstly, parcels to acknowledge—a packet of cigarettes from you and from Daddy, and also that box of Auntie Miriam's wodges, in very good condition. I shall be writing to thank her in the near future.

Could you send me some black darning wool as holes are gradually consuming more and more of my socks. Otherwise there is nothing I can think of that I want.

Yesterday I went over to do a job of work in Düsseldorf. The whole business was carried out in German and it really stood up to the strain quite well. On the way back I dropped in and saw Lee Walker, who was really very nice. She is tallish, and fair, and rather good-looking in a strong sort of way. She has got the same sort of mouth as Phyllis and was quite easily recognisable. I have asked her to come to our dance which she accepted with every show of pleasure. I think she is PA to practically the king-pin of North German Coal, which is a very good job. They work in what used to be Krupp's private house – a lovely spot. There is a squash court there and I have been offered the use of it, for which I am very grateful. She asked me to spend the weekend there, which seemed a friendly act, and although I was not able to accept, as I am to take over my new department by Monday, I might reciprocate by asking her over to Möhne one weekend in the near future.

(...)

My route yesterday took me right through the Ruhr and it is an amazing sight. Literally there is hardly a street for 50 miles in which at least 25 per cent of the houses are (not) bombed, and you can drive for miles through large towns without seeing signs of human habitation. Acres of factories, rusting away, and covered in weeds. My opinion for what it's worth is that Germany won't be able to wage war by herself for some 40 years.

No more news, I think.

My typing hasn't been too bad

With all my love,

Michael

(...)

'Wodges' were a wartime utility imitation of chocolate truffles, and although they clearly contained both sugar and cocoa powder, they were not covered by the sweet rationing which was to last for another six years. My aunt's source of wodges was the concierge at the Chatsworth Court Hotel in London where she resided. I wouldn't go so far as to say that there was a black market in wodges, but scarcity would have determined the price at which they were traded. Not that I recall our being much constrained by sweet rationing in the army in Germany, and nor were our brothers-in-arms in the US Zone of Occupation, for whom the Hershey Bar became a potent element as a means of exchange in the commerce between the sexes. For our soldiers the equivalent was the two-ounce bar of Cadbury's Dairy Milk and, more rarely, the plain Bournville chocolate bar, free from adulteration with powdered milk. One evening an unusually spruced-up Rifleman Barran passed my open office door on the way out of the headquarters building. 'Barran, where are you off to?' He turned to me, took a chocolate bar out of his battle-dress breast pocket and waved it at me, then put it back and went on his way. Words were superfluous. I wonder whether the rather straight-laced Quaker Cadbury family were aware of the extent to which their innocent product was being used to oil the wheels of social and sexual intercourse?

10

Spy Fiction and the State of the Nation
1950 - 1983

Guards feed the birds at the Berlin Wall, one of the most unnatural borders humankind has ever enforced.

BY THE EARLY 1950s the Western Allies had gone from viewing a German state as a threat to seeing it as a necessary expediency to halt the westward march of communism. After its creation out of the three Allied zones of occupation in 1949, the Federal Republic of Germany was rapidly integrated into the West, becoming a NATO member in 1955 and entering into the European treaties that would form the basis of the common market (and, later, the European Union).

Each step taking by the fledgling Federal Republic was matched by the East. The German Democratic Republic was proclaimed shortly after the FRG, and was a founding member of the Warsaw Pact in 1955. Yet while West Germany, bolstered by Marshall Plan money and profiting from sound economic policy and a traditionally stronger industrial base, raced ahead to become the world's third largest economy by the early 1960s, East Germany's growth was continually hampered by punitive Russia reparations demands, command-economy mismanagement and emigration to the West.

In 1961 the GDR decided to put a stop to the manpower drain, erecting the Berlin Wall almost overnight. With Cold War tension was running at an all-time high, Berlin was a clear flashpoint. The division of Germany into two states created a series of diplomatic problems, and staunchly conservative forces in the FRG refused to recognize or cooperate with the GDR. Even during the overall climate of Cold War *détente* in the early 1970s and the general swing to the left in West Germany in the wake of the 1968 student protests, the relationship between the two Germanys remained tense. The early 1980s then saw a return to the brinkmanship of earlier years, with a renewed arms race and the stationing of US Pershing missiles in West Germany. Protests against the deployment were socially divisive (very much the counterpart to Greenham Common in the UK) and led to the early electoral success of the Green Party in the German political system. By the early 1980s West German society was in many ways more open and more liberal than that of the Allied countries which had re-established democracy in it.

Despite the speedy rapprochement between West Germany and the Allies in diplomatic, economic and military terms from the 1950s onwards, the days when whole generations of British and American writers would be sent to Germany in their adolescence were well and truly gone. Gone too were the tourists in search of the sublime on the Rhine or in the Harz mountains, the latter bristling with tanks, artllery and watchtowers on the frontier between East and West.

With the exception of that trusty staple, letters, writing about Germany in this period is of another kind altogether, dominated by Cold War fiction, a genre beginning in the early 1960s, and the "quo vadis Germany?" strand of factual writing always looking in some way to answer the question as to whether the new and open German Federal Republic was likely to slip back into the bad habits of its dictatorial past.

Observers of the New Germany

British politician Anthony "Tony" Benn (b. 1925), from whose diary in 1957 the first extract is taken, visited Germany for the first time, coming back impressed not only by West German reconstruction, but by the open political attitude, a process that would take place time and time again with visitors to Germany initially wary of it due to its recent past. Benn finds a Germany that makes Britain in its post-war austerity look "down and out", but notices the scars of war. Meanwhile Anthony Sampson (b. 1926) had been in Germany in the immediate aftermath of the conflict and returned in 1962 to find a "scarcely believable" transformation. His *The New Europeans: The Vital Survey of Europe Today and Tomorrow*, although not limited to Germany, can be read as one of the first contributions to the "is Bonn the new Weimar?" genre.

Leon Uris' (b. 1924) *Armageddon: A Novel of Berlin,* written in 1963, deals with the final months of the Second World War and with the fragile peace that followed it up to the lifting of the Berlin Blockade in 1949. Uris, best known for the 1950s publishing sensation *Exodus*, constructed his historical novels following painstaking research, and gained access to much original documentation (his note of thanks includes the United States Army and Air Force). The resulting book was not only extremely detailed, but confronted many of the complicated moral questions involved in occupying Germany and cooperating with Germans in the wake of the Third Reich—questions that events such as the Eichmann trial were raising once again in the 1960s after the comparative amnesia of the 1950s.

Another 1963 publication in which the role of former Nazis in current defence policy is examined is John le Carré's (b. 1931, pen name of David John Moore Cornwell) masterpiece *The Spy Who Came in from the Cold*. Le Carré depicts the murky world of Berlin espionage at the height of the Cold War and, in the process, essentially founds a new genre: spy fiction. With his skilful evocation of divided Berlin—and of other parts of Germany—he rediscovered the country as a setting for imaginative fiction. His intricate plots and well-developed characters allowed him to tackle some of the key moral quandaries of the Cold War, above all the question of how far the end of preserving Western democracy can justify the amoral means his writing portrays.

Journalist Harry Flannery (b. 1900), who had already published on his experiences in Germany at the start of the Second World War (see Chapter 9), returned in 1968 to produce one of the defining works in the "quo vadis" genre, its title being the eponymous *Which Way Germany?* He examines the Federal Republic with a keen eye towards the dangers of a Nazi relapse and finds it healthy, due in no small part to its new (or newly-reawakened) political culture, which he describes through its satirical production.

With her famed "Ripley" series, Patricia Highsmith (b. 1921) produced something on the surface quite different to spy fiction; yet while her storytelling is not overtly political, but essentially character driven, it has the same primary plot concerns as spy fiction: passports, borders, identity, secrets and crime. In the 1980 instalment of her "Ripliad", *The Boy Who Followed Ripley*, Highsmith takes her characters on a gallivant across Europe that includes all of Berlin, from the concrete, glittery Kurfürstendamm and the drab East to the crime-ridden griminess of Kreuzberg.

A quite different vision of Germany is the depiction of Swabia given by Bob Larson in a kind of manual for US army families settling in the region, *Your Swabian Neighbours* (1981). In this guide, published only in Germany and aimed at a target demographic of Americans abroad, Larson explains the plush, predictable, sometimes stifling suburban Germany that developed following the economic miracle, a world away from the Berlin settings of fiction in these years.

A co-founder of the spy fiction genre was Len Deighton (b. 1929), whose *The IPCRESS File* became one of the most talked-about novels of the 1960s. In 1983, his *Berlin Game* espionage novel was published, a classic of the genre with its usual mix of bitter, lonely protagonists waiting at the Berlin Wall, and ethical questions woven into the plot. This well-paced story has remained exceptionally popular to this day.

From Excitement to Routine

When le Carré wrote *The Spy Who Came in from the Cold*, the Wall was barely two years old and the pre-Cuban Missile Crisis atmosphere of Armageddon could already be felt across the world. Any incident at the border seemed liable to lead to a Third World War: with its shoot-outs in glaring spotlights, the book is impregnated with the fear of the high-stakes, white-knuckle years in which it was conceived. The same is true of Uris' novel, examining the root of the discord between former Allies. At a time when the Cold War was reaching its second crescendo, it must have seemed apt to re-examine the edgy years leading to its first climax, the Berlin Blockade.

By the time Deighton finished his first Berlin spy novel twenty years later, however, the Wall had been in place for 22 years, and the fictional approach to it had to take into account that this abhorrent vacuum with the potential to ignite apocalypse had also become a decidedly everyday eyesore with its own boring routines. Patricia Highsmith, too, shows characters who have come to know the Wall as a feature of Berlin—an unpleasant and slightly unpredictable one, but a feature nonetheless—and gives her depiction of the city its piquancy by going to the then crumbling, criminal Kreuzberg district.

It is perhaps the boredom and stasis of suburban Germany so incisively described by Anthony Sampson that stifled other kinds of fiction about Germany in this period. While the years of the *Wirtschaftswunder* and the astonishing recovery of West Germany provided a rich field for economists, sociologists and journalists, many novelists may have seen nothing in them but slim pickings.

*

Tony Benn, *Diaries*

Sunday 13 January 1957
(...) To Frankfurt am Main in two hours. First impressions of Germany very mixed. The officials in uniform very reminiscent of the films. My Customs inspector looked the perfect Gestapo or SS Obergruppenführer – though very nice. It was a weird sensation of fear and hatred, no doubt accentuated by being a stranger and not very clear of where to go. By Pan American[1] to Tempelhof and there a tall, fat smooth man came up and introduced himself as Mr Kulf, my host. My heart sank as he told me we were going to the opera and then to dinner, I was so tired.

The performance was *The Marriage of Figaro* and it was most excellently done, the singing was beautiful and the staging superb, as was the design of the sets. The only trouble was that I was dog tired and dozed off fitfully.

Monday 14 January 1957
(...) Mr Trevor Davies and Mr Dees of the British Educational Commission collected me by car and we drove through the Tiergarten, under the Brandenburg Gate and along the Stalin Allee to the Soviet Cemetery. As Dees said, the Soviet sector is like Salford during a strike; compared with the lights and shops and buildings of the Western sector, the East was unbelievably dreary.

---

[1] Due to the strict access regulations made between the Allies and the Soviets, there were no direct flights to West Berlin: all planes had to take off in West Germany and use one of the three air corridors. Only airlines registered in the occupying nations of Britain, France, and the USA were permitted, meaning that Lufthansa was forbidden from flying into the city; this complicated access arrangement was kept to until the end of the occupation in 1990.

The rubble from the bombing still remained and the people looked tired and cold and ill-fed and ill-dressed.

Tuesday 15 January 1957
At 9:30 Herr Kulf collected me from the hotel and we drove in his car the Postdamerplatz. There we got out and walked across the Iron Curtain to the East Sector. The devastation was terrible and the gigantic electric news bulletin machine stood out against the skyline of ruins as a grim reminder of the Cold War. Loudspeakers from each side blare out the news at fixed times and the black market in East and West flourishes.

Caught the 1400 plane to Hanover.

Dr. Ronnebeck, the chairman of the Deutsche-Englische Gesellschaft, was at dinner and afterwards we talked in the hotel for half an hour. He feared that West Germany was mentally hypnotised by the boom. He thought that the heavy American investment in the Federal Republic had enabled the West Germans to escape lightly from the consequences of the war.

'Our children will have to pay for it,' he said. 'In the East at least the Germans are learning the lesson the hard way. Life is not easy for them. Now here we think we are the greatest nation again. The Americans are nouveau riche; the British are lazy, the French are stupid, we are hard-working respectable conscientious people.' This escapism and the apathy towards issues of personal freedom was a malaise.

Certainly the bright neon lights of Hanover and the enormous modern shops full of goods of all description gave an impression of prosperity that made Britain seem a very down and out country.

Thursday 17 January 1957
Bonn. Breakfast in my room and then to the Bundeshaus. I had to find Willy Brandt[2], the Speaker of the Berlin Parliament. We talked for nearly an hour in the spacious sunlit restaurant with its glass wall overlooking the Rhine (the aquarium, they call it). Brandt is young (39-42) and very intelligent. We discussed relations with East Germany and the frontier ('it can be negotiated at the right time'). I walked back to my hotel and was collected at lunch time for lunch given by the Secretary of the Anglo-German Parliamentary socialist group, Frau Hubert, a very charming woman.

---

[2] Brandt went on to take the national leadership of the Social Democratic Party in 1964, forming Germany's first left-wing democratically-elected government since the Weimar Republic in 1969. He pursued a policy of rapprochement with the Eastern Bloc, and is famed for dropping to his knees at the monument to the Warsaw Ghetto Uprising in 1970. In 1971 he was awarded the Nobel Peace Prize.

Monday 21 January 1957

The first working day at home after my visit to Germany. It certainly was extremely interesting though an exhausting visit. I am glad I went, for many reasons. First of all, there was a little cyst or boil of anti-German feeling in me which was lanced as a result of seeing the country. Obviously as an honoured guest getting the red carpet treatment, one cannot pretend to get more than a glimpse of a country or its political outlook. I was completely protected from the currents of opinion and the life of the average German. Nevertheless by constant talking and careful looking one got an impression of the place which was not without its value. The bomb damage was phenomenal. The scale of the reconstruction was also interesting. The shops, hotels and petrol stations were so modern and impressive that the visitor might think the country better off than we are. Yet no doubt millions still live in very poor conditions. Berlin was particularly tragic. The total destruction was enormous and the division of the city pathetically obvious. In the West the bright shopping streets and new architectural styles contrasted sharply with the poor and desolate Eastern sector. Of course, the Americans have poured money in to the West and the Russians are still taking it out of the East. One must make allowances for all that.

Anthony Sampson, *The New Europeans*

My first experience of the mainland of Europe was in Germany in the icy winter of 1946. For the Germans that was the *schlechte Zeiten,* the terrible times, worse for many of them than the war itself. I was in the British Navy at Cuxhaven, at the mouth of the Elbe: the harbour and whole Baltic Sea was frozen for three months. For Germans there was no fuel, little work, little food; but their obsessive craving was for cigarettes. The country was governed by a cigarette economy, so that anything could be bought for packets of fags – cameras, food, binoculars, girls; girls walked along the sea-front in high white socks, waiting to be picked up, and afterwards went back to their husbands to deliver the cigarettes. When we drove into Hamburg it seemed not a city but a group of camps among the ruins; the rubble was flat, there was no shape. People emerged from the rubble and hung on to the outside of trams and trains. The hub of the city, the centre of all patronage, was the Atlantic Hotel, the British officers' headquarters: inside the central heating was too hot, The Times was in the foyer, and the long bar was full of drunk officers. The British and Germans seemed equally corrupted by the chaos. The British occupation added to the confusion, split between two opposite policies – blowing up some things while patching up others. Only a few objects, like Leicas or Volkswagens, mysteriously emerged from the ruins.

(…)

Driving through Europe in the course of writing this book, twenty years after my first glimpse of the continent, I found the transformation still scarcely believable. I was travelling with my wife and baby daughter, staying in flats in suburbs, surrounded by sounds of cars and lawnmowers; the cosy society seemed to have no link with the wildness of the early post-war period. In Hamburg white villas and rich shopping centres had sprung out of the rubble; the Atlantic Hotel was the centre for cosmopolitan big business. All over western Europe a shiny and uniform superstructure had grown up, of supermarkets, skyscrapers, television towers, motorways. It was the kind of fantasy that post-war children had dreamt of, or glimpsed in Hollywood films. Yet the dream, having come true, had lost its magic; the things turned out to be no more than things, bringing their own problems – motorways brought traffic jams, travel brought tourism, suburbs brought boredom.

(…)

Volkswagen is the fading epic of the German economic miracle. The vast and symmetrical factory has, for the last fifteen years, been the showplace of German industry. It is not an easy pilgrimage: the factory stands in a bleak bit of country, at Wolfsburg, a few miles from the border with East Germany. As the train approaches you can see a solid mile of brick building, with four tall chimneys at one end, a skyscraper at the other and a neatly laid-out town across the railways with hundreds of Volkswagens parked nose to tail alongside the station. It is a pure company town, made by, for and with Volkswagens. As you enter the station a fruity American accent comes over the loudspeaker saying 'The Volkswagen factory welcomes you to Wolfsburg'.[3]

Inside, the building looks like a vast skeleton fairground, with familiar-looking bits of Volkswagen revolving from the huge roof, dangling like seats on the big dipper. Without much human interference, the bits of the beetle are fitted together; the climax comes when the front half meets the back half, and the two are automatically welded together with a clank, a hiss and a shower of sparks. A minute afterwards the roof, which has been waiting round the corner, is swung round into place and jammed on the top, in another shower of sparks; and then the whole body trundles on, while the chassis arrives, to be screwed on with automatic screwdrivers. At the other end of the works the cars come

---

[3] Volkswagen—literally, "people's car"—was founded by the Nazis using funds confiscated from trades unions. After the war British occupying forces allowed the company to reopen, but installed a model of union co-determination which went on to become one of the key elements of today's formidable German economy: union leaders control twenty per cent of the board of management in all large German industrials. In 2011 Volkswagen was the world's largest automotive concern measured by vehicle sales.

out into the open air, painted and polished at the rate of five a minute. They are tested, checked and driven on to special trains. This has been going on for two decades.

(...)

Each country, of course, has its own version of the consumer nightmare. It was in Germany, out of the post-war chaos of the cities, that the new world grew up most suddenly and immaculately, enveloping its inhabitants with all the trappings: staying in flats in German suburbs we became very aware of it. The traditional pride of the hausfrau – a justified cliché – was more intense after the years of desperate shortages, when a house could be found; for refugees from the east it was still more intense. The special relationship of a German family to their house or flat is unmistakable. A visitor is shown around the house as soon as he comes in; the objects, furniture and gadgets are laid out as if in a contemporary shop-window, or a Victorian front parlour. Young married couples when they move must always 'sich einrichten' – set themselves up – by buying all their suites, carpets and consumer durables, so that the scene will be ready for visitors. The completed stage leaves little room for development or disruption, and it helps to give that frozen look to German homes. There are no old sofas, junk or messy corners: and in this formal stage, people move uneasily, and the objects seem to acquire a power of their own.

(...)

The sterile world of the German suburbs, for those who were brought up in the earlier chaos, must remain something of a miracle, which must at all costs be preserved. But it would be surprising in the boredom had not produced a fierce reaction from the younger generation. The German students have not actually forsworn the benefits of washing machines and cars: but behind their fury with the 'fat-belly thinking' of their elders lies a deep-rooted sense of frustration and immolation in the luxurious prison of the consumer society, without knowing how to escape from it.

Leon Uris, *Armageddon*

Hansen picked up a document Sean recognized as a study he had completed the day before. TOP SECRET: PREROGATIVES OF MILITARY GOVERNMENT COMMANDERS IN GERMANY.

"This report was two weeks late."

"Lot more involved than I figured."

"What? The report?" Hansen thumbed through the pages, playing for fifteen seconds of tension-building silence. "You've got a real rod on against the Germans."

"If the General will be specific?"

"The General will be specific," he aped. He adjusted his specs for reading. "This choice morsel is on page fourteen, paragraph sixty-two. I quote Captain Sean O'Sullivan. 'In the event the orders of the local military commanders are not carried out by the civilian population, the commander is empowered to seize hostages from the German civilian population and execute them at his discretion until his will is enforced'." Hansen closed the report and snatched off his specs. "That's a hell of a thing for an American boy to write."

"I didn't know our function is to spread Americanism in Germany."

"Nor is it to continue Nazism. Now by hostages, Captain O'Sullivan, I take it you mean to define between Nazis and non-Nazis."

"If the General will tell me if the bullet that killed my brother came from a Nazi rifle or a non-Nazi rifle."

"So in judging all Germans as being the same, you mean to take hostages who are two, three, or four years old."

Sean baulked. "Well… perhaps we should limit the hostages to Nazis."

"There are fifteen million Nazis in Germany," Hansen pressed.

"We'll have room for them when we open their concentration camps!"

"Sit down, lad, don't get your Irish up on me. I want the explanation of the hostage paragraph."

Sean unclenched his fists and sank into his seat once again. Eric the Red meant business. "In my following comment I said it would never be necessary to use hostages because the Germans are orderly people and will respond to whoever represents authority. You know damned well, General, I've said over and over they won't conduct guerilla resistance. Quote Churchill. The Germans are at your throat or your feet. They'll be at our feet when we finish with them."

"Then why did you find it necessary to put this hostage thing in?"

"Because they've got their own little special missions sitting in Berlin writing their version of the same manual. You know their versions? All Germans, get under American protection at all costs where kindly GI's will supply you with cigarettes, chocolate, and short memories. We have to put that hostage rule into the record just to let them know it's there."

Hansen grunted. He opened the bottom drawer of his desk. His stubby fingers produced a bottle of rye whisky and a pair of glasses. He poured two oversized drinks and shoved one of them to Sean. He knew again why he had picked O'Sullivan for the Special Mission.

(…)

Rombaden gasped for life amidst its devastation. The full impact of defeat drove deeper with each passing day. No water, no food… ashes. Frightened movement stirred behind the charred walls as the armed Poles patrolled the streets.

The coming of Ulrich Falkenstein disturbed them deeply. The tyrannical but paternal rule of the von Romstein dynasty was over for the first time in history. Although Count Ludwig and his brothers had governed with an iron fist, they had worked for the solid status quo of traditional life. The von Romsteins were the father. The von Romsteins would take care of them.

Now Falkenstein, enemy of the Reich, scorned for two decades, sat at the right hand of the Allied governor.

Sean's first doubts about the meaning of Falkenstein's Germanness faded. Falkenstein would have no truck with the Nazis. Moreover, he could smell them. A few people from the whitelist and a few political survivors of Schwabenwald were placed in key civic positions. The Nazis were routed.

(…)

Neal Hazzard paced the living room of Sean's apartment angrily. "What the hell is the matter with General Hansen? Is he blind or something?"

"He is being hampered by a little system known as democracy," Sean answered.

"What about the treat of blockade? Why doesn't he know?"

"He knows. But he can't do anything until it is imposed. You know how it is, pal. The military cry 'wolf' and no one believes them. The only way it will be believed is when Berlin gets its Pearl Harbour."

Hazzard shook his head. "We have to stand here flatfooted waiting for the Russians to belt us."

"That's because we represent a society dictated by public opinion."

Hazzard had chewed his cigar beyond mercy, flung it into the fireplace. "Sean. I think I know the people of Berlin as well as anyone."

"I'll buy that."

"They've got strong nerves. If we could only give them our guarantee that we are going to stay."

"We can't do that, Neal."

"I know the Russians too. I know them from two hundred and fifty-eight meetings of the Kommandatura with Nikolai Trepovitch. They'll quit short of a fight."

"That's no secret."

"Goddammit, I'm going on RIAS and tell the people of Berlin this garrison is staying."

(…)

RIAS was the only radio planted deep inside the Russian Empire. A brilliant staff, which refused to be cowed, succeeded in obliterating the Russian propaganda assaults. RIAS was one of the few positions anywhere where the West took the offensive. Each day the reportage of Soviet atrocity was heard by millions of the enslaved. RIAS was a voice in the dark forest of Eastern Europe. To the Russians, the American Radio had become the most hated symbol of the West, and behind every move to get the West from Berlin was the plan to still its voice.

This station was so feared that six hundred Russian jamming stations tried to blot out its signal. To counter this, RIAS staggered its programmes to the Russian colonies. Then once a day the entire power output was combined and over a million watts thrown into a single programme, which nothing could jam. It is said that when RIAS went on full output it could be received in the silver fillings of your teeth two hundred miles away.

John le Carré, *The Spy Who Came in from the Cold*

It had taken a long time to build a decent East Zone network in Berlin, Leamas explained. In the earlier days the city had been thronging with second-rate agents: intelligence was discredited and so much a part of the daily life of Berlin that you could recruit a man at a cocktail party, brief him over dinner and he would be blown by breakfast. For a professional it was a nightmare: dozens of agencies, half of them penetrated by the opposition, thousands of loose ends; too many leads, so few sources, too little space to operate. They head their break with Feger in 1954, true enough. But by '56 when every Service department was screaming for high-grade intelligence, they were becalmed. Feger had spoilt them for second-rate stuff that was only one jump ahead of the news. They needed the real thing – and they had to wait another three years before they got it.

Then one day de Jong went for a picnic in the woods on the edge of East Berlin. He had a British military number plate on his car, which he parked, locked, in an unmade road beside the canal. After the picnic his children ran on ahead, carrying the basket. When they reached the car they stopped, hesitated, dropped the basket and ran back. Somebody had forced the car door – the handle was broken and the door was slightly open. De Jong swore, remembering that he had left his camera in the glove compartment. He went and examined the car. The handle had been forced; de Jong reckoned it had been done with a piece of steel tubing, the kind of thing you can carry in your sleeve. But the camera was still there, so was his coat, so were some parcels, belonging to his wife. On the driving seat was a tobacco tin, and in the tin was a small nickel cartridge. De Jong knew exactly what it contained: it was the film cartridge of a sub-miniature camera, probably a Minox.

De Jong drove home and developed the film. It contained the minutes of the last meeting of the Praesidium of the East German Communist Party, the SED.

By an odd coincidence there was collateral from another source; the photographs were genuine.

Leamas took the case over then. He was badly in need of a success. He'd produced virtually nothing since arriving in Berlin, and he was getting past the usual age limit for full-time operational work. Exactly a week later he took de Jong's car to the same place and went for a walk.

It was a desolate spot that de Jong had chosen for his picnic: a strip of canal with a couple of shell-torn pill-boxes, some parched, sandy fields and on the Eastern side a sparse pine wood, lying about two hundred yards from the gravel road which bordered the canal. But it had the virtue of solitude – something that was hard to find in Berlin – and surveillance was impossible. Leamas walked in the woods. He made no attempt to watch the car because he did not know from which direction the approach might be made. If he was seen watching the car from the woods, the chances of retaining his informant's confidence were ruined. He need not have worried.

Harry Flannery, *Which Way Germany?*

A character who looks like President Johnson stands with another who looks like Secretary of State Rusk before an intimate, sophisticated audience of 100 to 150 people.

Says the man who looks like the President: "How long has it been since we issued a statement saying we back West Germany's demands for re-unification?"

The man who looks like Rusk replies: "We haven't had such a statement for two weeks."

"That so? Better put out another one today. Send a copy to Chancellor Kiesinger[4], of course."

That's a typical excerpt from one of Germany's political cabarets, a distinctive and famous form of entertainment in which the artists run through an hour or two of skits, songs and patter making fun of people and issues in the news. The United States had a political cabaret group for a while when the English sent over "The Establishment," and television had "That Was the Week That Was," which survived air exposure longer that the German variety – one of which was cancelled late in 1965 even before it went on the Hamburg outlet of the

---

[4] Kiesinger was Chancellor of West Germany from 1966 to 1969, directly preceding Willy Brandt. He was famously slapped in public by the self-styled "Nazi hunter" Beate Klarsfeld, and the controversy about his Nazi past was emblematic of the circumstances which gave birth to the "1968 movement", when after two decades of silence, younger Germans started demanding answers from their parents and grandparents. This should also be seen as part of the wider youth movement across Europe and North America at the time.

First West German Television Network. The Germans have learned that such presentations are successful only when presented to a small, knowledgeable audience.

The German experience with political cabaret began in the twenties when two German humor magazines, *Die Fliegenden Blätter* and *Simplicissimus*, hired actors to present sketches from their pages once a week or month.

The names of the two magazines are difficult to translate. *Die Fliegenden Blätter* literally means "loose-leaf paper." It might be said, therefore, to be a collection of papers on all kinds of subjects, not presented in any order. The name *Simplicissimus* is taken from the title of a popular book by Hans Jakob Christofel von Grimmelshausen (1624-76), *Simplicius Simplicissimus*. Grimmelshausen, who is said to have done the most significant writing in Germany between Wolfram's *Parzival* and Goethe's Faust, criticized the militarism of the Thirty Year's War. (In later writings, as an interesting note, he advocated reunification of the Christian confessions.) *Die Fliegenden Blätter* and *Simplicissimus* were published in the period when the United States has similar magazines for the humor and satirical commentary like *Judge, Puck* and the original *Life*. One of the few survivors of the period is the British *Punch*. *Simplicissimus* made a comeback in 1954, after a failure to get through the Hitler years, but died its second death on June 3, 1967 – never able to regain the spirit of its old traditions.

The German political cabarets that began with *Die Fliegenden Blätter* and *Simplicissimus* continued for a while even after the Nazi regime began. While they were operating, Weiss-Ferdl ended his program each evening at the *Platzl*, a Munich music hall, with an anti-Nazi joke. One evening he told his audience, "Do you know I saw the biggest Mercedes car in Bavaria the other day in the Ludwigstrasse, and it didn't have a Nazi in it?" After that, he was sent to prison for a few days, as a warning. On the night he returned to the *Platzl*, Weiss-Ferdl ended with: "Do you know I was wrong about that Mercedes? There was a Nazi sitting in it after all."

Until Hitler forbade laughter at his government and its officials, political satire in Germany featured such persons as Georg Grosz, Bertolt Brecht, and Kurt Weil.

Today the most famous political cabarets are *Das Kommödchen* (The Little Commode, or chest of drawers), in Düsseldorf, Lach-und Schiessgesellschaft (roughly, Laugh Target), in Munich, and *Die Stachelschweine* (the Porcupine), in West Berlin. Sammy Drexel, famous as a sports reporter for international ice hockey, soccer, and other games, directs and stars in the Munich show, which sometimes travels to Bonn, Düsseldorf, and Hamburg. Drexel performs with stars from radio and television.

One of his sketches dealt with the new type of German worker who, through co-determination, sits on boards in some industries and buys stock in the company where he works. In the act, a spokesman for the workers demands an extra half hour off at noon.

"That's impossible," the manager replies. "We're already shorthanded. No unemployment these days, you know."

The spokesman threatened a strike.

"That would be blackmail. Why an extra half hour anyway?"

"Oh," replied the worker spokesman, "with all the shares we own now, we need time to watch the stock market. If anything happened to our shares, you've had it."

In these cabarets, President Lübke is characterized as an honest, stubborn man with a Westphalian peasant's accent. He's called *Linkisch*, a word that means leftist in German, and also, "not well-dressed, clumsy." [5] His wife, a former college teacher, who speaks three or four foreign languages fluently, is presented as Queen Wilhelmina. He, on the other hand, is portrayed as a person who always mispronounces foreign phrases. She calls him "her best *Heini*," an abbreviation for his real name that has other obvious meanings, such as "uncultivated and crude."

The Communist bloc comes in for its expected share of attention. One skit in *Die Stachelschweine* presented two old friends chatting in a government-owned East Berlin pub. They were interrupted by news that the son of one of the men has just fled to the West. While they are discussing the news, a policeman enters and arrests the man. Everyone else in the pub is worried, concerned. A few minutes later, he returns.

"You are back! They didn't hold you!" they say in astonishment.

"No."

"Well, what happened? Tell us."

He smiles and orders another drink.

"Oh, I just got a ten marks fine," he says. "You see, I was parked in a no parking zone."

Often the themes are serious, suggesting for instance that the Germans should use their heads and not trust their leaders, whoever they may be; that the Nazis were bad and ex-Nazis are even more so; and that a Germany which can fall for Hitler can never again be complacent about its public affairs.

The Berlin and Düsseldorf cabarets tend to reflect the local political climate and more liberal than those in Munich. Berlin entertainment guides list six

---

[5] The chronically maladroit Lübke is best remembered in Germany today for his (un)diplomatic faux-pas. He is said to have begun a speech on a state visit to Liberia in 1962 with the words: "Most esteemed ladies and gentlemen, dearest negroes…"

others in addition to *Stachelschweine*, and Munich has several. *Die kleine Freiheit* (the Small Freedom) is one. Dr. Dieter Hildebrand, dramatic art professor at Munich university, directs another on Occamstrasse in Schwabing, the Munich Greenwich Village.

Patricia Highsmith, *The Boy Who Followed Ripley*

Eric and Tom drove off in Eric's car for the Kreuzberg area of Berlin, which Eric said was less than fifteen minutes away. Peter had departed, promising to come to Eric's apartment around one a.m. Tom had said to Peter that he would be grateful if they could get an early start for the Lübars rendez-vous. Even Peter admitted that the driving, plus the finding of the place might take an hour.

Eric stopped in a dismal-looking street of reddish-brown, old four- or five-story apartment houses near a corner bar with an open front door[6]. A couple of kids — the word urchins sprang to Tom's mind — rushed up and begged pfennigs from them, and Eric fished in his pocket, saying if he didn't give them some coins, they might do something to his car, though the boy looked only about eight years old, and the girl perhaps ten, with lipstick messily applied to her lips and rouge on her cheeks. She wore a pavement-length gown which looked as if it had been fashioned from a brownish-red and pinned-together window curtain to create something like a dress. Tom erased his first idea, that the girl was playing with her mother's make-up and wardrobe: there was something more sinister going on here. The little boy bad a thick mop of black hair which had been whacked in places by way of a haircut, and his dark eyes were glazed or maybe simply elusive. His projecting underlip seemed to indicate a fixed contempt for all the world around him. The boy had pocketed the money that Eric had given the girl.

'Boy's a Turk,' said Eric, locking his car, keeping his voice low. Eric gestured toward a doorway they were supposed to enter. 'They can't read, you know? Puzzles everyone. They speak Turkish and German fluently, but can't read anything!'

'And the girl? She looks German.' The little girl was blonde. The strange juvenile pair were watching them still, standing by Eric's car.

'Oh, German, yes. Child prostitute. He's her pimp — or he is trying to be.'

A buzz released the door and they went in. They climbed three flights of badly lit stairs. The hail windows were dirty, and let in almost no light. Eric

---

[6] During the division of Berlin, Kreuzberg was a frontier district within sight of the wall, making it unpopular with many. Its buildings were left to crumble and rents stayed cheap, which made it attractive to low-earning immigrants and young people with alternative lifestyles. Today, it is one of the most sought-after areas to live in the whole city.

knocked on a dark brown door, its paint scarred as if from kicks and blows. When clumping footsteps approached, Eric said, 'Eric' at the door crack.

The door was unlocked, a tall, broad man beckoned them in, talking in mumbled German in a deep voice. Another Turk, Tom saw, with a swarthiness of face that not even dark-haired Germans ever achieved. Tom walked into a terrible smell of what he thought was stewing lamb mingled with cabbage. Worse, they were promptly ushered into the kitchen whence the smell originated. A couple of small children played on the linoleum floor, and an old woman with a tiny-looking head and fuzzy, thin grey hair stood at the stove, stirring a pot nervously. The grandmother, Tom supposed, and maybe German, as she didn't look Turkish, but he couldn't really tell. Eric and the burly man sat down at a round table to which Tom was urged also, and Tom sat down reluctantly, yet he meant to enjoy the conversation if he could. Just what was Eric doing here? Eric's slangy German, and the Turk's hash of it made it difficult indeed for Tom to understand anything. They were talking numbers. 'Fifteen.., twenty-three' and prices, 'Four hundred marks . . .' Fifteen what? Then Tom remembered that Eric had said the Turk did some work as go-between for the Berlin lawyers who issued papers to Pakistanis and East Indians, permitting them to remain in West Berlin.

'I don't like this nasty little work,' Eric had said, 'but if I don't cooperate to some extent, as go-between of papers myself, Haki won't do jobs for me that are more important than his smelly immigrants.' Yes, that was it. Some of the immigrants, illiterate even in their own language, and unskilled, simply took the underground from East Berlin to West Berlin, and were met by Haki who steered them to the right lawyers. Then they could go on relief, at West Berlin expense, while their claims to be 'political refugees' were investigated, a process that might take years.

Haki was either a full-time crook or on unemployment too — maybe both — otherwise what was he doing home at this hour? He looked no more than thirty-five, and strong as an ox. His trousers, which he had long ago outgrown as to belly, were now held together at the waist by a piece of string that bridged the gap. A few fly buttons showed, unfastened.

An awful white-lightning-type of home-made vodka (Tom was told) was brought forth by Haki, or would Tom prefer beer? Tom did prefer beer, after sampling the vodka. The beer arrived in a big half-empty bottle, flat and tepid. Haki went off to fetch something from another room.

'Haki is a construction worker,' Eric explained to Tom, 'but on leave because of some injury — at work. Not to mention that he enjoys the — *Arbeitslosenunterstützung* — the—'

Tom nodded. Unemployment benefits. Haki was lumbering back with a dirty shoebox. His tread made the floor shake. He opened the shoebox, and produced a brown-paper-wrapped parcel the size of a man's fist. Eric shook the parcel and it rattled. Like pearls? Drug pellets? Eric pulled out his wallet and gave Haki a hundred-mark note.

'Only a tip,' said Eric to Tom. 'Are you bored? We'll leave in a minute.'

Bob Larson, *Your Swabian Neighbours*

Dr. Walter Stahl, the Executive Director of the Atlantic Bridge Foundation in Hamburg, which puts on many seminars for the members of the US Forces in Germany and published *These Strange German Ways,* is a lawyer and a writer. He is the author of a series of guide books to major German cities, such as *Hamburg from Seven to Seven.*

I once asked Walter why he didn't write a guidebook to Stuttgart. His reply was, "Because I'd have to call it *Stuttgart from Seven to Seven-Thirty.*"

Is this north-German impression of Swabian entertainment true? Let's face it: it's tough for any German city to beat Hamburg, but Stuttgart isn't as dead as some people think.

My friend Wolfgang Hartmann of the Stuttgart Tourist Office recently assembled a 64-page, pocket-size information booklet in *English* with the Swabian title *Info-Päckle* (which means "Little Info Packet"), and subtitle *Stuttgart – What's Where: A Brief Guide.* For a "brief guide," it's very comprehensive, covering (in order of interest) sights and recreation, cultural activities, hospitality and entertainment, and general information "from A to Z." It is color-coded by major section and contains four handy maps.

Under "Night Clubs" he writes: "Although Stuttgart has no exclusive entertainment quarter like Hamburg's *Reeperbahn,* the passionate night-lifer can get his money's worth – in both senses." I'm not quite sure what he means by that, and I'll tell you what little I know about Stuttgart's "exclusive entertainment quarter" in a moment. (In this context the word "exclusive" doesn't mean "fancy," but rather "solely devoted to.")

Herr Hartmann wisely recommends that you spend DM 60 and sample Stuttgart's night life with a guided tour before striking out (I mean just that) on your own. Called "Stuttgart Nights" (*Stuttgarter Nächte*), the tour is conducted every Wednesday, Thursday and Friday from 2000 to 0130. You buy your ticket at the "i-Punkt" of the Tourist Office's outlet in the Klett-Passage and join the tour in front of the Hindenburg building across from the railroad station. You get to see the TV tower, several night clubs (including some strip tease), a drink in all five establishments you visit, and a light supper for your sixty Marks. (The current list of night spots on the tour includes the Königshof, Happy Night, Evergreen, and Four Roses.)

You probably have heard about "The Jungle" in downtown Stuttgart around Nesebachstraße, Weberstraße, and especially Leonhardstraße. You might also have been warned that you can drop sixty Marks in one of those joints faster than a B-girl can drop a hint that she's thirsty. (Most of the managers will take a credit card as quickly as the girls will take you, by the way.) Long considered a "thorn in the eye" of Lord Mayor Manfred Rommel, these places will be limited in the future to about a dozen on Leonhardsplatz, Leonhardstraße, Richtstraße and Weberstraße, instead of expanding to 40 in the so-called "Old City".

Strip joints are not the Swabian's bag, at least not on his home territory. And to judge by my father-in-law's comments when I showed him a directory of massage parlors I found in a motel in Richmond, I doubt if "erotic" massage parlors do much business with real Swabians in Swabia. ("The real *Schwob*," he told me, "helps himself through the night. The only things those girls massage is your wallet[7].") I hasten to add, however, that a few "sauna clubs" in Stuttgart do advertise "full-service and live-dancing" from midnight to four a.m., in addition to the swimming pool and the solarium.

There is an uncodified custom that the Swabian goes out on Wednesday night. I have no way to account for it except perhaps to note that most establishments are closed on Mondays, several on Sundays, and some on Tuesdays. If he likes to dance, he goes to one or more of Stuttgart's discos, or to the more conservative dance cafés scattered about the town.

I think it is indicative of local tastes and habits that there are more *Weinstuben* listed in the bi-monthly *Official Programof Events* published by the Stuttgart Tourist Office than night clubs, bars, cabarets, and places to dance.

Apart from frequenting *Weinstuben* (see chapter three for details), the Swabian will eat out with the family occasionally. This is usually combined with an invigorating, appetite-building walk through the woods of the Swabian Alb, or tramping through the Schönbuch Forest, on a Sunday morning before competing for seats in a Gasthaus or on benches around an authorized fireplace in the great outdoors for a do-it-yourself picnic.

Len Deighton, *Berlin Game*

"How long have we been sitting here?" I said. I picked up the field glasses and studied the bored young American soldier in his glass-sided box.

---

[7] Swabians are known in Germany as mean, somewhat like the avaricious Scot of the English imagination. Further attributes the stereotypical Swabian shares with the classic Scot are the use of impenetrable dialect and a strong dislike for central government. German Chancellor Angela Merkel has consistently referred to the proverbially penny-pinching "Swabian hausfrau" as her role-model in matters of macro-economic policy.

"Nearly a quarter of a century," said Werner Volkmann, His arms were resting on the steering wheel and his head was slumped on them. "That GI wasn't even born when we first sat here waiting for the dogs to bark."

Barking dogs, in their compound behind the remains of the Hotel Adlon, were usually the first sign of something happening on the other side. The dogs sensed any unusual happenings long before the handlers came to get them. That's why we kept the windows open; that's why we were frozen nearly to death.

"That American soldier wasn't born, the spy thriller he's reading wasn't written, and we both thought the Wall would be demolished within a few days. We were stupid kids but it was better then, wasn't it, Bernie?"

"It's always better when you're young, Werner," I said.

This side of Checkpoint Charlie had not changed. There never was much there; just one small hut and some signs warning you about leaving the Western Sector. But the East German side had grown far more elaborate. Walls and fences, gates and barriers, endless white lines to mark out the traffic lanes. Most recently they'd built a huge walled compound where the tourist busses were searched and tapped, and scrutinized by gloomy men who pushed wheeled mirrors under every last vehicle lest one of their fellow-countrymen was clinging there.

The checkpoint is never silent. The great concentration of lights that illuminate the East German side produced a steady hum like a field of insects on a hot summer's day. Werner raised his head from his arms and shifted his weight. We both had sponge-rubber cushions under us; that was one thing we'd learned in a quarter of a century. That and taping the door switch so that the interior light didn't come on every time the car door opened. "I wish I knew how long Zena will stay in Munich," said Werner.

"Can't stand Munich," I told him. "Can't stand those bloody Bavarians, to tell you the truth."

"I was only there once," said Werner. "It was a rush job for the Americans. One of our people was badly beaten and the local cops were no help at all." Even Werner's English was spoken with the strong Berlin accent that I'd known since we were at school. Now Werner Volkmann was forty years old, thickset, with black bushy hair, black moustache, and sleepy eyes that made it possible to mistake him for one of Berlin's Turkish population. He wiped a spyhole of clear glass in the windscreen so that he could see into the glare of fluorescent lighting. Beyond the silhouette of Checkpoint Charlie, Friedrichstrasse in the East Sector shone as bright as day. "No," he said, "I don't like Munich at all."

The night before, Werner, after many drinks, had confided to me the story of his wife, Zena, running off with a man who drove a truck for the Coca-Cola company. For the previous three nights he'd provided me with a place on a lumpy sofa in his small apartment in Dahlem, right on the edge of Grunewald. But sober, we kept up the pretence that his wife was visiting a relative. "There's something coming now", I said.

Werner did not bother to move his head from where it rested on the seatback. "It's a tan-coloured Ford. It will come through the checkpoint, park over there while the men inside have a coffee and hotdog, then they'll go back in to the East Sector just after midnight."

I watched. As he'd predicted, it was a tan-coloured Ford, a panel truck, unmarked, with West Berlin registration.

"We're in the place they usually park," said Werner. "They're Turks who have girlfriends in the East. The regulations say you have to be out before midnight. They go back there again after midnight."

"They must be some girls!" I said.

"A handful of Westmarks goes a long way over there," said Werner. "You know that Bernie." A police car with two cops in it cruised past very slowly. They recognized Werner's Audi and one of the cops raised a hand in a weary salutation. After the police car moved away, I sued my field glasses to see right through the barrier to where an East German border guard was stamping his feet to restore circulation. It was bitterly cold.

11

A Dying Dictatorship and Instant "Ostalgia"
1982 - 1999

The fall of the Berlin Wall surprised publishers as much as it did the wider world. Suddenly, decades' worth of writing about Germany was out of date.

ECONOMIC STAGNATION, CULTURAL PARALYSIS, totalitarian snooping: the situation of the population of the ironically-named German Democratic Republic in the 1980s was bleak. Despite the noises of *glasnost* and *perestroika* coming from Moscow, Erich Honecker in East Berlin remained as hard-line as ever. By the latter part of the decade the Cold War and the division of Germany had become seemingly so entrenched that what was to follow took most in the West by surprise.

Yet suddenly towards the end of the decade there was light at the end of the tunnel. The Soviet Union, increasingly preoccupied by its own decline, failed to intervene during the 1988 strikes in Poland, and by the summer of 1989 free elections had seen the oppositional Solidarity movement swept to power; in May, Hungary had not been prevented from opening its border with the West. It became clear to East Germans that, unlike in Budapest in 1957 or Prague in 1968, Soviet tanks were no longer standing between them and democracy. Their leadership looked weak, and sustained public pressure from demonstrations in autumn 1989 led, on 9 November, to the fall of the Berlin Wall.

Seismic political shifts were soon occurring on a daily basis: East Germany's first free elections on 18 March 1990, which gave a clear majority in favour of reunification; the extension of the Deutschmark to replace the rapidly disintegrating GDR currency; a full political union as of 3 October 1990—now the national holiday of today's reunited Federal Republic of Germany. Each step was fraught with risk: would not the East German police and secret services try to suppress demonstrations? Would Russia really stand by as the post-war geopolitical deep-freeze melted away under the tracks of its tanks battalions? Would the rest of the world—above all Britain's Margaret Thatcher (b. 1925)—agree to reunification and withdraw occupying forces? In the end, a reunited, democratic Germany became fully sovereign on 15 March 1991 under the entirely unthreatening aegis of Helmut Kohl (b. 1930) without a shot having been fired. Despite the economic challenges resulting from the overnight integration of the decrepit East, work began almost instantly on re-building Berlin as the German capital, and by the late 1990s, both there and elsewhere, it was often difficult at first glance to tell what had been on which side of the border.

It is perhaps surprising how limited the effect of the fall of the Berlin Wall and the Reunification of 1990 was on work about Germany. Publishing responds slowly enough to changes, and fiction especially is by its very nature often far further behind the times, but throughout the 1990s there was little by way of new writing on Germany. If anything, the fact that the country was, for the first time in almost a century, no longer a military powder-keg put an immediate end to non-fiction "state of the nation" writing on it beyond the academic sphere. What writing there was tended to be of the memoir kind, looking back to the last years of division and dictatorship just past.

Caught by Surprise in 1989

A publishing phenomenon about Germany in the 1980s illustrates the decade's atmosphere of stasis particularly well. First released in 1982, Gordon Craig's (b. 1913) *The Germans* was typical of the school of half-historical, half-sociological examination of contemporary German society, answering the overriding question of "could it happen again"? Not only did the book go through several editions in the 1980s, it was even updated in 1991 by a short afterword when much of it had already been rendered out-of-date by the Reunification. Perhaps the publishers alighted on Craig's work because its verdict on the prospects for a democratic Germany was positive? Some parts of it—like the section on language cited below—certainly retained their importance into the 1990s.

Another of the auditors of modern Germany was John Ardagh (b. 1928), a Europhile British journalist who made his name writing book-length analyses of continental societies. In *Germany and the Germans*, published in 1987, his mix of personal anecdote and profound research gives his view of the country currency way beyond the *Wende*—"change, turning"—of 1990. Many of the trends he observed were deep-seated enough to survive this radical change, and a few supplementary chapters written in 1994 were enough to keep the book serviceable up to the Millennium.

The same cannot be said of Michael Skinner (b. 1953), although this has far more to do with his subject matter than anything else. As a military journalist, Skinner conducted a thorough survey of the United States' armed forces in Europe, work which found its way into the bookshops in 1989 and was rendered hopelessly defunct by the Reunification the following year. Although his USAREUR: *The United States Army in Europe* may be little more than a historical curiosity today, in his introduction he gives an extremely concise and colourful picture of late Cold War Germany—and indeed the West of the period as a whole—on the very eve of its radical restructuring.

In *Neither Here nor There*, Bill Bryson (b. 1951) retraces the steps of his own first jaunt around Europe in his early twenties; here the American lover of all things British sets off around Europe again in 1991. He finds a Germany—or rather a Hamburg—completely at ease with itself in the wake of the unexpectedly successful Reunification and is, as such, a forerunner of more recent observers who are almost uniformly struck by the relaxed and luxurious lifestyle of urban Germany today.

Writing in 1992, Dave Rimmer (b. 1960) nonetheless takes us back to the late 1980s when he fled London in search of escape from Thatcherism, first in West Berlin and then in Eastern Europe, where he experiences the fall of communism. *Once Upon a Time in the East* is well worth reading for its depiction of West Berlin, whose closely-patrolled borders had, paradoxically, turned it into an enchanted island of sorts. It was the first English-language contribution to what German calls *Ostalgie*, a portmanteau of "East" and "nostalgia", and while Rimmer is not to be found idealizing communist regimes, he certainly mourns the way their demise led to the last backwaters of capitalism being swept into the mainstream.

There is sometimes a whiff of "Ostalgia" in Timothy Garton Ash's (b. 1955) *The File: A Personal History*, too, despite the disturbing nature of its contents. As a scholar of German history, Garton Ash lived in both West and East Berlin in the 1970s and 1980s, attracting the kind of attention from the *Staatsicherheitsdienst* or "Stasi" that this kind of cross-border life entailed. When the Stasi files were made accessible to the public following the fall of the Wall, Garton Ash decided to view his and publish the results in 1997. The principal value of his book lies in its detailed dissection of the sheer voyeuristic grubbiness of totalitarian regimes, and in this sense, it is anything but "Ostalgia".

The Return of Light-heartedness

It was the West that won the day, and both Bryson and Ardagh feel drawn to comment on the balanced, friendly and above all non-arrogant nature of modern Germany, with Ardagh specifically mentioning the death of the old Prussian stereotype. As in the previous decades following the Second World War, it takes extended visits before anti-German prejudice can be "lanced" (as Tony Benn put it in the chapter previous), and Bryson, with his caustic humour and concerns about historical responsibility, is a particularly tough case. Yet overall, writing of this period shows an English-speaking world becoming more and more open to having its prejudices removed, to allowing the pendulum of public opinion about Germans to start swinging back a little from the terrifyingly militaristic extreme.

With Bryson, and also with Rimmer, we have two examples of standard genre works of travel writing in which Germany plays a central role. With post-war commercial travel writing up to that point having been centred more or less entirely on southern Europe, books like theirs heralded a diversification that would gather speed throughout the 1990s. Driven in no small part by the ever-growing total number of books written and published, especially in the travel sector, this proliferation nevertheless also suggested a broader shift in the general understanding of Germany from being Europe's greatest unsolved problem towards being just another European country.

✳

Gordon Craig, *The Germans*

At the outset, it may be remarked that a Mark Twain *redivivus* would find German newspapers less impenetrable than they were in the nineteenth century. It is true that interminable sentences that he complained of can still be found in journals like the *Frankfurter Allgemeine Zeitung* or the *Süddeutsche Zeitung*, although far less frequently than was once the case. But papers like Axel Springer's chief organ *Die Welt* cultivate a more succinct style , and the popular press, of which *Bild-Zeitung* is the most widely read example, go in for short sentences, one-paragraph stories, and a lively but simple idiom.

But this is misleading. The greatest barrier confronting the foreigner who seeks an understanding of contemporary German by reading its journals and books is that there seems to be no universally accepted standard High German anymore. A mastery of the dignified and somewhat stuffy style of the *Frankfurter Allgemeine Zeitung* does not prepare one to unravel the complexities of *Der Spiegel*, a weekly journal that is written in radical-chic German that is designed to be outrageous and abounds in unusual combinations and linguistic inventions; and the problems awaiting the foreigner in the world of scholarship are even more formidable. The professorial style was always, as we have seen, an obstacle to easy comprehension, but at least it was true, in the days before Hitler, that there was a rough uniformity of view in the attitudes that university faculty members held regarding social and political problems. This can no longer be counted on, and the result has been a perceptible increase in the amount of general theorizing that has crept into contemporary scholarship. It is not easy to find a recent book in history in which the author applies himself to his subject without writing a fifty-page theoretical preface first. Moreover, the theorists always seem to belong to schools, and the schools have private languages that have to be understood if the works of their members are to be properly appreciated. This is not easy for the foreigner who may not have learned to recognize, from the employment of terms like *systemimmanent* and *umfunktionieren*, what wavelength he is supposed to tune into. He is apt to feel the same inadequacy as earlier foreigners did when confronted with the symbols and the charged words and the flights into music of the Romantics.

To gain an understanding of the variability of political view and position in the German Federal Republic is no easier, particularly if one intends to try to learn something about the attitudes of the extreme critics of the existing political and social system. Here again a special language is encountered, that of the *Chaoten* and the *Spontis*, of the anarchists and the *Flipperlebensgemeinschaften*, an idiom called *Rotwelsch*, made up of liberal borrowings from the jargon of the underworlds and from the Marxist theoreticians, in which the police are always *Bullen* or a *Faschistenpack* and political awareness requires participation in *Befreiungsaktionen*, at the risk of being *geklaut* and forced to sit in the *Knast*, in order to undermine that *verlumpte Staat* and to achieve a *höhere Lebensqualität*.[1] Here again the nuances and shadings implicit in the terms used are not easily perceived by the outsider.

Finally, there is the problem of the German Democratic Republic, which has a totalitarian regime and a totalitarian theory of language, which means that 18 million Germans in the East, who use the same language as their brothers in the Federal Republic, are being taught systematically to use it in a different way and for a different purpose. Georg Klaus, one the DDR's leading philosophers of speech, makes no bones of the fact that, in the eyes of the East German regime, the purpose of language is to change "attitudes of people in production and public life and their moral behaviour, so that the goals of Socialism may be maximally achieved."

To promote this end, language is controlled and manipulated – in much the same way as it was during the Third Reich – by regulations formulated by the government and imposed upon the school system, the news agency AND, and the central organ of the Socialist Unity Party, *Neues Deutschland*. The emotional charging of words, the excessive use of superlatives, the preference for terms taken from the military vocabulary, the sharp schematization that eliminates neutral valuations in favour of black-white dichotomies, the insistent use of invective, and the constant repetition of stereotyped epithets that were the stock-in-trade of Goebbels are in use once more. So, moreover, are words that are also used in the West but have, in the DDR, a profoundly different meaning – words beginning with the prefix "peace" or the adjectives "people's" and "popular," words like "coexistence" and "relaxation of tension" and "human rights" and "democracy." It is for this reason that, when agreements have been made with the German Democratic Republic, Western diplomats have sometimes been unpleasantly surprised by the meaning later assigned by the government of the DDR to wording that they had accepted and had thought they understood.

When Willy Brandt met Willi Stoph in Erfurt in 1970, they had two private

---

[1] Many of these items of Marxist vocabulary are still in general slang use today, especially *Bullen* and *Knast*. Others, however, are hopelessly outdated: *verlumpter Staat*, for instance, would mark its user out as a tragically unreconstructed communist, while *Spontis* is only used by political journalists to describe the rapidly-ageing radical wing of the Green Party.

talks, with no one else present. There was no need for an intermediary or interpreter, they decided, Stoph remarking, "We both know German." This was accurate, as the sequel showed, only in the most formal sense. The fact is that German – the same German – is not the language of all Germans. This does not make things easy for the foreign student of the contemporary German scene.

John Ardagh, *Germany and the Germans*

I lived in Germany four ten months in 1984-5, part of the time in Stuttgart with Katinka but most of it on tour with her by car to the other main West German cities and to the GDR. For this field research we spent several weeks each in Munich, Frankfurt, Bonn, Hamburg, and Berlin, with shorter visits to Cologne, Düsseldorf, the Ruhr, Bremen and many smaller towns and rural areas. In France too I have always tried to concentrate on the provinces rather than Paris: but in Germany this is ten times more imperative, for Bonn is a tedious little place and nearly all the interest is in big real cities. So I have got to know those fearsome *Autobahnen* all too intimately, and in my sleep I could retrace every curve of those giddy gradients in the Schwäbische Jura or the hills south of Kassel, with the BMW 700s flashing arrogantly by. Apart from this hazard, I find Germany a very pleasant and easy country to travel and work in – cosy little hotels, good simple food always well served, attractive scenery (at least in the south), relative absence of urban traffic jams, efficient public services, telephone kiosks that have seldom been vandalised. Everywhere I felt very much at home; even the average industrial city, though outwardly no beauty with its anonymous concrete blocks and officious ringways, is very civilised in its way and far less drab than in Britain. Some foreigners get irritated by German tidiness and efficiency: for the visiting reporter they do carry advantages.

This today is a very open society, and using the normal techniques of the journalist I found it easy to see the people I wanted and obtain the information I needed. If I have nonetheless found Germany a harder country to write about vividly than France, I do not think this is really because my background knowledge goes less deep, nor because the Germans are a more complex and baffling people. Rather it is that Germany is a less lively place, at least on the surface, without the same Latin sense of show. The Germans are more methodical but less innovative than the French: there is endless talk, and even some violence, but constructive reforms and changes take place in so muted and legalistic a way that it is much harder to spotlight them than in France with its penchant for pioneering and confrontation. Above all, the number of really colourful or outspoken personalities in public life is amazingly small – and I am thinking not just of politicians but of the leaders of industry, the trade unions, the farming lobbies, local government or education, or indeed autonomous figures who have risen from the rank-and-file to champion some cause. The French love an eccentric show-off who has wit and originality, and the will rally to him; the Germans are more wary. In politics, a Franz-Josef Strauss is rare; and in other fields the flamboyant stars tend to be not in positions of formal responsibility but lone outsiders (Werner Herzog and the late Josef Beuys have been prime examples). Those who become the elected heads of organisations or even of private pressure-groups may well possess drive, ability and real qualities of leadership: but they also tend to conform to a standard that is sedate, reassuring, and not too startling. One explanation could be the prudent desire to avoid any new Nazi-style personality cult (before Hitler's day, showy individualism was much more readily accepted).

Younger Germans in particular – apart from a stubbornly bigoted minority – I have found to be more than averagely thoughtful, concerned, gentle, modest, and internationally-minded. The Germans may still be a shade too earnest, but they are less pompous than they used to be. And their old tendency towards arrogance and lofty superiority, once associated with the Prussian upper classes, took such punishment from wartime defeat and Nazi shame that today it is very little present, at least in their dealings with foreigners, on whom they are still generally keen to make a favourable impression. I encountered very little arrogance, noticeably less than in Paris – the only exceptions being possibly the haughty executives of some of the big industrial firms, who are so successful and confident that presumably they can afford not to worry what foreigners think.

There may still be other aggressive and domineering instincts lurking somewhere beneath the surface of this polite and placid new Germany – or that is certainly the impression one gains from observing the German behind the steering wheel.

Certainly the Germans would seem to have changed radically since their Nazi aberration of 1933-45. But how deep does the change go, and are there still some danger signs? In very many ways the picture since the war has been extremely positive. The Germans have developed a new and open society that is far less class-divided than it used to be, or than Britain and France still remain; here the labour relations have blossomed in remarkable harmony,[2] and democratic

---

[2] The legal framework of workers' representation, as well as the behaviour of the unions themselves, has been a major contributing factor in Germany's post-war industrial success. Labour laws in Germany stipulate works councils for firms above a certain size, and in larger companies representatives from these councils sit on the boards of management. Yet despite this legally enshrined position of power and their collective bargaining rights, unions in Germany have tended to be moderate in their demands, especially during recessions, helping manufacturing to remain competitive internationally. During the work and welfare reforms of the early 2000s and most recently following the financial crisis, German unions have often refrained from demanding pay rises for their members for years at a time.

reasonableness has put down firm roots, helped by the stability afforded by economic success. If it has proved to be rather a conformist society, this in a sense has been an unconscious result of the attempt to tame the wild streak that led to Nazism by putting the premium on decent dull codes of conduct, practical rather than idealistic. It has proved to be a very legalistic society, festooned with a million petty rules and regulations and obsessed by the need to abide by them. This is by no means a new German trait, but the law-making has intensified since the war, and this too many in a sense have been a price paid for the new stability: the post-war Germans seem to have felt instinctively that the necessary way to safeguard a fledging democracy is to hedge it about with laws that direct the citizens on how to behave in it, and thus prevent a return to past excesses.

It is true however that the trait of automatic obedience has begun to weaken in recent years, and this is one of a number of significant new changes now emerging. Under the impact of the ideas of 1968, society has started to become a little more socially informal, less deferential to authority, and perhaps more tolerant. A new generation has arrived with new values, and although some of the wilder ideas of the Greens may be altogether too fanciful, even dangerous, there is undeniably a sympathetic side to many of the new trends – not only the concern for nature and quality of life, but the renewed interest in tradition. The links with the better side of the German heritage were smashed by the Nazi experience which after the war led to a blanket rejection of the entire past, in the bid for a clean new start. This was understandable, but in the longer term it could be harmful.

Michael Skinner, *USAREUR: The United States Army in Europe*

There's a war outside the Tower Motel. Holed up inside, I've got everything I need: bad German food and worse German cable TV. Turn up the volume and you hardly notice the 155mm artillery shells rattling the thin windows, rolling like Texas thunder across the farm fields between the range and me.

You can try to ignore the booming, but you can't stop it. Grafenwohr is ground zero in the Central European cockpit. They've been pounding this particular piece of real estate for about a hundred years, popping off small arms, cranking the tanks, yanking the lanyards on main guns pointed east, west, north, south. It's a firing range. It's *supposed* to sound ominous.

From the balcony, day and night, you hear the war, the continuous war, the war between Us and Them, the good guys and the bad. This generation the players line up west and east: NATO, all hope and cavalry, pacing "the trace." On the other side of the cut, the Russians and their dim allies squat, leaning forward in their armored cynicism. You can't hear their guns from here, but I don't imagine they sound much different than ours.

Start anywhere you want—politics, history, the humanities—this is where you'll end up, listening for guns in the German night. It's the largest piece of unfinished business on the planet. Everything else is a peripheral theatre. (…)

On April 25, 1945, Soviet and American troops met and shook hands, perhaps for the last time, at Torgau, about sixty miles south of Berlin. Roads and bridges into Soviet-occupied Germany were blocked two weeks later. The victorious Western armies withdrew into their zones of occupation, determined long before the end of the war. Germany, meant to be temporarily divided into four parts, was permanently divided into two. A pencil mark on a map, drawn more or less casually by war-weary allies, trusting and naive, became a bayonet scar dragged through the ashes of Germany. And we've been staring at each other across that line ever since.

It is an imaginary line drawn across the heart of Europe, splitting Germany, and the world, ideologically and militarily. The greatest armies the earth has ever known — could ever know — are facing off there, ready to torch the planet over what is, essentially, a 700-mile-long scratch in the dirt.

Unlike most national borders, no natural barriers separate East and West Germany. Except for a brief stretch of the Elbe near Hamburg and some rough country to the south, there are no great rivers or mountain ranges to deter invasion; only politics divides what has become the German Democratic Republic and the Federal Republic of Germany (FRG). (…)

To the governments of the two Germanies, the "inner German border" (IGB) is, officially, no big deal. Legally, the Federal Republic of Germany and the German Democratic Republic consider the IGB no more formidable than a state line, say, or the boundary between two provinces. In theory, citizens of both countries can go freely back and forth, with just a short check at any number of "blue" autobahn crossings. In practice the border is only semipermeable.

But to the officers and men of the United States Army in Europe, who are pledged to shed their lives for this intellectual construction, the border is simply as "the trace." It is one of those rare, perfectly suited military terms, evoking, as it does, images of range wars, cavalry sorties from frontier outposts, and long riders, lonely, cold, and ever watchful, checking stretches of wire in a dulling and dangerous routine. That's life on the border today.

For more than forty years, USAREUR troops, the British Army of the Rhine, the resurgent Bundeswehr, the reluctant French, and resentful allies have been keeping a wary eye to the east. Through moods alternating between neglect and paranoia, NATO strives to keep the unfinished business of World War II from combusting into World War III. It is a bad peace, but the most peace Central Europe has ever known.

(…)

To most travelers, Fulda, West Germany, is a hundred-kilometer blur off the E70 autobahn. The little city rates only a footnote in the guidebooks. There really is not much to see.

Saint Boniface, the English missionary who anointed King Pippin and brought the gospel to the Franks, is buried there. He did it the hard way. Near his tomb are all that's left of the good saint: his head, his sword, and a book of scriptures with which he tried to protect himself from his murderers. The codex is half cut through. The second thrust brought sainthood to Boniface. The futility of attempting to ward off armed force with the written word has never been so graphically illustrated. Yet, today, 1,200 years later, the last lesson of Saint Boniface must still be taught anew to each generation.

Surrounding the crypt, a cathedral and its grounds form the heart of Fulda. There are stone balustrades and towers, and huge doorways and imposing stairs that don't lead to anything anymore. They are baroque memories of little wars long gone. There will be no more little wars for Fulda.

Visitors do flock to the city, not so much for *what* it is as *where* it is. To the north is Kassel. To the south, Wurzburg. To the west, Frankfurt and the industrial Ruhr valley. To the east lies World War III.

Fulda is perhaps the only spot in the world where people come to walk a battlefield that has never seen conflict. And what they come to see doesn't exist. They're searching for nothing, the absence of something, a hole, a hollow, a gap. Future historians, overachieving reporters, journalists of the cataclysmic — they've all been here, making the mandatory, preapocalyptic pilgrimage to the famous Fulda Gap.

And they are invariably disappointed. There is nothing to see. Those looking for Armageddon staring out of tank slits should head on farther east, to Berlin. Fulda is no garrison town. The 11th Armored Cavalry minds its manners, its most noisy presence confined to well outside the city center. And as for the Russians, they are not welcome here.

"Fulda's a nice town," says a Blackhorse officer. "Catholic, conservative, a real German town, full of staunch, true Germans. Russian-hating Germans. They like the Americans here."

(…)

"The people here usually refer to us as 'the Fulda Regiment,' rather than the 11th ACR or whatever," explains a Blackhorse major. "They consider us their unit."

Perhaps the greatest reason the cav and the city are so chummy, however, is the presence of danger so near. It has a way of bringing people closer. There is an axiom in USAREUR that the closer you get to the border, the friendlier the Germans are. Or more supportive, at any rate, especially the older ones. The protests one sees against NATO in general, and the American military presence in particular, usually center around college campuses in the larger cities in the west and the north, well back from the line.

(...)

Besides constant quibbles about levels of military spending and command slots, the biggest dilemma for NATO centers around two related questions: Where do we make a stand? When do we go nuclear?

These are important questions. The answers depend on where you're standing. To the French, the nuclear tripwire seems to run along their border at the Saar. The British would probably stand to see the continent overrun before risking a nuclear exchange. Living on the line gives you a particularly nihilistic attitude, however, and the Germans might be ready to "Go Ugly Early," as they say in the F-111 bomber squadrons; after all, what's the difference between a conventional fire storm and a nuclear fire storm? When you're dead, you're dead.

Bill Bryson, *Neither Here nor There*

I walked a few hundred yards inland and uphill to the Reeperbahn, that famed mile-long avenue of sin. It looked disappointingly unlusty. Of course, sinful places never look their best in daylight. I remember thinking even in Las Vegas that it all looked rather endearingly pathetic when viewed over a cup of coffee and a doughnut. All that noise and electric energy that is loose at dusk vanishes with the desert sun and it all suddenly seems as thing and one-dimensional as a film set. But even allowing for this, the Reeperbahn looked tame stuff, especially after Amsterdam. I had envisioned it as a narrow, pedestrianized street packed on both sides with bars, sex-shops, peep-shows, strip-clubs and all the other things a sailor needs to revive a salty dick, but this was almost a normal city street, busy with traffic flowing between the western suburbs and the downtown. There was a fair sprinkling of seamy joints, but also a lot of more or less normal establishments – restaurants, coffee shops, souvenir stores, jeans shops, even a furniture store and a theatre showing the inescapable *Cats*. Almost the only thing that told you this was a neighbourhood of dim repute was the hard look on people's faces. They all had the gaunt, washed-out look of people who run fairground stalls.

(...)

It was getting on for midday and people were sitting out in the sunny plazas having lunch or eating ice-creams. Almost without exception they looked healthy and prosperous and often were strikingly good-looking. I remembered German cities from twenty years before being full of businessmen who looked just as Germans were supposed to look – fat and arrogant. You would see them gorging themselves on piles of sausages and potatoes and gulping with full mouths from litre tankards of golden beer at all hours of the day, but now they seemed to be picking delicately at salads and fish, and looking fit and tanned – and, more than that, friendly and happy. Maybe this was just a Hamburg trait. Hamburg is after all closer to Denmark and Sweden and even England than it is to Munich, so perhaps it is atypical of Germany.

At all events, this relaxed and genial air was something that I hadn't associated with Germans before, at least not those aged over twenty-five. There was no whiff of arrogance here, just a quiet confidence, which was clearly justified by the material wealth around them. All those little doubts we've all had about the wisdom of letting the Germans become the masters of Europe evaporated in the Hamburg sunshine. Forty-five years ago Hamburg was rubble. Virtually everything around me was new, even when it didn't look it. The people had made their city, and even themselves, rich and elegant and handsome through their cleverness and hard work, and they had every right to be arrogant about it, but they were not, and I admired them for that.

I don't think I can ever altogether forgive the Germans their past, not as long as I can wonder if that friendly old waiter who brings me my coffee might have spent his youth bayoneting babies or herding Jews into gas ovens. Some things are so monstrous as to be unpardonable. But I don't see how anyone could go to Germany now and believe for a moment that that could ever happen again. Germans, it struck me, are becoming the new Americans – rich, ambitious, hard-working, health-conscious, sure of their place in the world. Seeing Hamburg now, I was happy to hand them my destiny – happier, at any rate, that leaving it to those who have spent the last forty years turning Britain into a kind of nation-state equivalent of Woolworth's.

Dave Rimmer, *Once Upon a Time in the East*

In those days the East began at the Hook of Holland. You crossed the North Sea, cleared Dutch controls and walked out on to the station platform to find a string of East German rolling stock, nicely drab and dilapidated next to local trains in gleaming kingfisher colours. This was the North-West Express, a slim tendril of the communist world which, twice every twenty-four hours, would slither all the way out to this western edge of the continent. There was just enough on board to stir something in the soul of the Cold War romantic. In the dingy Mitropa car you could order an East German breakfast of hard bread, pale cheese and bitter coffee from a menu printed on some smudgily antiquated duplicating machine. You'd sprinkle salt on your far-too-soft boiled egg from an orange plastic cruet and watch Holland passing primly by through windows framed with grimy lace. (…)

It wasn't until mid-afternoon, when the train reached Helmstedt, that the fun and games began. After the tedious haul across the Federal Republic, here the train would pause and take on East German officials. Outside, a watchtower or two rose above what appeared to be a great, brown slagheap. Border guards came into the carriage bearing trays with shoulder straps – much like those of cinema ice-cream salespeople, except in place of popcorn and ices they'd be full of rubber stamps, rule books and blank transit visas, and instead of a shaded bulb to illuminate the wares, they'd have a little UV light to show up any hidden marks some colleague might previously have placed on your documents. (…)

The point was emphasised by the corridor the train would now be inching through, barbed wire to left and right, tall grey lamps standing every few yards. Presently it stopped at Marienborn on the other side. After squeaky clean West Germany you'd notice how much shabbier everything looked. Outside was a hard currency Intershop. There were no branches of C&A here, would be none for over a hundred miles, and then only in the fortified outpost of capitalism that was West Berlin. (…)

If you arrived in West Berlin by air, it was possible to miss the point completely. Just as New York or London yield none of their glamour until long after touchdown at JFK or Heathrow, so the experience of flying into the sleepy West Berlin airport of Tegel offered no hint of the city's tense situation. Maybe travellers would notice that they could not fly in by Lufthansa, only on carriers from the allied countries; maybe also that along the air corridor over the Zone the plane would be flying at about a third of normal cruising height – and hangover from the days when the rules were negotiated and unpressurised airliners couldn't venture much higher. The astute observer, looking down over the East German landscape on a rare clear day, might even notice the effect collectivisation of agriculture had on land use.

But the Inter-German Border, as the Allies used to call it, looked like nothing from the air. I never once managed to spot it flying in from the West. Coming down low into Tegel it was possible to catch a glimpse of the Wall, if you knew where to look. And then it was gone as you descended over lakes, forest, neat red-roofed housing laid out around inner courtyards, tree-lined avenues ploughed by cream double-deckers. Finally you emerged from your anti-sceptic aircraft into a bright, efficient airport where the uniformed officials gave you a minimum of fuss. It could have been any normal city.

Not so coming in by road or rail. On the journey along the transit routes you were accompanied by a perceptible heightening of tension. Berliners were used to it, but West Germans would often get a little edgy. I once hitched a ride out of Berlin with a woman on her way back to Cologne. For the whole 188 kilometres between one border post and the other, this woman was a bag of nerves: speeding up and slowing down, serving between dawdling Trabants, careering from one lane to the other, torn between anxiety about lingering too long in this dreadful place and feat of being stopped for speeding by disagreeable Volkspolizei. The minute we emerged into the West at Helmstedt she was calm again – right after pointing out how, on a little fringe of the DDR just beyond their border controls, three armed solider guarded two dungareed workmen who were cutting the grass, just yards away from the freedom to choose between C&A and Benetton.

I was no stranger to the train. On my first trip this way, eight years before, I'd hung out of the window all the way across the Zone, fascinated by any glimpse of smoking factories, seedy farmhouses, funny little cars at level crossings. We'd stopped briefly at Magdeburg, the only town of any consequence between the border and Berlin. It was rush-hour. Over the heads of the guards blocking off our train from the others in the station, I watched local commuters and noted the Eastern cut of imitation leather jackets, the stiffly shaped briefcases, the peculiar design of their double-decker trains: my first glimpse of communist life.[3]

Timothy Garton Ash, *The File*

I sit down at a small plastic-wood table in Frau Schulz's cramped room in the Federal Authority for the Records of the State Security Service of the former German Democratic Republic: the ministry of the files. As I open the binder, I find myself thinking of an odd moment in my East German life.

One night in 1980, when I was living as a student in East Berlin, I came back with a girlfriend to my room in a crumbling Wilhelmine tenement house in the borough of Prenzlauer Berg. This was a room with a view — a view into it. Large french windows gave directly on to a balcony and, were it not for the net curtains, people living across the street could look straight in.

---

[3] The double-decker carriages are about the only surviving element of the GDR in use in Germany today. Especially around Berlin, there are double-decker trains with both Western and old communist stock, albeit now in the same livery. In the early part of the new millennium there was a trend towards reviving old Eastern products with Proustian *madeleine* potential such as toothpaste or milkshake powders as part of the overall *Ostalgie* (portmanteau of "East" plus "nostalgia") phenomenon.

As we embraced on the narrow bed, Andrea suddenly pulled away, finished undressing, went over to the window and threw open the net curtains. She turned on the glaring main light and then came back to me. Had this been, say, Oxford, I might have been a little surprised about the bright light and the open curtains. But this was Berlin, so I thought no more about it.

Until, that is, I learned about the file. Then I remembered this moment and started wondering whether Andrea had been working for the Stasi, and whether she had opened the curtains so we could be photographed from the other side of the street.

Perhaps those photographs are lurking in this binder, which Frau Schulz has already inspected. What was it she said? 'You have a very interesting file.'

Hastily turning the pages, I'm relieved to find that there are no such photographs here and that Andrea does not appear as an informer. But there are other things that touch me.

Here, for example, is an observation report describing a visit I apparently paid to East Berlin on 06.10.79 from 16.07 hours to 23.55 hours. The alias given me by the Stasi at this date was, less romantically, '2468 i6'.

16.07 hours
'246816' was taken up for observation after leaving the Bahnhof Friedrichstrasse frontier crossing. The person to be observed went to the newspaper stand in the upper station concourse and bought a 'Freie Welt', a 'Neues Deutschland' and a 'Berliner Zeitung'. Then the object [that's me] walked questingly around the station.

16.15 hours
in the upper station concourse '246816' greeted a female person with handshake and kiss on the cheek. This female person received the code-name 'Beret'. 'Beret' carried a dark brown shoulder bag. Both left the station and went, conversing, to the Berliner Ensemble on Brechtplatz.

16.25 hours
both entered the restaurant
Ganymed
Berlin-Mitte
Am Schiffbauerdamm
After c. 2 minutes the persons to be observed left the restaurant and went via Friedrichstrasse and Unter den Linden to the Operncafé.

16.52 hours
'246816' and 'Beret' entered the restaurant
Operncafé
Berlin-Mitte
Unter den Linden
They took seats in the café and drank coffee.

18.45 hours
they left the café and went to Bebelplatz. In the time from
18.45 hours
until
20.40 hours
they both watched with interest the torchlit procession to honour the 3oth anniversary of the GDR. Thereafter '246816' and 'Beret' went along the street Unter den Linden
[and] Friedrichstrasse to the street Am Schiffbauerdamm.

21.10 hours
they entered there the restaurant Ganymed. In the restaurant they were not under observation.

23.50 hours
both left the gastronomic establishment and proceeded directly to the departure hall of the Bahnhof Friedrichstrasse frontier crossing, which they
23.55 hours
entered. 'Beret' was passed on to Main Department VI for documentation. The surveillance was terminated.
Person-description of object '24 68i 6'
    SEX: male
    AGE: 20—25 years
    HEIGHT: C. I.75m
    BUILD: slim
    HAIR: dark blond
    short
    DRESS: green jacket
    blue polo-neck pullover
    brown cord trousers
Person—description of connection 'Beret'
    SEX: female
    AGE: 30—35 years

HEIGHT: I.75m—I.78m
BUILD: slim
HAL R: medium blonde
curly
DRESS: dark blue cloth coat
red beret
blue jeans
black boots
ACCESSORIES: dark brown handbag

I sit there, at the plastic-wood table, marvelling at this minutely detailed reconstruction of a day in my life and at the style that recalls a school exercise: never a sentence without a verb, the pretentious variation of 'gastronomic establishment'. I remember the slovenly gilt-and-red Ganymed, the plush Operncafé and the blue-shirted, pimpled youths in the thirtieth anniversary march-past, their paraffin-soaked torches trailing sparks in the misty night air. I smell again that peculiar East Berlin smell, a compound of the smoke from old-fashioned domestic boilers burning compressed coal-dust briquettes, exhaust fumes from the two-stroke engines of the little Trabant cars, cheap East European cigarettes, damp boots and sweat. But one thing I simply can't remember: who was she, my little red riding-hood? Or not so little: 1.75 — 1.78 metres, nearly my height. Slim, medium blonde, curly hair, 30—35, black boots? I sit there, under Frau Schulz's inquisitive eye, sensing an awful disloyalty to my own past.

12 Berlin Hype, Globalization and the Role of History
2000 -

Burned down, played in front of by everyone from David Bowie to Phil Collins, and now both a functioning parliament and a tourist attraction courtesy of Norman Foster: the Reichstag.

GERMANY ENTERED THE NEW millennium in better geopolitical shape than it has ever been. For the first time in European history, there is a country called Germany with no breakaway regions or disputed peripheries which is surrounded entirely by friendly neighbours: with the exception of neutral Switzerland and Austria, all of the countries with which it shares a land border are members of the same military alliance, NATO; all of its neighbours (again excepting Switzerland) are in the European Union.

This simple fact explains why Germany is still one of the most pro-European countries in the EU. It is noteworthy that, despite the mind-boggling sums of money the Germans have had to throw at the Eurozone since the 2008 financial crisis, Germany remains the only major European country without a far-right anti-European protest party to speak of. Since the Second World War, the Federal Republic worked at buying itself a peaceful international neighbourhood full of good customers for its exported goods, and its citizens seem by and large ready to keep shelling out for this comparatively advantageous situation.

With little serious disagreement on the foreign policy front, the debate in Germany has turned increasingly inwards in recent years. The electorate is split down the middle. There are those who see the key to the country's postwar success as change-averse, consensus-orientated conservatism, preferably with a seemingly uncharismatic moderator who keeps ugly machinations behind the scenes and governs for long enough to become a national treasure. Adenauer (1949-1963) and Kohl (1982-1998), both from the CDU, played this role to perfection, and Angela Merkel (2005-) is following in this "safe pair of hands" tradition with bravura.

The other half of the electorate is one of the most radical in Europe, and when it does occasionally gain the upper hand, it has a tendency to vote for iconoclastic alpha males on the left of the political spectrum: Willy Brandt (1969-1974) was the first example, and Germany saw in the year 2000 with the brusque, bustling social democrat Gerhard Schröder (1998-2005) in charge of the first national government coalition in the world with a Green party element. The Federal Republic today is largely the result of his administration: even if measures such as rationalisation of unemployment benefit and the decision to abandon nuclear power were polarizing and unpopular ten years ago, they have now become part of the consensus conservative voters have elected Merkel to curate – as her volte-face following Fukushima showed when, having just decided to reinstate nuclear power, public opinion forced her to re-abandon it. Like a duck gliding across the

European lake, Germany's political legs paddle rapidly below the waterline to produce a generally stable economy and society.

If the 1990s saw comparatively little by way of writing about or literature set in Germany, the period following 2000 has quickly compensated for this. With a well-preserved welfare state and strong economy, an open and no-holds-barred approach to cultural barriers, and its capital Berlin open for business – and yet scarred enough by its past to offer attractive rents for Bohemians – Germany in the new millennium has once again became a destination of choice for many writers. Convincingly democratized, attractively civilized, and cushioned by wealth, life in a country called Germany has never been as free and pleasant as it is now, and yet the proximity of its dark (but literarily exciting) history means that there is no shortage of subject matter. In short, Germany today is a promised land for writers.

A promised land, and a big one, offering a variety of places, themes, and times. Writing about Germany since 2000 has become very diverse, ranging from typically light "Englishman abroad" or "American in Europe" romps to historical genre fiction, or from popular history to literary novels: much of the best writing today borrows liberally from all of these categories. An interesting trend, too, is the proliferation of new voices writing about Germany, especially from North America, opening up unexpected parts of its history.

Academics, Journalists, Authors

In 2003, Robert Ford (b. 1975) produced a typical example of the new literary, historical novel about Germany. Set just before the reunification, *Rhapsody* (US: *The Student Conductor*) follows the fortunes of a young American arriving in Karlsruhe to be taught conducting by an old maestro. It also uses the freedom of its student protagonist to roam around the old West Germany and includes an enthralling border crossing just after the reunification and a brief view of an East Germany already melting away. By working with music, the book nevertheless often goes back beyond the usual aspects of modern German history into a more timeless cultural space.

Another modern-historical literary novel from 2003 featuring Americans abroad is James Carroll's (b. 1943) *Secret Father*. Set in early 1961 and told from the perspective both of an expatriate bank manager and his son enrolled at the American military school in Wiesbaden, this novel takes a detailed look at the American presence in southern Germany and interaction with the local population. There is a daring journey to Berlin just before the wall goes up and a frantic search for missing children carrying missing documents in typical Cold War thriller style. As a decidedly literary novel, however, Carroll's text plays with other genres while remaining itself strangely elusive, as the extract below shows.

The year 2004 saw two excellent books on Germany written by East Coast academics. Steven Ozment's (b. 1939) history *A Mighty Fortress*, takes an important step forward in its treatment of the German people, allowing the author to look back at Germany before it was named so, and before the unpleasant associations still widespread in the Anglo-American world could even start to develop. Ozment reframes the static, circular, sometimes infuriating historical and popular debate about Germany and its guilt, rather than entering into it on its own terms.

In *The Bells and Their Silence,* Michael Gorra (b. 1957) too is trying to break out of the restricting emphasis on Germany's modern crimes, and also goes far back into the country's medieval history to do so. As a personal account, half travel writing and half essay, Gorra's work documents his own efforts to reach a fresh perspective; it is a piece of writing on Germany about the very act of writing on Germany. It asks what can be written about Germany in the light of its history, and how, questions to which several answers are given in the years following.

The Times correspondent Roger Boyes (b. 1952), for example, produces a light-hearted travel account of the popular kind, treating Germany to a large extent just like any other country in which a typically jokey, self-ironic, knowingly clueless British writer may find himself. His *A Year in the Scheisse* of 2006 is uncompromisingly modelled on *A Year in the Merde*, a wildly successful account by an Englishman living in France, which picks up and plays with the usual Gallic clichés. Boyes applies the model to Germany, making him as fearless as he is generous about tackling taboos in German history.

In a similarly fearless, fun and decidedly male-oriented vein is Ben Donald's *Springtime for Germany* (2007). Nevertheless, it finds itself repeatedly tackling the cultural detritus of the twentieth-century British-German animosity, and some readers find it difficult to tell to what extent Donald is making fun of jingoistic British attitudes or himself falling victim to them—despite the preface in which he explicitly sets out to sell Germany just like any other destination. Whatever the tone, Donald is certainly the first in a wave of recent non-academic British Germanophiles who distinguish themselves by their research into German customs and traditions, having been followed by Simon Winder (*Germania*, 2010) and Peter Watson (*The German Genius,* 2011) onto the British book market – and feeding and fanning the rekindling interest in Germany there. Most recently, Guardian journalist Philip Oltermann, born near Hamburg and resident in the UK since the age of 16, has contributed his cross-cultural perspective by charting Anglo-German encounters in *Keeping up with the Germans* (2012), a thoroughly knowledgeable and entertaining read.

American novelist Anna Winger (b. 1970) finds an entirely different way of getting round the difficulties of writing in the wake of German history. Although very aware of the history of its setting, Berlin, and of modern German culture, her 2008 novel *This Must Be the Place* is essentially just that: a novel. Rather than pushing the fact that it is set in Germany into the foreground, Winger presents us with an engaging story and skilfully weaves in the peculiarities, difficulties and fascination of Germany as a setting into its fabric.

With his genre-fiction series, Philip Kerr (b. 1956) spent the early 1990s founding a the specific literary form known as "Berlin Noir". His 2008 instalment in this long-running crime novel series, *A Quiet Flame,* shows the continued success of his approach, which is to tackle all of Germany's darkest hours at once—the Weimar Republic, the rise of the Nazis and the Cold War—from the perspective of a likeable German hero: "I think something happened to Germany after the Great War. You could see it on the streets of Berlin. A callous indifference to human suffering. And, perhaps, after all those demented, sometimes cannibalistic killers we had during the Weimar Years, we ought to have seen it coming." Conversely, by focusing on appalling crime at an individual level, Kerr finds a way of dealing with crime on a national, historical scale. The true star of Kerr's detective series, though, is not the unswervingly anti-Nazi protagonist Bernie Gunther, but Berlin itself.

As it is for Ingrid Anders, whose 2009 look at international student life in Berlin pays as much homage to the relaxed, liberal city of today as Kerr's books to its anything-goes Weimar predecessor. Anders' book is significant because it is the first literary document of something that is set to become a defining experience of a whole generation of young university students across the world: a semester abroad in Berlin. She tells this story—with all of its predictable and less predictable pitfalls—with quirky verve and is clearly writing for a young market in the know.

Germany's renewed attractiveness as a destination, especially for artists, authors and academics, has been drawing in more and more people from abroad, especially to Berlin, which has an expatriate writers' scene comparable in number to the 1920s. Esi Edugyan, born in Canada of Ghanaian parents, has recently spent time in Germany on a fellowship, and returns in spirit to that older international Berlin in the company of a forgotten element of those years: African-American jazz musicians. In his 2011 *Half Blood Blues*, Edugyan has her protagonist, an old Baltimore "gate", return to Berlin today while telling the story of his time there in the 1920s and 1930s. It is an ambitious, fascinating look at a well-known piece of history from a very unique perspective, and is as such a telling example of what new writing about Germany is becoming today.

*

Robert Ford, *Rhapsody*

Barrow woke to the hard yank of an oncoming train and caught the whisper of the last orange car as it passed. Outside, the German sun flung itself in all directions, glanced from the rails, perfected clouds. It was the kind of day they polish steel for.

An elderly woman sat across from him in the compartment—gray hair, black raincoat, and striking blue eyes. "Pretty sun," he said in German. *Schöne Sonne.*
"Ja."

Her eyes did not leave the empty headrest to his left.

He tried giving himself over to the clip of passing utility poles, their near-rhyme. The intervals were not quite fixed, which only fed his anxiety.

He glanced back at the old woman. "One sees the Rhine on this trip?" he asked, still in German.

"Where are you going?"

"Karlsruhe."

"No."

She turned to stare out the window. He noticed the severity with which her hair had been clawed back into a bun, the particular gray of her skirt. She could be a nun. He considered her profile, pictured her as a little girl—and older, at the age of her decision, her commitment or whatever they call it, standing before the altar at the head of a long line of other girls, her blue eyes angled down so as not to astonish the priest.

He wandered between awake and stupid, the kind of stupid induced by trains. Farm fields chased by his window, some harvested and trailing smoke, fires running lengthwise in banked rows—he'd read somewhere that ash was good for the soil.

Inches from his cheek, the safety glass was warm from the sun. When the conductor announced the Karlsruhe station, he was half asleep.

Another spark from the intercom—*Nächste Station Karlsruhe Haupt bahnhof.*

He was on his feet, pulling down bags. The nun's murmured "Good luck" surprised him, and he muttered something back. In the station he pondered food, but his stomach rejected the idea. He found a locker for the larger of his two bags, bought an English-language newspaper and a map, and worked out a walking route to the Karlsruhe Festplatz.

A wide boulevard called Ettlinger Strasse led to the heart of the city, and he strode its tree-lined sidewalk, working his calves to muscle out the excess adrenaline. Tram tracks split the broad avenue, and he sought distraction in the geometry of the electric lines slung overhead, the quiet shim of passing streetcars. The Festplatz came up. He checked his watch and walked for another three blocks, doubled back, and dropped to a bench by a circle of fountains surrounded by flowers bright as lemons. He surveyed the brick-paved acreage, followed the lazy progression of a two-baby family attired for a stroll through the city zoo.

It was his accursed gift to know that his heart rate was just over 116 beats per minute. He stared into the fountain and closed his eyes, thinking to lose himself in the steady smack of water on water—the consolation of pure noise—but it didn't work.

It was too early, but he got up, adjusted his pack and headed for the massive limestone building that held down the far corner of the square. The Konzerthaus. Wrecked by war, and now, forty-something years later, back on its feet. A verandah of trees hid the rear quarter of the building, where Barrow had been assured over the phone—a brief word with the people at the music school, the Badische Hochschule für Musik—that he'd find a certain door unlocked. It was unusual, they had said, but the maestro liked to audition his pupils in the concert hall.

James Carroll, *Secret Father*

The Russian Chapel was visible from everywhere in the Rhine River valley. A sepulchral shrine with three golden onion domes, it sat on top of a small mountain on the eastern edge of the city. A local duke had it built a hundred years before, in memory of his wife, a niece of the czar, after she died giving birth to her first child. I had seen the chapel only from a distance, but I needed no taxi driver to tell me where it was. I'd had it pointed out on practically every visit to Wiesbaden. None of my host ever seemed to know if the child, whether boy or girl, had lived or died.

The surprise in actually visiting the chapel was to find that it stood with its back to the view. In the valley I had been admiring from behind. A small Orthodox church, the entrance faced a gravel circle that was ringed, in turn, by an oval grove of birch trees, the tops of which fell short of the troika domes. The life-size veiled head of a woman, carved in stone, stared blankly out from the meter-wide medallion above the portal. More than inert, she seemed vividly dead.

I pulled the heavy door open and stepped inside. While my sense of sight failed at once, my sense of smell came alive. The pungent odors of stale incense, candle wax, dust, and perhaps the leavings of small animals all combined to evoke an airless musk of religion. What I took to be a sanctuary lamp burned above me, but then I realized the red glow was from the glass of a rose window strategically placed to illuminate the otherwise dark reaches of a very high ceiling.

As my eyes adjusted, I saw what a cramped space it was: an altar, a grilled screen before it, a half-dozen pews, and on the wall to the right below the rose window, a gilt-framed icon whose face I could not make out.

A rack of squat, mostly burned-out candle stubs stood before the icon. Altogether, the shrine might not have been entered in the century since its princess died, and suddenly it seemed more mausoleum than church. I backed out, feeling like a profaning interloper.

Aare of the crunch of my shoes on gravel, I circled around the building to the small fenced plaza behind. I took in the vista of the city spread below, the needle spire of Wiesbaden's Lutheran churches, the brick tower of the Rathaus, the town hall. A line of haze hung over the Rhine, an otherwise invisible river perhaps five miles distant. From that direction – ultimately, from the North Atlantic – storm clouds marched steadily overhead, having overrun the sun again, I took the driving wind squarely in my face, the way a deck officer does.

I studied the view as a way to avoid looking at my watch. The taxi had dropped me at the bottom of a curving gravel road that marked the limit of the secluded site. Odd that the chapel should be so visible across the province yet so isolated. A Saturday morning, but there were no other visitors. The it hit me that Mrs. Healy would have known that.

Not for the first time, I wondered what Gerhard would be making of my having vanished. A decade or two later, expatriate American executives holding positions like mine would be at risk for kidnapping, even in Europe, but not then, when we Yanks were still unvanquished. I knew that before calling the police at my disappearance, Gerhard would call Butterfield, my assistant, back in Frankfurt. So from Hainerberg, I had called Butterfield first, and told him to have Gerhard wait for me at the station.

And I, precisely what was I making of the melodrama into which I had been conscripted? I had never been a man for mystery novels or spy thrillers, and if you had told me that I would take seriously a warning of being followed, whispered by a woman with an accent, I would have laughed at you. But that ways before mystery had come to define my life, the mystery of what Michael was becoming, the mystery of what Edie's absence had done to both of us. (...)

Shacks and tumbledown huts in the shadows of dusk one moment, a bejeweled early-evening skyline the next: to come out of the postwar wasteland of Soviet Germany into the frantic brilliance of West Berlin was to cross a line on the earth. To see that demarcation of the world-historic argument was to glimpse the trench into which each side was poised to plunge. Of such instants is the structure of a mind made, and after that I was a sucker for dualism, if in nothing but politics.

But here is the odd thing: I arrived in West Berlin, with its propped opulence, prepared to see it as I'd been told to, as a showcase of freedom. Berlin was the urban proof text of free enterprise. *From each according to his ability, to each according to what he can grab.* It is not as if I did not link arms with Kit and Ulrich, our triune phalanx advancing on the train platform in an exuberant spirit of American arrival, the exhibitionism of the entitled young. But the human tide against which we pushed back, forcing us out of our little bubble to see – really *see.*

All around us was the bustle of far more complex comings and goings. The train station was the terminus of major supply routes for the island city. Raw materials were offloaded in the yards outside, but here along each platform, and on the broad terrace into which each platform ran, were stacked hundreds of pallets holding cartons, bundles, and mailbags. Moving among all that were throngs of travelers, not giddy like us but grim-faced, eyes fixed, coursing to and from trains with the air of those for whom transit itself was the thing to survive. Greeters and senders-off clutched handkerchiefs, some weeping openly. Vendors stood at sawhorse benches and pushcarts selling wurst, newspapers, bottles of milk. Their customers included roughly dressed women and men mystified by the currency they held – a crowd that reeked, as one creature, of body odor. Later I would understand that many of these people had come down from the elevated train platform above, the S-Bahn line that ran from East Berlin to West Berlin, stopping first here at the *Hauptbahnhof.* These were refugees who, as fugitives, had just dared to step off the city train in this forbidden sector, part of the tide of thousands that the Wall would break in August.

The S-Bahn was the easiest way to flee the East, and if there were grave expressions on the faces of certain of the men and women around us, it was not for the danger they were in, but for the sure jeopardy into which they had just plunged their relatives at home. For those left behind, there would be loss of jobs, loss of housing, possible arrest, or banishment to the distant countryside near Poland. In that time and place, the supremely selfish act was defection.

Others of those around us were arrivals from the West, disembarking trains that had come from Hamburg and Munich and Düsseldorf. These were the young men looking for draft exemptions and training slots at Telefunken and Siemens, industrial giants that had made West Berlin the electronics center of Europe. They were girls coming for the artificially high-salaried jobs in hotels and offices. They were continental beatniks coming for the jazz clubs and cafés. And that evening, they were young Social Democrats coming for the May Day celebrations that would take place the next day on both sides of the city. All had come, in one way or another and however gravely, of what in America we thought of as the thrill of the frontier. Us too.

GERMANY: BEYOND THE ENCHANTED FOREST

Steven Ozment, *A Mighty Fortress: A New History of the German People*

Over much of the postwar period, any general discussion of Germany has begun and ended with Hitler and the Nazi seizure of power in 1933. More recently new generations of historians have replaced the role of great men with those of greater structural forces (industrialization, economics, domestic politics), now telling a longer and more complex German story. Also mirroring this historiographical shift is a new generation of German political leaders determined to project their nation as one among others acting in tandem with the great powers of Europe and the world. The result, both historically and in the present, is the promised emergence of a normal Germany.

Despite this more optimistic direction, the legacy of the 1930s and 1940s has proved impossible to shake, its inexplicability, pain and fascination still stopping people in the tracks, so that the history of Germany remains by and large that Nazis and Jews. Even today a tour of German history can be a circular journey around a magnetic Nazi pole, mesmerizing the general public and distracting historians and politicians eager to move on. This enduring perspective has also turned Germany's pre-twentieth-century past into a hunting ground for fascist forerunners and defeated democratic alternatives to the absolute territorial state.

Not surprisingly, then, there is popular opinion, even within Germany, which appears to believe that Germans have always been cryptofascists, if only the surface of their history is scratched deeply enough. To that false impression both academic historians and the media contribute, first by continuing to treat the two centuries between Prussia's rise to power and the defeat of the Third Reich as the history of Germany, and second, by reading that history backwards from the Nazi seizure of power in 1933. In the United States, the History Channel is popularly known as the "Hitler Channel," so often are *der Führer* and the Third Reich the subjects of its programming, and not a few Americans still unthinkingly interchange Nazis and Germans. Among biographies of historical figures, Adolf Hitler still holds a lock on the most copies in print.

The study of Germany today places one at the crossroads of two contradictory approaches, each looking for precursors and precedents that brought Germany to its twentieth-century pass. The first, older and waning, searches German history for shadows extending to the Third Reich and finds abnormality at seemingly every turn. The other looks instead for the dawning lights of the postwar German Federal Republic of 1949, pointing to numerous precedents and signs in the German past and present. Neither approach, however, has shown much interest in a deep German past before the modern age, to which older generations, academic and non-, had more trustingly turned for clues.

Some historians even caricature the effort to examine modern Germany from the perspective of the distant past, calling it the "Tacitus hypothesis". By that is meant a misguided belief that one can properly know a part of German history only as one knows the whole of it – in this case going all the way back to the first historian of Germany, the Roman Cornelius Tacitus, who lived from A.D. 55 to 120.

(…)

Over most of their history Germany have embraced ideals of order and authority without totalitarianism, and pursued freedom and equality without democracy. The German difference from the American, British and French models of society and politics does not lie in any German rejection of individual freedom in favor of absolute, or totalitarian, rule. Historical experience has instead left Germans more fearful of anarchy than of tyranny, inclining them to hedge, if hedge they must, on the side of good order. This they have done in a compelling belief that it is not freedom, once attained, but discipline, carefully maintained, that keeps a people free.

For Germans the Weimar Republic and National Socialism were novel twentieth-century experiments, not familiar historic lifestyles. Emerging from the failure of its first democratic government, whose lifespan was a mere fourteen years, 1919-33, Germany's first totalitarian government endured for only twelve, 1933-45. While historians see parallels to the former in the revolution of 1848-49, and to the latter in Wilhelmine Germany, modern Germany's most prominent feature remains the novelty of democracy and totalitarianism in its historical experience.

Michael Gorra, *The Bells in Their Silence: Travels Through Germany*

If in travelling we are to (…) think of a country in terms of those things that mark it out from other, then Germany's most easily discernible distinguishing features assume the shape not of architecture or cuisine or manners but of history. The metonymy with which it is still most surely identified is that of the Third Reich.

Whether after more than fifty years of the *Bundesrepublik* and NATO and the *Wirtschaftswunder*, after the European Union and the Wall and Willy Brandt and the Greens and the *Wende*; whether now that we all use German-made countertop coffee machines and wish that we could afford to drive German cars – whether that's *fair* is, of course, a different question. But it's also moot; I suspect that such a metonymy will hold for as long as any of us have a living memory of those for whom the war was a living memory. It is surely a superficial judgement, and as with Leigh Fermor it may not – I hope it does not – affect our, my, relations with individual men and women. Still, there it is, and that peculiarity presents the traveler with a curious problem. It ought in one sense to be simple to write about Germany. In a country where the young and well-educated often use the adjective "German" pejoratively, one can have an easy conscience in drawing on national stereotypes, the travel writer's old and now discredited stock-in-trade. Yet in another sense it's very hard.

(...)

I find Hamburg as attractive and easy a city to live in as any I know, and I have been as happy sitting in its cafés and walking along its streets as I have been at any point in my life. But there seems to me something risible, even something scandalous, in that sentence as I write it. For what role should we give to pleasure here? Or to put it another way, can one write about Germany without also writing about, concentrating on, and worrying away at The German Problem?

(...)

In an earlier age, what was perhaps most peculiar about Germany was its maze of local exceptions to a rule so vague it could hardly be called general. Most of the people living within the borders of the nation-state that Bismarck put together in 1871 would not, as the historian Michael Stürmer argues, "have described themselves... as Germans but... Bavarians, Prussians, Badeners," a diversity rooted in the differences of "bread and beer, in custom, language, and the local law." And, of course, Hamburg had – has – its own peculiarities. It is an Anglophiliac port city, where even now people speak English with a British accent; Bavarians tend, in contrast, to have an American one. Though it lies eighty miles up the Elbe, it turns out toward the Atlantic, rather than in upon Germany itself, and has always taken pride in its openness to the world outside; so open, in fact, that to many nineteenth-century observers it hardly seemed a part of Germany at all.

Stürmer writes that the Hamburger – the name itself offers a spurious provenance for American fast food – would instead identify himself as "*Hanseaten*", referring to the medieval glories not only of Frankfurt and Cologne but also to Riga, Amsterdam and that provincial capital called Berlin. Such self-descriptions, he adds, "always had an undertone, and still have, setting those using them apart from the German nation at large." You claim a regional identity as a way of dodging a national one,[1] and in the early nineteenth century the memory of the Hanseatic League was revived as a mercantile alternative to other

---

[1] Many surveys in recent years have shown that a large minority of Germans, when asked with which geographical and geopolitical entities they most identify, will answer first with their hometown, home region or state, then with Europe—and finally with Germany. A brief tot-up of the flags German homeowners or allotment-holders fly is more than enough to confirm these results. The only occasions on which large numbers of German flags and flag-merchandise can be seen are at international sporting events, especially football tournaments.

forms of German unification, an assertion of North German independence in the face of Prussia's ever-increasing territory. Some commercial treaties still obtained between the independent city-states of Hamburg, Lübeck, and Bremen, and so they set to work inventing tradition, referring to themselves once more as the "Hanseatic towns", and managed to keep a measure of autonomy even after they signed on with Bismarck's Germany. Hamburg still maintained a Berlin embassy in 1902, and even now newspapers will use "Hansestadt" as a synonym for the city itself, and without the sense of slang with which an American tabloid mentions Beantown or Gotham.

(…)

For if the rhetoric of Germany appears to discourage some kinds of writing, it seems to encourage others. One writes with (or perhaps against) the belief that one must somehow "cover" the country: must go East to report on the internal borders that belie the absence of other boundaries, must worry about immigration and unemployment and their effect on the local elections. About everything, in short, that Germans do themselves.

Most Anglo-Americans manage, in contrast, to treat Italy's internal problems as a form of local color: corruption and incompetence and even the Mafia can still be made to seem charming. But a discussion of Germany's national vices leads somewhere else, and insofar as its history makes you think that its problems are yours as well, the country effectively elides the distinction between the traveler and the native, as though its *Sonderweg* were universal after all. (…) Yet (…) as I confess my interest in what, at times, Germany doesn't make me think or feel, I have to acknowledge that I've been caught once again by the peculiarities of its past.

Roger Boyes, *A Year in the Scheisse*

My relationship with Frau Beckenbender – that is, her role as an informal tutor in all matters German – was based largely on food and its memories. We would sit round her table in Hamburg, an Anglophile city that had been bombed flat by British pilots like my father. The language books would be open and from the stove would come the smell of potato soup. Whatever text we studied, Frau Beckenbender would return to the subject of the war. It seemed quite normal to me: the generations of my parents and my grandparents were in constant time-travel, commuting to a past that was more vivid and more real. Sometimes, I thought: war is their drug. It wrecked them physically and mentally but they became hooked on the fear, the intensity of life, the making-do, the warmth. The short-term. For Frau Beckenbender, teaching German to an Englishman was not so much about language, or even culture, but about therapy, about surviving in the absence of a father, about a life centred on the kitchen rather than the living room or the bedroom. I had come to understand her when we had a lesson on cooking vocabulary. Her brown eyes lit up when she described the sixteen dishes that could be made out of potatoes. Suddenly I remembered that my family too had grown up with the memory, real or inherited, of meals based on potatoes, on Swedes and turnips. They were war vegetables and to eat them was a patriotic duty. Great Aunt Mabel would sing to me as a child:

Potatoes new, potatoes old
Potato (in a salad) cold
Potatoes baked or mashed or fried
Potatoes whole, potatoes pied
Enjoy them all, including chips
Remember spuds don't come in ships!

Potatoes were home grown. Neither England nor Germany needed to import them. For the English, potatoes were an act of resistance, they made us less vulnerable to Hitler and U-boats, which were attacking the food convoys over the Atlantic. For the Germans, potatoes grown in scruffy allotments were an act of independence from rationing Nazis and blockading Russians.

'Seventeen,' I told Frau Beckenbender, remembering a recipe from Great Aunt Mabel for potato fingers. 'You make some mashed potato, add flour, shape them like fingers and put them in an oven.'

'Eighteen,' retorted Frau Beckenbender and gave me the recipe for potato pastry.

Our potato ping-pong continued over the years. By the time I had finished my studies we had reached eighty-nine potato recipes. Now that I was back in Germany, this time as a correspondent, I felt it was time to take our relationship to another level: cabbage. So, no instant potatoes. I had somehow to re-invent burned cabbage as an edible alternative. And time was running out. I wrenched open the fridge: there was some ancient low-fat cream, a jar of capers, a few rashers of bacon and a bottle of chilli. I t would just have to do. The bacon was thrown into a pan and deep-fried while I used an old toothbrush to paint the cream on the black bits of the cabbage. The capers were scattered round, the crispy bacon sliced and mixed into the cabbage and three drops of chilli covered up more fire-damage. If in doubt, says one of England's top and relentlessly optimistic chefs, add colour. The doorbell rang and I took one last look at the dish. It was certainly colourful, but then so were car accidents.

Frau Beckenbender stood beaming at the threshold. Her bird-like figure was dwarfed by a huge swollen marrow. 'I thought it was time to move on from our potato obsession,' she said, 'and I have dozens of marrow recipes. But then I caught the smell of cabbage in the courtyard and I know you had the same idea.'

I took the marrow. 'Thank you. Yum-yum. Though I like flowers too you know, Frau Beckenbender. I'm not short of food. Rationing ended a while ago. You can buy all sorts of things in the shops nowadays.'

'You're teasing me.'

'No, really, rationing is over.'

'Rationing is never over,' she said, with a sudden Hanseatic gloom. 'Life is rationing.'

'Well, you can eat as much cabbage as you like today,' I said, quietly admiring my own nerve, 'I've conjured up something very special for you.'

Frau Beckenbender's crinkled face lit up. She handed me her coat and immediately sat down at the kitchen table. 'Cabbage is my favourite.' I believed her because she was in love with same memory of poverty and deprivation that the rest of my apartment block hated. It was a typical tenement in Berlin's Prenzlauer Berg district, built for workers in the early twentieth century, bombed, refurbished, but still essentially a place for people who counted their money carefully at the end of the month. The neighbours included a car dealer who spent long hours in the solarium, a female teacher who was having an affair with a sixteen-year-old pupil, a Serb who wore false beards (Fridays: black specked with grey; Thursdays: red and bushy) whenever he went to the supermarket for fear of being caught by investigators from the International War Crimes Tribunal. Average Berlin. What they had in common was a distaste for cabbage: it was the smell of social decline. There was no other incident in the daily rhythm of the house that aroused so much collective anger: not the incontinent terrier, not the drunk who rang the doorbells after midnight. Cabbage, however, was a cause for official complaint. The concierge would knock on the door, clear his throat and put in a formal request to open the windows or deodorise the corridor or to stop cooking and eat somewhere else. On one occasion he brought me a voucher for a McDonald's Maxi Meal, sponsored by my neighbours.

Ben Donald, *Springtime for Germany*

And what about the women? I had in my mind huge, slightly hirsute, buxom waitresses of indeterminate sex, looking mostly like eastern European weightlifters and dressed in lace-fringed gingham tablecloths, their considerable embonpoint to the fore and used for parting the crowds. What girl would wear a *Dirndl* – the word means both the costume and a girl in Bavaria by choice? Surely it could not be made to look flattering or sexy? Well, clearly these things were a matter of personal taste. But, looking more closely at Munich's young wenches dressed in their traditional finery, I saw I had been wrong. The lace and check patterns had a childishness that on the adult female form oozed a naughty, Heidi-like innocence, especially given the plunging neckline and trussed-up chest *à la Liaisons Dangereuses*. The European Union, that great leveller and arbiter of fun and good taste, had in 2004 threatened to make excessively décolleté necklines illegal at the Oktoberfest. Munich's mayor was so outraged he is reported to have said, 'A waitress is no longer allowed to wander around a Biergarten with a plunging neckline? I would not enter a Biergarten under these conditions.' Like the mayor I was now convinced the *Dirndl* was in fact made for frolicking. The more ties there were to pull, the sexier. In our flesh-obsessed age – and no more so than on the Baltic coast – I sensed that previous, more conservative eras had a better understanding of the power of suggestion. A thought that was no doubt anathema to members of FKK Jugend!

So, was I becoming a *Lederhosen* convert, or just a fetishist?

All in context, of course. You wouldn't want to be seen dead in *Lederhosen* outside the Oktoberfest. For this latest generation of partying Münchners, *Lederhosen* were just a party uniform. And this had rubbed off on international visitors. While there were plenty of boring party-poopers in normal clothes, a huge majority of non-German party-goers treated the Oktoberfest as an excuse to dress up in one form of national costume or another.

Ubiquitous among these was the kilt, which, it occurred to me, is the British equivalent of *Lederhosen*: faintly ridiculous, outmoded and full of sexual connotation, pointlessly patriotic and so displayed with great pride by natives, but much parodied or worn as mocking fancy dress by the rest. Standing next to me was a case in point: a group of five fat blokes dressed in those identical one-clan-fits-all tartan kilts you can buy on Oxford Street. On the front of their boys-on-tour T-shirts they had printed, 'Bangor Gynaecology Hospital – Oktoberfest 2005' and on the back, 'Jesus loves you – the rest of us think you're a twat'.

But there were more erudite takes on national dress. I saw several groups of English people dressed up like toffs out for a day's fly-fishing or grouse-shooting: plus fours, yards of tweed, Sherlock Holmes cap and the same hues of brown and murky green. On the first sight I was inclined to agree with the boys from Bangor. But on reflection I found their attire to be quite a good judgement of equivalent sartorial cultures. Like tweed plus-fours and their associated jackets and hats, *Lederhosen*, I knew, have their origins in hunting and country pursuits. If anything, this was proof of a link, not a difference, between Germany and Britain. I thought of those market towns in England with their timeless sporting shops, 4x4s parked outside, that sell Barbour gear, Pringle jumpers, check tweed and unspeakable red corduroy trousers better suited for reading the property section of the *Sunday Times*. The clothes were always window-dressed with the veneer of guns, fishing rods and a plethora of other sporting accessories equally unlikely to ever be purchased. This nostalgia for a more rural and noble hunting past seemed to be common to both countries.

Apparently, no evidence can be found that Bavarians wore *Lederhosen* any earlier than the late eighteenth century. So their invention seemed to me more the fruit of Romantic nation building.

Anna Winger, *This Must Be the Place*

"It's hard to imagine anything bad ever happening here."

"Because bad things don't happen to rich people?"

"Maybe. Maybe because I can't imagine that anyone even lived here before me. I know this is an old apartment, but the walls are so white and perfect. It seems completely new."

"Americans are the greatest customers in the world. You're so easily sold."

He had been facing her, standing in the middle of the room, and now he walked to the nearest wall by the window and ran his hand over it as if feeling for the latch of a secret door.

"What are you doing?"

She took a step toward him. His finger moved vertically and then across the wall from side to side, as if drawing boxes on the plaster.

"I'm just trying to prove a point. Come here."

His finger was pink and slim, the nail bitten ragged. At the point in the wall where it rested was a nearly invisible seam, where one sheet of paper appeared to have been glued against another. The seam ran from the ceiling to the floor.

"White *Raufasertapete*," said Orson. "It means rough, textured wallpaper. It's a special German invention. Looks like plaster at a distance. It's a faster and much cheaper way to cover things up."

"Is it all over my apartment?"

"Of course. It's all over the walls of every apartment in Berlin. When one tenant leaves, the owner just wallpapers over his mistakes and starts again with the next one. Check this out."

With what was left of the nail on his finger, he picked at the seam until he was able to lift the edge, then quickly pulled away a chunk of it about the size of a quarter to reveal a glimpse of bright orange wallpaper underneath it.

"What is that?"

"The good taste of the people who lived here before you did, obviously."

"They left up the old wallpaper?"

"God knows how many layers there are underneath. That's my point."

"That's disgusting."

Up close, it smelled of old smoke, she thought. She could practically hear it exhaling through the hole in the white top layer. Long, sour breaths held in for years. Then she realized it was Orson she smelled. His arm was almost touching hers, as if they were trapped together in a telephone booth at a bar. Did they still have telephone booths in bars, or anywhere else anymore? She stepped back trying to remember the last time she had actually been in a proper bar in any city.

"Don't worry, the crew can fix the hole when we're finished," said Orson. "Along with anything else we move around. We'll leave the place looking exactly as we found it."

When he turned to make a telephone call, Hope stared at the orange spot. From a few feet away it was hard to tell if it lay on top of the white wallpaper, like a stain, or was actually a hole, sucking the brightness of the room in toward it. But when she touched it, she could feel its depth against her fingers, and was struck by the sense of reaching through a portal, as if, when her finger pushed into the orange wallpaper, it might pull her hand with it, her arm, the rest of her. She looked up at the white wall, stretching to the ceiling, that only moments earlier had seemed flat and lifeless, but now rippled with the possibility of layers beneath it.

Philip Kerr, *A Quiet Flame*

We drove back to the Alex which, with its cupolas and arched entranceways, was as big as a railway station and, behind the four-storey brick façade, in the double-height entrance hall, very nearly as busy. All human life was in there. And quite a bit of pond life, too. There was a drunk with a black eye who was unsteadily awaiting being locked up for the night; a taxi driver making a complaint about a passenger who had run off without paying; an androgynous-looking young man wearing tight white shorts who was sitting quietly in a corner checking his make-up in a hand mirror; and a bespectacled man with a briefcase in his hands and a livid red mark across his mouth.

At the bunker-sized front desk we checked through a file containing a list of missing persons. The desk sergeant who was supposed to be assisting us had a big handlebar moustache and an eleven o'clock shadow that was so blue it made his face look like a house-fly's. This effect was enhanced because he eyes were bulging out of his head at the sight of the two tall boot girls a cop had shooed in off the street. They were wearing thigh-length, black leather boots and red leather coats which, thoughtfully, they had left undone, revealing to anyone who cared to look that they were wearing nothing underneath. One of them was carrying a riding crop that the arresting officer, a man with an eye patch – a man I knew, named Bruno Stahlecker – was having a hard job persuading her to give up. Clearly the girls had had a drink or two, and probably quite a bit else besides and while I flicked through the missing persons reports, half of me was listening to what Stahlecker and the girls were saying. It would have been hard not (to – sic) hear it.

"I like a man in uniform," said the taller of the leather-booted Amazons. She snapped her riding crop against her boot and then fingered the hair at the base of her belly, provocatively. "Which one of Berlin's bulls wants to be my slave tonight?"

Boot girls were the city's outdoor dominatrices. Mostly they worked west of Wittenberg Platz, near the Zoological Gardens, but Stahlecker had picked up this pair of whores in Freidrichstraße (sic) after a man had complained of being beaten and robbed by two women in leather.

"Behave yourself, Birgit," said Stahlecker. "Or I'll throw the rules of the medical profession at you as well." He turned to the man with the red mark on his face. "Are these the two women who robbed you?"

"Yes," said the man. "One of them hit me across the face with a whip and demanded money or she'd hit me again."

The girls loudly protested their innocence. Innocence never looked quite so venereal and corrupt.

Finally I found what I'd been looking for. "Anita Schwarz," I said, showing Heinrich Grund the missing persons report (…) But Grund was hardly paying attention. (…)

"I know that man," murmured Grund.

"Who? Schwarz?"

"No. That man there." Leaning back on the front desk he flicked his snout at the man with the whip mark on his face. "He's an Alphonse." An Alphonse was Berlin criminal underworld slang for a pimp. One of many slang words for a pimp, like Louie, Oiler, Stripe Man, Ludwig, and Garter Handler. "Runs on of those bogus clinics off the Kudamm. I think his racket is that he poses as a physician and then 'prescribes' an under-age girl for his so-called 'patient'." Grun called out to Stahlecker. "Hey, Bruno? What's the citizen's name? The one wearing spectacles and the extra smile."

"Him? Doctor Geise."

"Doctor Geise, my eggs. His real name is Koch, Hans-Theodor Koch and he's no more a doctor than I am. He's an Alphonse. A medicine man who fixes old perverts up with little girls."

The man stood up. "That's a damn lie," he said indignantly.

"Open his briefcase," said Grund. "See if I'm wrong."

Stahlecker looked at the man who held the briefcase tightly to his chest as if he really did have something to hide. "Well, sir? How about it?"

Reluctantly the man allowed Stahlecker to take the briefcase and then to open it. A few seconds later there was a pile of pornographic magazines lying on the desk sergeant's blotter. The magazine was called Figaro and on the cover of each copy was a picture of seven naked boys and girls, aged about ten or eleven, sitting in the branches of a dead tree, like a pride of small white lions.

"You old pervert," snarled one of the boot girls.

"This puts rather a different complexion on things, sir," Stahlecker told Koch.

"That is a naked culture magazine," insisted Koch. "Dedicated to the cause of free life reform. It doesn't prove anything of what this vile man has alleged."

"If it proves one thing," said the boot girl with the whip, "it proves you like looking at dirty pictures of little boys and girls."

We left them all in a heated argument.

"What did I tell you?" said Grund as we went back to the car. "This city is a whore and your beloved Republic is her pimp. When are you going to wake up to that fact, Bernie?"

Ingrid Anders, *Earth to Kat Vespucci*

The *Plattenbau* isn't nearly as ugly on the inside as it is on the outside.[2] The apartment consists of a long corridor with three bedrooms and a common kitchen and bathroom. The walls are painted a sterile white, and the furniture is all the same pastel blue. I walk into my room and set my luggage down on the bed. It feels odd to be given an actual apartment, with my own room all to myself. At Rutgers, I live in a miniscule dorm room with another student and share a communal bathroom with the whole floor.

I meander into the kitchen, which has a tiny refrigerator, half as high as a fridge in the States, and a stove, but no oven. The kitchen grants access to a concrete balcony. I walk out onto it and notice that I is identical to the concrete balconies of all the other apartments.

The view from the balcony is actually pretty good. The centerpiece is the *Berliner Fernsehturm*. It is an eye-catching, smokestack-like television tower, triple the height of any other building in view, with a blinking glass ball three-quarters of the way up, and a large, candy-striped, antenna on top. To me, it looks like a massive, psychedelic, hypodermic needle. It is also the only landmark in the Berlin skyline, making it the polar opposite of the New York skyline,

---

2 Plattenbau is the word for the trademark concrete-slab blocks of flats found in the old communist East. In Berlin this typical feature of the ex-GDR can be seen close to the centre: Frankfurter Allee is one of the most striking examples. In other eastern cities the Plattenbauten often form an imposing ring around the older core (Leipzig, Magdeburg).

in which hundreds of skyscrapers compete for attention. The simplicity of the Berlin skyline, with the TV tower floating above a vast expanse of human-sized buildings, makes me feel less intimidated by the city than I was this morning.

I actually know a thing or two about the TV tower from school. It built by the East German government during the Cold War as a "naa naa na-naa naa" to the West. When the city had been divided, the TV tower was one of the only structures in the East that could be seen over the Wall, and East Germans were proud of it. The only problem was that the panes of the glass ball, perched high atop the chimney-like stack, were arranged in such a way that when the sun shines on it, a glare appears in the shape of a cross. This was unacceptable to the East German government, who was trying to run an atheist country, and very acceptable to West Berliners, who chuckled and called it "the Pope's revenge." No amount of painting or scratching the surface of the TV tower on the part of the East German government would drive the ironic cross away, and the only saving grace for the Communist regime was that it is rarely sunny in Berlin.

The other thing I notice on this first look at Berlin from my balcony is directly below me, in what I guess would be considered the backyard of the *Plattenbau*. There is another factory, questionably defunct, which serves as a hub for several of the gangly green pipes that I noticed on the walk from the *S-Bahn*. Nine of these tubular serpents emerge from the side of the low, flat building and then slither out into the community to disperse their mysterious contents. I still cannot fathom a guess as to what could be inside these pipes. My imagination runs the gamut from radioactive waste to human fat, though I hope neither is the case.

The thought overwhelms me suddenly, and I notice that I have a pounding headache. The excitement of the day has made me forget that I am utterly and completely exhausted. I totter back in from the balcony, push my bags off of my bed, and collapse with a heavy frump. Ahh, sleep – the best thing that's happened to me all day.

Esi Edugyan, *Half-Blood Blues*

(…) The city's new hugeness shook me. It'd always been big, but not like *this* – the war opened great holes all those decades ago and I could see them even now. Green parks broke up the sea of cement, and so many concrete lots sat empty, all gone to weed. The streets looked wider than I remembered, too. As we passed the Berliner Dom, I got a vague itch all high up in my throat. My god. That vast pillared Renaissance church – it'd shrunk. Looked timid, apologetic, like a man brought down in the world.

Chip set one big grey hand on my seat and leaned forward as the cabbie turned up the broad avenue of Unter den Linden. 'You know where we are?' he said quietly.

A weird feeling rose up in me. Last I seen Unter den Linden, they torn out all them linden trees that gave the boulevard its name, tossed up white columns in their place, sanded the pavement so their damn jackboots wouldn't slip.

All that was gone like it ain't never been. I got a shock of recognition, of half-recognition, and heaven knows why but I recalled the night I seen my ma's body laid out in her coffin. As I leaned lower over her, her features seemed the same, arranged in familiar calm, but there was a trace of something not her, a watermark left by the undertaker. A whimsy to her lips maybe. As if in dying she'd learned a whole new kind of irony, a contempt for what she'd left behind.

'This ain't our Berlin, Sid,' said Chip.

(...)

The quiet just swallowed me up. It was like being cottoned by moss. Oh Berlin, our beautiful Berolina, our charcoal life. What a city this was, after that first war. And all of us poor, antsy, fetching to know what more life held. I been a latecomer, didn't hit these streets till '27, but man was she beautiful. Hundreds of gates flocked here, dragging their instruments. Hundreds of stage hens.

Every joint felt famous then. The Barberina. Moka Efti. The Scala. In the Romanisches Café, the great brains of the age gathered like grapes to trade ideas over beer. I saw Kästner there, and Tucholsky,[3] even Otto Dix. Dix maybe dreaming up some nightmares for his paintings, pausing over his glass as something new struck him. That famous one he did of Anita Berber, the dancer, her hair and dress red as torn flesh.

That Berber girl, hell. We used to flock to watch her dance at the White Mouse. She'd slither half-nude through the packed tables, bring her dance to a climax by breaking champagne bottles over fellows' heads. Broke one over Big Fritz's head, he ain't hardly noticed. I remember her working the Eldorado, too, that pansy club so dark you couldn't hardly see the stage. And all her flexing and shivering to the dry old tunes of Camille Saint-Saëns – man, did she ever bring it down.

In the craziest days, there was more than twenty cabarets. For real. Damn near every casting agent become a Colombus – new talent was everywhere to

---

3 Satirist, writer and journalist Kurt Tucholsky is a figure who, while little known even to German studies students abroad, has an exceptional stature in modern Germany. The left-wing activist is remembered today for his aphoristic, often ironic style (famous quotations include exhortations such as "Language is a weapon—make sure you keep it sharp" and satirical nuggets such as "Germans: buy German lemons!") and his commitment to fighting right-wing extremism. In 1930 he left for self-imposed exile in Sweden, inconsolably disappointed at the developments in Germany and (correctly, as it turned out) convinced that National Socialism would not be a simple flash in the political pan. He died of an overdose of sleeping pills in 1935.

discover. Marlene Dietrich at the The Two Cravats; Ursula Fuller at the Red Feather. Who'd have reckoned Fuller – so dainty, an angel on earth – would cut her chops in that lowdown joint? Cause The Feather, man, it left *nothing* to the imagination. We only ever been there once but I ain't never forget it.

Bibliography and Further Reading

The works cited are listed in the same order as they appear in the anthology. Where I have become aware that there are editions available online, either scanned or as text files, a link is provided (these are not necessarily the editions used; all links last accessed in September 2012).

Chapter 1

Pearsall Smith, Logan (ed.), *Sir Henry Wotton: Life and Letters* (vol. 1, Oxford: Clarendon, 1907) – p. 229-231, 233-234

Moryson, Fynes, *Fynes Moryson's Itinterary* [1617] (Glasgow: University Press, 1907) – p. 4-5

http://archive.org/details/fynesmorysons01moryuoft

Coryat, Thomas, *Coryat's Crudities* [1611] (London, 1776) – p. 345-346, 350-355

http://books.google.co.uk/books?id=2k5Liv-LrMkC&source=gbs_book_other_versions

Taylor, John, *Taylor his travels: From the City of London in England, to the Citty of Prague in Bohemia* (London, 1620) – p. 8-10, 15-17

Chapter 2

Graham, Walter (ed.), *The Letters of Joseph Addison* (Oxford: Clarendon, 1941) – p. 36-39 http://books.google.co.uk/books?id=lU4VAAAAYAAJ&dq=joseph%20addison%20letters%20stepney%201703&hl=de&pg=PR18#v=onepage&q&f=false

Wortley Montagu, Mary, *The letters of Lady Mary Wortley Montagu 1710-1718* (London, 1762) – p. 6-7

Creig, J. V. T. (ed.), *The Letters of David Hume* (vol. 1, Oxford: University Press, 1932) – p. 119-122, 125-126

http://books.google.co.uk/books?id=f-YghlmN108C&lpg=PP1&hl=de&pg=PP1#v=onepage&q&f=false

Danziger, Marlies K. (ed.), *James Boswell: The Journal of his German and Swiss Travels 1764* (New Haven: Yale University Press, 2008) – p. 14, 26-29, 34, 117-118

Kahrl, George M. & Little, M. (ed.), *The Letters of David Garrick* (vol. 2, London: Oxford University Press, 1963) – p. 422-425

Moore, John, *A View of Society and Manners in France, Switzerland and Germany (with Anecdotes relating to some Eminent Characters)* (vol. 1, 1780) – p. 100-103

Wraxall, Nathaniel, *Memoirs of the Courts of Berlin, Dresden, Warsaw, and Vienna, in the years 1777, 1778, and 1779* (vol. 1, 1799) – p. 94-103

Chapter 3

de Selincourt, Ernest, Rev. L. Shaver, Chester (ed.), *The Letters of William and Dorothy Wordsworth, The Early Years* – *1787-1805* (Oxford: Clarendon, 1967) – p. 220, 223-224, 229-230, 250-251, 254-255

Griggs, Earl Leslie (ed.), *Collected Letters of Samuel Taylor Coleridge volume 1* – *1785-1800* (Oxford: Clarendon, 1954) – 417-419, 431, 438-440

Morley, Edith J. (ed.), *Crabb Robinson in Germany 1800-1805* (London: J. M. Dent, 1929) p. 17-18, 19-20, 22-25

Bysshe Shelley, Percy, *History of a Six Weeks' Tour through a part of Switzerland, France, Germany, and Holland* (London, 1817) – p. 62-73

Wollstonecraft Shelley, Mary, *Frankenstein: or, The Modern Prometheus*, [1818] (1823, London) – p.104-106

Chapter 4

Meredith, William, *A Tour to the Rhine – with antiquarian and other notices* (London, 1825) p – 55-59, 73-75

Ray, Gordon N., *The Letters and Private Papers of W. M. Thackeray* (vol. 1, Cambridge: Harvard University Press, 1945-46) – p. 111-118, 57-59, 125-126

Bond Head, *Francis, Bubbles from the Brunnens of Nassau by an Old Man* (London, 1834) – p. 35-37, 57-59, 69-70

Morgan, Peter F., *The Letters of Thomas Hood* (Toronto: University Press, 1973) – p. 287-293

Hood, Thomas, *Up the Rhine, Second Part* [1840] (New York, 1857) – p. 3-10
http://books.google.com.au/
books?id=cGk4AAAAYAAJ&hl=de&pg=PR1#v=onepage&q&f=false

Chapple, J. A. V. & Pollard, Arthur, *The Letters of Mrs. Gaskell* [1966] (Manchester: University Press, 1997) – p. 40-44

Melville Metcalf, Eleanor, *Herman Melville: Journal of Visit to London and the Continent,1849-1850* (Cambridge: Harvard University Press, 1948) – p. 25-29

Haight, Gordon (ed.), *Letters of George Eliot* (vol. 2 New Haven & London: Yale University Press, 1954) – p. 184-186, 194-195

Chapter 5

Edel, Leon (ed.), *Letters of Henry James* (vol. 1 Cambrdige: Belknap Press of Harvard, 1974) – p.25,30-31, 296-297, 398-399, 457-460

Twain, Mark, *A Tramp Abroad* [1880] (Oxford: University Press, 1996) – p.28-31, 43-47

Stevens, Thomas, *Around the World on a Bicycle – Volume 1: From San Francisco to Teheran* (Cambridge, Mass., 1887) – p. 121-145
http://archive.org/details/aroundtheworldon05136gut

Bagby, Albert Morris, *Miss Träumerei: A Weimar Idyll* (New York, 1895) – p.7-12

Jerome, Jerome K., *Three Men on the Bummel*, [1900] (London: Penguin, 1994) – p. 90-94

Chapter 6
Lawrence, D. H., "The Prussian Officer", *The Prussian Officer and other stories* [1914] (London: Penguin, 1995) – p. 1-2, 11-12
Eliot, Valerie & Haughton, Hugh, Haffenden, John (ed.) *Letters of T. S. Eliot* [1988] (vol. 1, London: Faber and Faber, 1999) – p. 52-54
Princess Blücher, Evelyn, *An English Wife in Berlin* (London: Constable & Co, 1920) – p. 5-6, 11, 46-47, 253; 295-297
Madox Ford, Ford, *The Good Soldier* [1915] (London: Penguin, 2002) – p. 13-28
Conrad, Joseph, *Notes on Life and Letters* [1921] (Cambridge: University Press, 2004) – p. 129-130
Graves, Robert, *Goodbye to All That* [1929] (London: Penguin, 2000) – p. 21-35

Chapter 7
Spender, Stephen, *The Temple*, [1988] (London: Faber & Faber, 1989) – p. 107-111
Isherwood, Christopher, *Goodbye to Berlin* [1939] (London: Penguin, 1958) p. 16-18
Hamilton, Gerald, *Mr. Norris and I* (London: Alan Wingate, 1956) – p. 128-139
Leigh Fermor, Patrick, *A Time of Gifts: On foot to Constantinople – From the Hook of Holland to the Middle Danube* (London: John Murray, 1977) – p. 47-48, 50-51
Dodd, Martha, *My Years in Germany,* (London: Harcourt, Brace (New York), 1939) – p. 21-27, 124-26; 1939 (US title: Through Embassy Eyes)
Mosley, Charlotte, *The Mitfords: Letters Between Six Sisters* [2007] (London: Harper Perenniel, 2008) – p. 47-48, 63-65, 68-69

Chapter 8
Bell, A. O. (ed.) *The Diary of Virginia Woolf Volume IV: 1931-1935* (Boston: Houghton Mifflin Harcourt,1982) – p. 310-312
Beckett, Samuel, *German Diaries* (unpublished, Reading University special collections) – p. 15-23
Holman, C. Hugh, "I Have a Thing to Tell You", *The Short Novels of Thomas Wolfe;* [1937] (New York: Scribner,1961) – p. 233-250
Dubois, W. E. B., "Forum of Fact and Opinion", *Pittsburgh Courier* [1936] (articles September 19, October 10, December 12 and 19, 1936 in PittCat archive)
Hillary, Richard, *The Last Enemy* [1942] (London: Vintage, 2010) – p. 17-19
Shirer, William L., *Berlin Diary: The Journal of a Foreign Correspondent, 1934-1941* (New York: Knopf, 1941) – p. 142-143, 197-199

Chapter 9

Smith, Howard K., *Last Train from Berlin* (New York: Knopf,1942) – p. 81-97

Flannery, Harry, *Assignment to Berlin* (New York: Knopf, 1942) – p. 86-87, 110-113, 262-263

Burn, Michael, *Yes, Farewell* [1946] (London: Jonathan Cape 1947) – p. 19-22

Bielenberg, Christabel, *The Past is Myself* [1968] (London: Corgi, 1993) – p.192-195

Davie, Michael (ed.), *The Diaries of Evelyn Waugh* [1976] (London: Phoenix, 1995) – p. 645-646

Howard, Michael, *Otherwise Occupied;* (Exeter: Old Street,2010) – p. 53-55

Chapter 10

Benn, Tony, *Years of Hope (Diaries)* [1994] (London: Arrow, 1995) – p. 130-135

Sampson, Anthony, *The New Europeans* [1962] (London: Panther, 1971) – p. 19-20, 146-147, 248-250

Uris, Leon, *Armageddon* [1963] (London: Corgi, 1966) – p. 18-19, 253-254

le Carré, John, *The Spy Who Came in from the Cold* [1963] (London: Hodder & Stoughton, 1994) – p. 74-75

Flannery, Harry & Seger, Gerhardt Heinrich, *Which Way Germany* (New York: Hawthorn, 1968) – p. 205-207

Highsmith, Patricia, *The Boy Who Followed Ripley* [1980] (London: Vintage, 2001) – p. 155-157

Larson, Bob, *Your Swabian Neighbors* (Stuttgart: Schwaben International, 1981) – p. 29-30

Deighton, Len, *Berlin Game* [1983] (London: Harper Collins, 2010) – p. 1-4

Chapter 11

Craig, Gordon, *The Germans* [1982] (London: Penguin, 1991) – p. 341-343

Ardagh, John, *Germany and the Germans* (London: Hamish Hamilton, 1987) – p. 4-7

Skinner, Michael, *USAREUR: The United States Army in Europe* (New York: Presidio, 1989) – p. ix – x, 2 – 7, 10 – 15

Bryson, Bill, *Neither Here nor There* [1991] (London: Black Swan, 1998) – p. 115-125

Rimmer, Dave, *Once Upon A Time In The East* (London: Fourth Estate,1992) – p. 23-26

Garton Ash, Timothy, *The File: A Personal History* (London: Random House, 1997) – p. 3-10

Chapter 12

Ford, Robert, *Rhapsody* [2003] (London: Atlantic, 2004) – p. 1-4 (US title: The Student Conductor)

Carroll, James, *Secret Father* (New York, Houghton Mifflin Harcourt, 2003) – p. 46-47, 108-109

Ozment, Steven, *A Mighty Fortress: A New History of the German People*; [2004] (New York: First Perennial, 2005) p. 2-3, 14

Gorra, Michael, *The Bells in Their Silence: Travels Through Germany*; (Princeton: University Press, 2004) – p. 40-43, 93-94

Boyes, Roger, *A Year in the Scheisse* (Chichester, Summersdale, 2006) – p. 25-29

Donald, Ben, *Springtime for Germany* (London: Little, Brown, 2007) – p. 82-84

Winger, Anna, *This Must be the Place* [2008] (New York: Riverhead, 2009) – p. 206-208

Kerr, Philipp, *A Quiet Flame* (London: Quercus, 2008) – p. 52-55

Anders, Ingrid, *Earth to Kat Vespucci* (Bloomington, IN: iUniverse, 2009) – p. 37-39

Edugyan, Esi, *Half-Blood Blues* (London: Serpent's Tail, 2011) – p. 42-45

Further Reading

I am greatly indebted to a number of authors for pointing me in the direction of interesting material, or for providing general background information. Worthy of special mention are Matthew Jeffries *Hamburg: A Cultural and Literary History* (also Signal, 2011) and *Travels in the Reich* by Oliver Lubrich (Chicago University Press, 2010), as well as the ever-valuable Routledge *Traveller's Dictionary of Quotation* (1983). Simon Winder's *Germania* (Picador, 2010) and Philip Oltermann's *Keeping up with the Germans* (Faber & Faber 2012) both provided a wealth of ideas and knowledge not only about Germany, but about the relationship of English-speakers to it.

On the internet, I came across several pieces of writing that informed and inspired me, including "The Sorcerer's Apprentice: English Travellers and the Rhine in the Long Nineteenth Century" by Hagen Schulz-Forberg (http://blog.oup.com/2012/07/medieval-pogrom-origin-20th-century-anti-semitism-germany/) and several articles on SlowTravelBerlin.com by or about Christopher-Isherwood-expert Brendan Nash.

Acknowledgements

Despite considerable efforts, the editor and the publisher regret that they were not able to locate all of the owners of copyright material in this book. In many cases, we were successful in our search and would like to acknowledge and thank the following for permissions granted to use material in this book: Faber & Faber for T. S. Eliot's letters; A. P. Watt for *Goodbye to All That*; the estates of Christopher Isherwood (*Goodbye to Berlin*) and Evelyn Waugh (diaries), as well as to the Wylie Agency for handling these requests; the Ed Victor agency for *The Temple*; A. M. Heath Agents for *The Last Enemy*; the Random House Group for the Tony Benn diaries, *The Berlin Game*, and *Neither Here nor There*; Little, Brown for *Springtime for Germany*; Princeton University Press for *The Bells in Their Silence*; and Quercus for *A Quiet Flame*.

Two publishers were kind enough to waive fees for material they hold rights to: Old Street Publishing, for the excerpt from *Otherwise Occupied* and Atlantic Books for an extract from *Rhapsody*. The editor and publisher gratefully acknowledge this.

Several of the authors featured in the last chapter of this book were also kind enough to personally grant me the right to use their work without a fee: Ingrid Anders, Roger Boyes, Steven Ozment, and Anna Winger are all deserving of thanks.

Thanks

Producing an anthology is a group project in every respect. Not only is this collection built on the work of 76 authors over a period of more than 400 years, but it certainly would not have been possible without the help of many, many others.

I would like to thank the staff at the British Library in London, the Bodleian and the English Faculty Libraries at Oxford, the University of Reading's special collections reading room, and the London Borough of Sutton and Hamburg library services for helping me find the material I was looking for.

I would also like to thank Lara Ehrenhofer at Oxford for helping me to track down some of the older and rarer works in this collection; her knowledge of the University library systems was simply invaluable.

Above all, I am indebted to James Ferguson, who had the initial idea for this anthology, guided me through the process of creating it, and is of course publishing it.

No vote of thanks is ever complete without a mention of friends and family: Tomas Furlong, as well as Esmerelda Francés and Berny Sèbe, were kind enough to provide accommodation close to some important libraries; my partner Nicole Runschke put up with my constant research trips, repeated ravings about odd bits of forgotten writing and the occasional whiff of midnight oil; and, as ever, I couldn't have done this without my mother.

Index

Aaron's Rod (Lawrence, D. H.) xvi, 131
A Mighty Fortress (Ozment, Steven) 205, 211
A Quiet Flame (Kerr, Philip) 206, 219
A Time of Gifts (Leigh Fermor, Patrick) 111, 113, 118
A Tour of the Rhine (Meredith, William G.) 52, 54
A Tramp Abroad (Twain, Mark) 79
A View of Society and Manners in France, Switzerland, and Germany (Moore, John) 17, 29
A Weimar Idyll (Bagby, Albert Morris) 69, 86
A Year in the Merde (Clarke, Stephen) 205
A Year in the Scheisse (Boyes, Roger) 205, 214
Aachen (Aix la Chapelle) 64
Addison, Joseph (b. 1672) 17, 18
Adenauer, Kondrad (b. 1876) 203
Adlon, Hotel, Berlin 149, 182
air raids (on Germany) 143, 152, 153, 155-157, 161, 167-169
Aix (les Bains) 54
Albania, Albanian 119
Aleman (Alman, Almaign, Allemaigne) 4
Algarotti, Francesco (b. 1712) 20
All Quiet on the Western Front (Remarque, Erich Maria) 112
Alps 108, 137
Alsace 29, 74, 82, 137, 145
Alster 8, 132, 133, 153
Altona 41
Amsterdam 11, 195, 213
An English Wife in Berlin (Blücher, Evelyn Princess) 94, 98
Anders, Ingrid 206, 221
Anne, Queen of the United Kingdom (b. 1665) 39
Antwerp (Antwerpe) 5, 64, 69
An Itinerary (Moryson, Fynes) 3, 6
Ardagh, John (b. 1928) 186, 187, 190
Armageddon: A Novel of Berlin (Uris, Leon) 165, 169, 171
Around the World on a Bicycle (Stevens, Thomas) 82
Assignment to Berlin (Flannery, Harry) 146, 150, 154

Athens 91, 145
Atlantic 53, 93, 214
Atlantic Hotel, Hamburg 169, 170
Auden, W. H. (b. 1907) xv
Auerbach, Berthold (b. 1812) 54
Augsburg 86, 132
  Peace of 2
Austerlitz 33
Australia, Australian x, 155
Austria, Austrian 16, 29, 33, 51, 55, 73, 77, 109, 130, 132, 137, 145, 203
  Anschluss 128
Austro-Hungarian Empire 98
Aryanism 136, 151

Baden, Badener 213
  Margrave of 18, 29-31
Baden-Baden 77, 78, 79
Baedeker 159
Bagby, Albert Morris 69, 74, 86
Baltic 27, 40, 169, 217
Baltimore 206
Baring, Maurice (b. 1874) xiv
Basel (Basill) 5
Batty, Robert (b. 1789) 52
Bauhaus 111
Bavaria, Bavarian 2, 16, 23, 33, 86, 93, 95, 104, 108, 109, 138, 176, 182, 213, 216-218
Beckett, Samuel (b. 1906) 129, 132, 133
Beckford, William (b. 1760) 35
Beethoven, Ludwig van (b. 1770) 98, 132
Belgium 69, 101, 107, 118, 149
Benn, Anthony 'Tony' Neil Wedgewood (b. 1925) 165, 167, 187
Berlin xvi , 18, 24, 25, 27-29, 36, 69, 89, 94, 99-102, 111-118, 121-124, 134-136, 138-139, 141, 142, 146, 147-153, 156-159, 165, 166-169, 172-178, 182, 183, 185, 187, 190, 193, 197-201, 204, 206, 209, 210, 213, 216, 218-223
Berlin Diary: The Journal of a Foreign Correspondent (Shirer, William) 130, 141
Berliner Zeitung 199
Berlin Game (Deighton, Len) 166, 181
Blockade (1948-49) xv, 165, 166, 173, 174,

214
Checkpoint Charlie 182
Television Tower (Fernsehturm) 221, 222
Unter den Linden 89, 91, 101, 136, 146,
149-152, 222, 223
Wall 164, 166, 182, 185, 187
Wall, Fall of 185-187
Beuys, Joseph (b. 1921) 191
Bielenberg, Christabel (b. 1909) xvi, 147, 156
Bild-Zeitung 188
Bildungsroman 146
Bismarck, Otto von xii, 73, 152, 155, 213, 214
Black Forest 74, 75, 79, 83, 84, 158
Blaubeuren 85
Blücher
    Evelyn Princess (b. 1876) 94, 95, 98, 112
    SMS *Blücher* 100, 101
Bohemia (Beame) 3, 4, 12-14, 19, 145
Bohemia (non-geographic) 113, 117
Bond Head, Francis (b. 1793) xvi, 52, 59, 94
Bonn 22, 47, 58, 62, 165, 168, 176, 189
    Bundeshaus (parliament) 168
    University of 57, 77
Bordighera 103
Boswell, James (b. 1740) 17, 24
Boyes, Rogert (b. 1952) 205, 214
Bolzano/Bozen (Botzen) 77
Brandenburg 16, 136, 137
    Elector of 16
    Gate 91, 101, 102, 149, 153, 167
Brandt, Willy (Herbert Frahm, b. 1913) 168,
176, 189, 203, 212
Braunschweig (see Brunswick)
Brecht, Berthold (b. 1898) 176
Bremen (Breme, Breame) 3, 5, 138, 190, 214
Brentano, Clemens (b. 1778) 34
Breslau (see Wroclaw)
Brielle (Brill) 11
Britain, British x-xiii 31, 33, 34, 51, 54, 73,
81, 84, 93, 99, 100, 106, 113, 128, 142,
146, 147, 148, 155, 158, 159, 164, 168,
185, 190, 191, 196, 205, 212, 213-217
    Battle of 129, 150
    armed forces of 147, 164, 169, 174, 193
Brocken 36, 39
Brothers Grimm 75
Brunswick (Brunswicke)   5, 11, 12,
28, 38
Bryson, Bill (b. 1951) 186, 187, 190, 195

Bubbles from the Brunnens of Nassau by an Old Man (Bond Head, Francis) 52, 59, 94
Bundesrepublik (see Federal Republic)
Burn, Michael "Micky" (b. 1912) xvi, 125,
146, 154
Burschenschaft (student fellowships) 58, 65, 66,
81, 98
Byron, Lord George Gordon (b. 1778) 35, 52,
56, 64

Cabaret 112
Carlyle, Thomas (b. 1795) 70, 87
Carroll, James (b. 1943) 204, 208
Chancellery (Reichskanzlei) 141, 153
Charlemagne (Carolus Magnus) 9, 65, 67, 118
Charlottenburg 135
Charterhouse (school) 109
Chemnitz (Chemniut) 13
Childe Harold's Pilgrimage (Byron) 35, 46, 64
Churchill, Winston (b. 1874) 150, 151, 172
Clarke, Edward Daniel (b. 1769) xiv
Clausthal-Zellerfeld 39
Cleves 21, 22
Coblenz (Coblentz) 22, 53, 56, 57, 61, 67,
68, 119
Colditz xvi, 125, 146
Cold War 164-168, 185-187, 193-197, 204,
206, 222
Coleridge, Samuel Taylor xii, 34, 39, 64
Cologne (Collin, Cologn) 2, 11, 20-23, 46, 47,
52, 56, 62, 64, 66-69, 112, 114, 115, 138,
148, 190, 198, 213
    Cathedral 56, 67, 69
Conrad, Joseph (b. 1857) 95, 106
Coryat (Coryate), Thomas (b. 1577) xi, 3, 9,
17
Continental Blockade 35
Coswig 25
Courland 145
Crabb Robinson, Henry (b. 1775) 33, 34, 36,
41, 52
Cracow 137
Craig, Gordon (b. 1913) xv, 186, 188
Crudities (Thomas Coryat/Coryate) 3
Cuxhaven 132, 169
Czech (people, country, Republic) 3, 128, 141,
145

Dahlem 182

Danube 24, 85, 86, 119, 138
Danzig (Dantzic) 27
Deisenhofen 108
Deighton, Len (b. 1929) 166, 181
Denmark (Denmarke) 7, 73, 196
Der Spiegel 188
Deutsch-Britische Gesellschaft (Deutsche-Englische Gesellschaft) 168
Die Fliegenden Blätter 176
Die Welt 188
Dietrich, Marlene (b. 1901) 223
Dilke, Charles Wentworth (b. 1789) 53
Dix, Otto (b. 1891) 223
Dresden (Dreason) 3, 14, 18, 27, 57, 90
Dodd, Martha (b. 1908) 113, 120
Donald, Ben 205, 216
Drachenfels (Drackenfels) 35, 56-58, 62, 64, 77
Dubois, W. E. B. (b. 1868) 129, 130, 136
Dunkirk (Dunkerke) 6
Durlach 9, 29
Düsseldorf 161, 176, 177, 190, 210
Dutch (see Netherlands)
Dutch (High, Low, dialect, language) 4, 5

Earth to Kat Vespucci (Anders, Ingrid) 221
East Germany (see German Democratic Republic)
Edugyan, Esi xv, 206, 222
Ehrenbreitstein 56, 57, 68
Eichmann, Adolf (b. 1906) 165
Eifel 147
Eisenach 40, 59
Elbe (Elve) 3, 6, 14, 38, 40, 62, 107, 120, 138, 153, 169, 193, 213
Eliot, George (b. 1819) 53, 68, 95
Eliot, T. S. (b. 1888) 93, 97, 99, 112
Ems, Bad 54, 57, 140
Erfurt (Erdforde) 5, 189
Euro (currency) 203
European Union 164, 203, 212, 217
Exodus (Uris, Leon) 165
Expressionism 111

Faust (Goethe, Johann Wolfgang von) 36, 176
Federal Republic of Germany
FRG (1949-1990) 164, 165, 168, 182, 183, 185, 188, 193, 196, 198, 204, 211, 222
Federal Republic of Germany (post 1990)

185-187, 203, 211
Ferdinand, Archduke Franz (b. 1863) 98
First World War xi, xvi, 93, 95, 98, 148, 206
Flanders 8, 64
Flannery, Harry (b. 1900) 146, 149, 150, 165
Florence 78
Ford, Robert (b. 1975) 204, 206, 207
forest (woods) xii-xv, 8, 39,47, 48, 54, 55, 64-66, 75, 78, 79, 80, 87, 89, 96, 97, 102, 107, 108, 113, 119, 120, 132, 136, 140, 147, 154, 174, 175, 181, 197
Forum of Fact and Opinion (Dubois, W. E. B. in Pittsburgh Courier) 129, 136
France x, 16, 22, 24, 25, 30, 34, 44, 51, 73, 82, 83, 84, 128, 142, 145, 148, 157, 168, 190, 191, 193, 205, 212
Franco-Prussian War 1870-1871 73, 112
Franconia 119
Frankenstein: or, The Modern Prometheus (Shelley, Mary Wollstonecraft) 35, 47
Frankfurter Allgemeine Zietung 188
Frankfurt (Franckforde, Frankfort) 5, 21-23, 41, 43, 44, 51, 55, 56, 57, 69, 76, 114, 138, 167, 190, 194, 209, 213
Frankfurt an der Oder 138
Frederick I, King in Prussia 16
Frederick I, King of Prussia 16, 18
Frederick II, King of Prussia, the Great (Frederic, Friedrich) 20, 24, 25, 27, 62, 89, 155
Frederick William IV of Prussia 51
Freie Welt 199
Freudenstadt 84
French Revolution 33, 51
Friedrichstraße 152, 182, 199, 200
Frisia 2
Fry, Roger (b. 1866) 160
Fulda 194

Gardnor, John (b. 1729)
Garton Ash, Timothy (b. 1955) 187, 198
Garrick, David (b. 1717) 17, 26
Gaskell, Elizabeth (b. 1810) xii, 21, 53, 54, 64, 75
George VI, King of United Kingdom (b. 1895) 150
German Confederation 73
German Democratic Republic (GDR) 12, 164-170, 174, 177, 182, 183, 185, 189, 193,

196, 198-201, 221, 222
Communist Party of (SED) 174, 185, 189
German Reunification 1990 (see Reunification)
Germania (Winder, Simon) 205
Germany and the Germans (Ardagh, John) 186, 190
Gestapo 128, 167
Geyde, Eric xv
Godesberg (Godeberg) 57, 58, 76, 118
Goebbels, Joseph (b. 1897) 124, 149, 189
Goethe, Johann Wolfgang von (b. 1749) xii, 33, 34, 36, 39, 52, 69, 87, 130, 152, 176
Goodbye to All That (Graves, Robert) 95, 108
Goodbye to Berlin (Isherwood, Christopher) 112, 115
Göring, Hermann (b. 1893) (Goering) 129, 140, 141
Gorra, Michael, (b. 1957) 205, 212
Goslar 38
Gotha 59
Goths 103
Grand Tour, the 35
Graves, Robert (b. 1895) xvi, 95, 108
Green Party (Germany) 164
Grosz, Georg (b. 1893) 176
Grunewald 182

Halberstadt (Halverstadt) 12
Half Blood Blues (Edugyan, Esi) 206, 222
Hamburg (Hamburgh, Hambrogh, Hambourg, Hambro) xiii, 5, 7, 8, 11, 14, 19, 34, 37, 39-42, 107, 112, 114, 120, 121, 132, 138, 152, 153, 169, 170, 175, 176, 180, 186, 193, 195, 196, 210, 212-214
Reeperbahn 133, 180, 195
Hamilton, Gerald (b. 1888) 113, 114, 117
Hanover/Hannover xi, 29, 39, 41, 137, 168
Hanoverian Kings of the United Kingdom xi, 39
Hanseatic League 7, 137, 213
Hapsburg 16, 33
Harburg 40
Harz (Hartz) 39, 164
Heemstra, Ella van (b. 1900) xvi, 125
Heidelberg (Heidelberge, Heydleberge) 3, 5, 6, 7, 9, 13, 14, 53, 54, 64, 65, 79, 80, 132
University of 81, 132
Heimat 95, 102, 158
Heine, Heinrich (b. 1797) 51

Heligoland (Holyland, Heiligland) 3, 6, 107
Helmstedt 197
Hemingway, Ernest xv, 147, 148
Hepburn, Audrey (b. 1929) xvi, 125
Hervey, Baron John (b. 1696) 24
Herzog, Werner (b. 1942) 191
Hesse, Hessian 23, 104
Hesse, Hermann (b. 1877) 93
Highsmith, Patricia (b. 1921) 166, 167, 178
Hildesheim (Heldeshim, Heldesheim) 11
Hillary, Richard (b. 1919) xvi, 129, 130, 139
Hindenburg, Paul von (b. 1847) 111, 152
History of a Six Weeks' Tour (Shelley, Mary Wollstronecraft, Percy Bysshe) 35, 45
Hitler, Adolf (b. 1889) 111, 113, 118, 122, 124, 125, 128, 132, 138, 141, 146, 148-152, 176, 190, 211, 214
Hitler Youth 152
Hocheimer 55
Hohenzollern 16, 111
Holland (see Netherlands)
Holland, Hook of 196
Holstein (Hoist, Holste) 7
Holy Roman Empire xi, 2, 7, 16, 33
Homburg 78, 104
Honecker, Erich (b. 1912) 185
Hood, Thomas (b. 1799) 53, 54, 62
Howard, Michael (b. 1925) 147, 160
Howell, James (b. ca. 1594) xiv, 4
Hungary, Hungarian 139, 185
Hume, David (b. 1711) xii, 17, 21, 95
Hürtgen Forest, battle of (Hurtgen) 147

I Have a Thing to Tell You (Wolfe, Thomas) 129, 133
Ingelheim 9
Inner German Border 193, 196, 197
Innsbruck 77, 132
Instructions and Directions for Forren Travel (Howell, James) xiv, 4
Isar 108
Isherwood, Christopher (b. 1904) xv, 112-117
Italy, Italian 22, 25-27, 35, 43, 44, 77, 78, 109, 129, 214

James, Henry (b. 1843) 73, 75, 112
Japan, Japanese 139, 151
Jerome, Jerome K. (b. 1859) 74, 75, 89, 95
Jewish (population of Germany and Europe)

extermination of 145, 159, 160, 196
persecution of 121, 128, 129, 132, 138, 211
prejudice against 138, 139
Journal of a Visit to London and the Continent
(Melville, Herman) 53, 66

Kaliningrad (Königsberg) 16
Kaltenbrunner, Ernst (b. 1903) 160
Kant, Immanuel (b. 1724) xii
Karlsruhe (Karlsruch) 29, 45, 204, 207
Kassel (Cassel) 43, 55, 59, 190, 194
Keeping up with the Germans (Oltermann,
Philip) 205
Kerr, Philip (b. 1956) 206, 219
Kiel 100
Kiesinger, Kurt Georg (b. 1904) 175
Klarsfeld, Beate (b. 1939) 175
Klaus, Georg (b. 1912) 189
Kleist, Heinrich von (b. 1777) 33
Klopstock, Friedrich Gottlieb (b. 1724) 37, 38
Koblenz (see Coblenz)
Kohl, Helmut (b. 1930) 195, 203
Köln (see Cologne)
Kreuzberg 166, 167, 178
Kristallnacht 128
Kulturnation 33
Kurfürstendamm 134, 149, 166
Knight, Dame Laura (b. 1877) 160

Lahn 54, 97, 98
Larson, Bob 166, 180
Las Vegas 195
Lawrence, D. H. (b. 1885) 94, 95, 96, 132
le Carré, John (Cornwell, David, b. 1931) 165,
166, 174
League of Nations 128
Leiden (Leyden) 11
Leigh (Liegh) 4, 6
Leigh Fermor, Patrick xii, 111, 113, 118, 212
Leipzig (Leipzic) 13, 61, 114, 221
Lessing, Gotthold Ephraim (b. 1729) 39, 71
Letters from Turkey (Wortley Montagu, Mary)
17
Liaisons Dangereuses, Les (Laclos, Choderlos
de) 217
Liège 22, 69
Lietzensee (Litzensee) 153
Liszt, Franz (b. 1811) 69, 70, 74, 87-89
Litoměřice/Leitmeritz (Leutmeritz) 14

London xvi, 4, 6, 16, 17, 21, 25, 27, 28, 34,
40, 42, 48, 52, 53, 61, 99, 109, 117, 150,
151, 159, 161, 187, 197
Lübeck (Lubeck, Lubecke, Luebeck) 7, 138,
214
Lübke, Heinrich (b. 1894) 176
Lufthansa 167, 197
Lüneburg (Luneburg) 7
Lusitania (RMS) 101
Luther, Martin 2, 59
Lutheran 42, 97, 209

Maas (Maze) 11
Madox Ford, Ford 93, 95, 102
Magdeburg 157, 158, 198, 221
Main (Maine) 23, 43, 167
Mainz (Mentz, Mayence) 10, 23, 45, 48, 52,
55, 69, 138
Mann, Thomas (b. 1875) xiv, 93
Mannheim (Manheim) 29, 46
Marburg 94, 97
Marienborn 197
Marienburg 13
Marshall Plan 164
Maxwell Fyfe, Sir David (b. 1900) 160
Mecklenburg 137
Medici, Mary de 67
Melville, Herman (b. 1819) xii, xvi, 53, 66
*Memoir of the Courts of Berlin, Dresden, Warsaw
and Vienna* (Wraxall, Nathaniel) 17, 27
Meredith, William G. 52, 54
Merkel, Angela (b. 1954) 181, 203
Metternich, Prince Klemens von 68
Miss Träumerei (Bagby, Albert Morris) 74, 86
Mitford, Unity (b. 1914) xiv, xvi, 113, 124,
146
Möhnesee 161
Molotov, Vyacheslav (b. 1890) 142, 160
Moore, John (b. 1729) 17, 29, 56
Moravia 145
Moryson, Fynes (b. 1566) xi, 3, 17
Moscow 145, 185
Moselle 23, 57, 68
Mr. Norris and I (Hamilton, Gerald) 113, 117
Mr. Norris Changes Trains (Isherwood,
Christopher) 113
München (see Munich)
Munich (Munick) xvi, 26, 108, 124-126, 136-
138, 146, 148, 158, 176, 177, 182, 190,

196, 210, 216, 217
My Years in Germany (Dodd, Martha) 113, 120

Namur 69
Napoleon 33, 155
Nassau 23, 52, 54, 60
NATO (North Atlantic Treaty Organization)
  164, 192, 193, 195, 203, 212
Nauheim 103, 104
Nazi
  Brownshirts xii, 119, 122
  bureaucracy 130
  censorship 137, 176
  ideology 113, 130, 146
  Party (NSDAP) 111
  Party headquarters, Munich 124
  persistence after 1945 165, 172
  propaganda 148-151, 191
  regime 128, 129, 134, 145-147, 176, 191,
    206, 211, 212, 223
  SS 123, 124, 167
  war crimes 147, 148, 159, 160, 190
  winter collections 138, 151
Neckar (Necker) 64, 65, 79, 80, 132
Neither Here nor There (Bryson, Bill) 186, 195
Netherlands, the xvi, 2, 4, 22, 33, 44, 117,
  131, 145, 196, 197
Neues Deutschland 189, 199
New York 197, 221
New York Times 146
Nijmegen (Nimeguen) 20
Nonnenswerth 63
Nordhausen 38
North Sea 107, 129, 137, 196
Norway 45, 145
Notes on Life and Letters (Conrad, Joseph) 95,
  106
Novalis (Georg Philipp Friedrich Freiherr von
  Hardenberg, b. 1772) 33
November Revolution (1918) 93
Nuremberg (Norremberge) xvi, 5, 20, 125,
  146, 147, 159
  Rallies 125, 146, 147
  Trials 159, 160
Nürnberg (see Nuremberg)

Oberkirch 82, 83
Oder 138
Oktoberfest 217

Olympics (1936) 136, 138
Once Upon a Time in the East (Rimmer, Dave)
  187, 196
Oppenau 83
Ostalgie 187
Otherwise Occupied (Howard, Michael) 147,
  160
Owens, Jesse (b. 1913) 136
Ozment, Steven (b. 1939) 205, 211

Palatinate (Pallatinate) 2, 11, 104
Paris 26, 27, 61, 79, 103, 109, 117, 125, 139,
  150, 190, 191
Parzival (Eschenbach, Wolfram von, b. ca.
  1170) 176
Pascal, Blaise (b. 1623) 71
Peterstal (Petersthal) 83
Pirna 14
Pittsburgh xi, 130
Pittsburgh Courier 129, 136
Poland, Polish 51, 94, 128, 137, 142, 145,
  172, 185, 210
Potsdam (Potzdam) 24, 27, 29, 62, 89
Potsdamer Platz 152, 167
Prague 3, 4, 13, 14, 19, 128, 185
Prenzlauer Berg 198, 216
Prussia, Prussian xii, 16, 20, 21, 29, 31, 33, 34,
  51, 55, 57, 58, 73, 75, 79, 111, 137, 145,
  191, 211
Prussian Officer, The (Lawrence, D. H.) xvi,
  94, 96

Quebec 68

Rastatt (Rastade) 29
Ratzeburg 38, 40
Ravenna 9
Ravensbrück (concentration camp) 147
Reformation 2
Reich, Third 128, 130, 134, 139, 152, 165,
  173, 189, 211, 212
Reichstag 91, 122, 142, 153
Rheinberg (Reinberg) 20
Rheinsberg 20
Rench (Bench) 84
Reunification, German (1990) 149, 152, 167,
  185, 187
Rhapsody 204, 206, 207
Rhine xii, xvi, 16, 19, 21-23, 35, 36, 43,

46-48, 52-58, 62, 64, 67-69, 75-77, 82, 113-115, 119, 131, 132, 138, 157, 164, 208, 209
Confederation of the 33
legends surrounding 119
Up the Rhine 53, 62
Rhineland
  French occupation of 111, 128
Ribbentrop, Joachim von (b. 1893) 160
Riga 213
Rilke, Rainer Maria (b. 1875) 93
Rimmer, Dave (b. 1960) 187, 196
Röhm, Ernst (b. 1887) 122-124
Rolandseck 63
Romanticism, Romantics xii, 34, 36, 51, 52, 54, 64, 73-75, 188, 218
Rome 103
Rommel, Manfred 181
Rothenburg 84
Rotterdam 11, 48
Round the World in Any Number of Days (Baring, Maurice) xv
Rowohlt, Ernst (b. 1887)147
Rubens, Peter Paul (b. 1577) 67, 105
Ruhr (area) 161, 190, 194
Rusk, David Dean (b. 1909) 175
Russia, Russian 16, 79, 89, 99, 122, 145, 155, 156, 164, 168, 173, 174, 185, 192, 208, 214

Saar, Saarland 128, 195
Sampson, Anthony (b. 1926) 165, 167, 169
Sand, George (b. 1804) 70
Sanssouci, Palace of (Sans Souci) 24, 62, 89, 90
Sarajevo 98
Saxe-Coburg-Gotha, Prince Albert of (b. 1819) xi
Saxony, Saxons x, 2, 3, 13, 14, 19, 33, 40, 61, 104, 137
Saxony, Lower 44
Scapa Flow 93
Scenery of the Rhine (Batty, Robert) 52
Schiller, Friedrich (b. 1759) 33, 34, 76, 111, 152
Schleicher, Kurt von (b. 1882) 122, 124
Schröder, Gerhard (b. 1944) 203
Schwabing 178
Schwalbach, Langen 55, 60
Second German Empire 72, 82, 93

Second World War xi, xiii, xv, 113, 128-130, 145-148, 155, 156, 165, 166, 187, 192, 193, 203, 214
Secret Father (Carroll, James) 204, 208
Serbia, Serb 98, 216
Shelley
  Mary Wollstonecraft xii, 35, 45, 47, 56, 95
  Percy Bysshe 35, 45, 95
Shirer, William (b. 1904) xv, 130, 141, 149
Siebengebirge (Seven Mountains) 63, 77
Silesia, Silesian (Schlesien) 16, 106, 137, 145
Simplicius Simplicissimus (Grimmelshausen, Hans Jakob von b. 1621) 176
Simplicissimus 176
Skinner, Michael (b. 1953) xiv, 186, 192
Slovakia 145
Smith, Howard K. (b. 1914) 146, 149, 148
Soviet Union 128, 142, 167, 173, 185, 193, 209
Spa (Belgium) 26, 54
spa towns (cure, Kur) 17, 52, 75, 78, 79, 83, 94, 95, 101, 104-106
Spain 2, 145
Spanish Civil War 128, 136
Spender, Stephen (b. 1909) xv, 112, 113, 114
Springtime for Germany (Donald, Ben) 205, 216
St. Boniface, legend of 194
St. Petersburg (Petersburgh) 27, 28, 89
Staatsicherheitsdienst (Stasi) 187, 198
Stade (Stode, Stoade) 4, 5, 7
Stauffenberg Plot xvi , 147
Stevens, Thomas (b. 1854) 74, 82, 95
Stockholm 29
Stoph, Willi (b. 1914) 189
Strasburg (Strasburgh, Strasbourg) 45, 47, 138
Strauss, Franz (b. 1822) 69
Strauss, Franz-Josef (b. 1915) 191
Student protests (1968) 164, 175, 192
Sturm und Drang 34
Stürmer, Michael (b. 1938) 213
Stuttgart (Stugard) 25, 138, 157, 180, 190
Süddeutsche Zeitung 188
Sudetenland 128
Swabia 94, 119, 166, 180, 181
  Swabian Alb 181, 190
Sweden 16, 79, 196, 223
Switzerland, Swiss 35, 43, 45, 48, 76, 77, 109, 146, 203

Tacitus, Cornelius (b. 55) xii, xiii, 212
Tales of the Black Forest (Auerbach, Berthold) 54
Taunus 104
Taylor, John (b. 1578) xvi, 3, 11
Taylor his travels (John Taylor) 3, 11
Tegernsee 108
Tempelhof 167
Tennyson, Lord Alfred (b. 1809) 53
Teplitz 36
Thackeray, William Makepeace (b. 1811) xii, 21, 52, 54, 56
"The Awful German Language" (Twain, Mark) xv, 74
The Bells and their Silence (Gorra, Michael) 205, 212
The Boy Who Followed Ripley (Highsmith, Patricia) 166, 178
The File: A Personal History (Garton Ash, Timothy) 187, 198
The German Genius (Watson, Peter) 205
The Germans (Craig, Gordon) 186, 188
The Good Solider (Madox Ford, Ford) 94, 102
The IPCRESS File (Deighton, Len) 166
The Journal of his German and Swiss Travels (Boswell, James) 24
The Last Enemy (Hillary, Richard) 129, 130, 139
The Last Train from Berlin (Smith, Howard K.) 146, 148
The Natural History of German Life (Eliot, George) 53
The New Europeans: The Vital Survey of Europe Today and Tomorrow (Sampson, Anthony) 165, 169
The Past is Myself (Bielenberg, Christabel) 147, 156
The Revolver Republic (Geyde, Eric) xv
The Rise and Fall of the Third Reich (Shirer, William) 130
The Spy Who Came in from the Cold (le Carré, John) 165, 166, 174
The Student Conductor (Ford, Robert, see Rhapsody)
The Temple (Spender, Stephen) 112, 114
The Times (of London) 34, 111, 169, 205, 217
Thirty Years' War 2, 16, 176
This Must Be the Place (Winger, Anna) 206, 218
Three Men on the Bummel (Jerome, Jerome K.) 74, 75, 89
Three Months in Weimar (Eliot, George) 53
Through Embassy Eyes (Dodd, Martha, see My Years in Germany)
Thuringia, Thuringian 86, 104, 138
Tiergarten 102, 123, 151, 153, 167
"Tintern Abbey" (Wordsworth, William) 49
Torgau 193
Travels in Various Countries of Europe (Clarke, Edward Daniel) xiv
Travemünde (Travemunde) 40
Trier (Treves) 23
Tromsø 145
Tucholsky, Kurt (b. 1890) 223
Turkey, Turkish 17
  Turkish migration into Germany 178, 179, 182
Turlowe (see Durlach)
Twain, Mark (b. 1835) xii, xv, 74, 75, 79
Tyrol 77

Ulm 85, 86
United States of America, American x, xi, 51, 73, 74, 76, 81, 93, 98, 99, 113, 129, 131, 137, 139, 142, 146, 148, 150, 155, 164, 166, 168, 175, 176, 196, 205, 21, 212, 213, 221
  armed forces of 147, 157, 159, 164, 165, 180, 181, 186, 192, 193-195
Uris, Leon (b. 1924) xv, 165, 169, 171
Ursula, St., bones of the virgins of 20, 21, 56, 64
USAREUR: The United States Army in Europe (Skinner, Michael) 186, 192
Utrecht 4, 25

Varus, Quintilius xii, 119
Venice 2, 9, 10, 20
Verona 78
Versailles 59, 73, 89, 104
  Treaty of 111, 128, 137, 138, 155
Vienna 17, 19, 24, 25, 27 33, 138
  Congress of 33
Volkswagen 169, 170
Voltaire (Arouet, François-Marie, b. 1694) 90
Vormärz (1848) 51

Wall Street Crash (1929) 111, 138
Warsaw Pact 164

Warsaw Ghetto, Monument to 168
Wannsee (Wansee) 123
Waterloo, Battle of 155
Watson, Peter 205
Waugh, Evelyn (b. 1903) 147, 159
Westphalia, Westphalian 57, 58, 77, 137, 177
Weil, Kurt (b. 1900) 176
Weimar 33, 34, 36, 40, 52, 53, 59, 69, 74, 86,
    87, 165
    Republic xv, 111-113, 117, 122, 165, 168,
    206, 212
Wende (1990) 186, 212
Weser 138
West Germany (see Federal Republic of
    Germany)
Western Allies 145, 155, 164, 167, 185, 193
Which Way Germany? (Flannery, Harry) 166,
    175
Whythorne, Thomas (b. 1528) 4
Wieland, Christoph Martin (b. 1733) 39
Wiesbaden (Weis Baden, Wisbaden) 23, 55,
    76, 204, 209
William I, King of Prussia 73
William II, Emperor of Germany (Wilhelm,
    the Kaiser) xii, 100-102, 155, 160
Winder, Simon 205
Winger, Anna (b. 1970) 205, 218
Wirtschaftswunder (economic miracle) 167, 212
Wittenberg 62
Wodehouse, P. G. (b. 1881) 159
Wolfe, Thomas (b. 1900) 129, 130, 133
Wolfsburg 170
Wolfenbüttel (Wolfenbuttle, Wolfunbuttle) 12
woods (see forest)
Woolf
    Leonard (b. 1880) 129
    Virginia (b. 1882) xvi, 129-132
Wordsworth
    Dorothy (b. 1771) 34, 36
    William (b. 1770) 34, 36
Wortley Montagu, Mary (b. 1689) 3, 17, 20
Wotton, Henry (b. 1568) xvi, 2, 4, 9
Wraxall, Nathaniel (b. 1751) 17, 27, 34, 89
Wroclaw 137, 138
Württemberg (Wurtemberg) 84, 86, 137
Würzburg (Wurtsburg, Worzburg, Wurzburg)
    21, 59, 120, 194
Wuppertal
    Eberfeld (Eberfeldt) 59

Year of Revolutions (1848) 51
Yes, Farewell (Burn, Michael) 154
Yiddish xi
Your Swabian Neighbours (Larson, Bob) 166,
    180

Zerbst 25